Personality Development in Adolescence

Challenge and conflict are an integral part of adolescent life here in the West. This intriguing book looks at adolescence from a cross-cultural perspective, including research presented here for the first time, from Canada, the United States, Norway and Japan.

The roles of morality, family contexts, social change, and gender are considered in adolescent personality development by contributors well known in their respective fields. In three parts, *Personality Development in Adolescence* begins with a look at related studies of adolescent development of individuation, ego, identity and moral orientation related to family context in several countries, with a focus on family communication and adolescent personality. *Personality Development in Adolescence* examines development in differing cultural contexts and concludes with an exploration of life span issues of moral development, separation–individuation, and psychosocial issues, focusing on Henrik Ibsen's *Peer Gynt*.

This book will be of central importance to developmental and clinical psychologists, sociologists and criminologists, and valuable to social workers, teachers, nurses and all those working with young people.

Eva Skoe is Professor of Developmental Psychology at the University of Tromsø in Norway. She is renowned for her work on the ethic of care, identity and gender which is widely published.

Anna von der Lippe is Professor of Clinical Psychology at the Center for Research in Clinical Psychology at the University of Oslo. Her work on personality development in young women has appeared previously in journals.

Adolescence and Society
Series editor: John C. Coleman

The Trust for the Study of Adolescence

The general aim of the series is to make accessible to a wide readership the growing evidence relating to adolescent development. Much of this material is published in relatively inaccessible professional journals, and the goals of the books in this series will be to summarise, review and place in context current work in the field so as to interest and engage both an undergraduate and a professional audience.

The intention of the authors is to raise the profile of adolescent studies among professionals and in institutions of higher education. By publishing relatively short, readable books on interesting topics to do with youth and society, the series will make people more aware of the relevance of the subject of adolescence to a wide range of social concerns.

The books will not put forward any one theoretical viewpoint. The authors will outline the most prominent theories in the field and will include a balanced and critical assessment of each of these. Whilst some of the books may have a clinical or applied slant, the majority will concentrate on normal development.

The readership will rest primarily in two major areas: the undergraduate market, particularly in the fields of psychology, sociology and education; and the professional training market, with particular emphasis on social work, clinical and educational psychology, counselling, youth work, nursing and teacher training.

Also available in this series

Fathers and Adolescents
Shmuel Shulman and Inge Seiffge-Krenke
Adolescent Health
Patrick C.L. Heaven
Identity in Adolescence
Jane Kroger
The Nature of Adolescence (second edition)
John C. Coleman and Leo Hendry
Growing up with Unemployment
Anthony H. Winefield, Marika Tiggermann, Helen R. Winefield and Robert D. Goldney
Young People's Leisure and Lifestyles
Leo B. Hendry, Janet Shucksmith, John G. Love and Anthony Glendinning
Sexuality in Adolescence
Susan Moore and Doreen Rosenthal
Adolescent Gambling
Mark Griffiths
Youth, AIDS, and Sexually Transmitted Diseases
Susan Moore, Doreen Rosenthal and Anne Mitchell
Adolescent Coping
Erica Frydenberg
Social Networks and Social Influences in Adolescence
John Cotterell

Personality Development in Adolescence

A cross national and life span perspective

Edited by Eva Elisabeth Aspaas Skoe
and Anna Louise von der Lippe

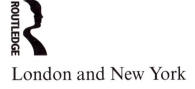

London and New York

читатель

First published 1998 by Routledge
11 New Fetter Lane, London EC4P 4EE

Simultaneously published in the USA and Canada
by Routledge
29 West 35th Street, New York, NY 10001

© 1998 Eva Elisabeth Aspaas Skoe and Anna Louise von der Lippe, selection and editorial matter; individual chapters, the contributors

Typeset in Times by Routledge
Printed and bound in Great Britain by Redwood Books, Trowbridge, Wiltshire

British Library Cataloguing in Publication Data
A catalogue record for this book is available from the British Library

Library of Congress Cataloguing in Publication Data
Personality development in adolescence : a cross national and life span perspective / [edited by] Eva Skoe and Anna von der Lippe.
"Primarily papers presented at the seminar . . . May 1994, at the University of Tromsø"—Introd.
Includes bibliographical references and index.
1. Personality in adolescence—Cross-cultural studies. I. Skoe, Eva.
II. Lippe, Anna Louise von der. III. Series.
BF724.3P4P47 1998
155.5'1825—dc21 97-37966
CIP

ISBN 0-415-13505-2 (hbk)
ISBN 0-415-13506-0 (pbk)

For my parents Evelyn Vera and Jens Aage Dybwad Aspaas (ES)

For my grandchildren Martine, Mathias, Julie and Kai (AL)

Contents

Part III Life Span Development

Illustrations

Contributors

Mary Louise Arnold, University of Toronto

Catherine R. Cooper, University of California, Santa Cruz

Harold D. Grotevant, University of Minnesota

Torild Hammer, The Norwegian Institute for Social Research NOVA

Susan M. Hilbers, Wilfred Laurier University

Jane Kroger, University of Tromsø

Siv Kvernmo, University of Tromsø

James E. Marcia, Simon Fraser University

Michael W. Pratt, Wilfred Laurier University

Eva Elisabeth Aspaas Skoe, University of Tromsø

Anna Louise von der Lippe, University of Oslo

Lars Wichstrøm, University of Trondheim

Preface

This book contains primarily papers presented at the seminar held at the inauguration of the doctoral program in psychology in May 1994, at the University of Tromsø, which is the youngest university in Norway and the northernmost university in the world (if one discounts the university branch on Svalbard at 88 degrees north). In fact, the University of Tromsø is situated on a coastal island in the North Sea, north of the Arctic Circle. The Gulf Stream makes this polar part of the world habitable. This is the land of extremes–from midnight sun in the summer to darkness in the winter. The Psychology Department was established in 1989 to meet demands for psychological services in northern Norway. The first group of psychologists all graduated successfully in 1995.

In this unique setting, the seminar provided a special opportunity for national and international scholars to meet and to discuss with post-graduate students and with each other various theories, research, and thoughts about personality development in adolescence and across the life span. It has been noted that "developmentalists often are not interested in the outcome of a developmental process in adulthood . . . or additional development past adolescence (or sometimes even past infancy)" (Eisenberg, 1995, p. vii). This is clearly not the case with the contributors in this volume; all have worked extensively with developmental issues in adolescence and beyond.

We arranged this seminar because we believe adolescence to be an important phase with regard to personality development. Adolescence was long an underresearched area, seen to be unstable and little related to the periods before and after (Block, 1971). The last 20 years have, however, seen a blossoming of research and the starting of scientific journals. The way adolescence is negotiated between the young and his or her environment has become to be viewed as far reaching in its later consequences. Adolescence also has its sensitivities, not least for girls, who suffer set-backs which need to be understood. In Norway, adolescence has received some research attention by criminologists and sociologists, but considerably less by psychologists. In 1990 a cross-disciplinary research program was started to stimulate research. Central to this program was a longitudinal nationwide project with 12,000 youth, which is now nearing completion. Two of the contributors to this volume are active in this program. Its initiation stimulated the choice of personality development in adolescence as topic for the seminar. An additional reason was the hope to put together the proceedings in a volume by inviting internationally renowned researchers in the field to the conference and later asking them to contribute to the book, both for their excellence, but also to add a cross-cultural perspective. An offshoot of this effort was that one of these contributors (Jane Kroger) is now professor at the University of Tromsø.

Generally, this book is cross-cultural in nature. The chapters discuss research conducted with many different cultural groups: for example, Canadian, American, Japanese, Chinese and European. Although most of the writers are to some degree psychodynamically inclined, all agree that context effects, such as culture, family, peers, and the social as well as physical environment, are important for explaining and understanding personality development. We also all seemed to agree that we would like to meet again at such a seminar. Perhaps because we were a relatively small group (about 20 people), the atmosphere throughout the three days the seminar lasted was especially warm and conducive to genuine discussion and sharing of ideas as well as feelings and experiences. Another reason for the good atmosphere may be that we Norwegians appreciated and valued the presence of the three distinguished international speakers, Harold Grotevant, Jane Kroger, and James Marcia, all who had traveled very long distances to be with us.

In the chapters ahead, contributors address various issues and topics examined in a variety of nationalities, which we hope that both students and professionals will find useful for gaining greater insights into the complex processes of personality formation. The first three chapters consider primarily influences of the family context on identity, ego development, and moral orientation, stressing the interactional aspects of the parent–child relationship. In their extensive and informative chapter "Individuality and connectedness in adolescent development: review and prospects for research on identity, relationships, and context " (Chapter 1), Harold D. Grotevant and Catherine R. Cooper argue that central to all human relationships is the transactive interplay of the two dimensions of individuality and connectedness; such transactions influence both individual and relational development. Their developmental model assumes that security in the parent–adolescent relationship will be predictive of the adolescent's ability to explore his or her sense of identity and the future. Also, in their view, historical, cultural, and economical contexts have significant bearing on the nature of family processes and the development of identity. In this chapter the key approaches used and the findings from a study of 121 two-parent families with adolescents are described. Studies with several different cultural groups, such as Mexican, Chinese, Filipino, Vietnamese, Japanese and European, are also discussed. Grotevant and Cooper highlight methodological and conceptual advances and close with a description of new directions their work will be taking.

The importance of the parent–child relationship is further assessed by Anna L. von der Lippe (Chapter 2: "Are conflict and challenge sources of personality development? Ego development and family communication"). von der Lippe discusses the "optimal growth" hypothesis, that environmental challenge and conflict are potential contributors to personality development when they take place in a benign atmosphere. She reviews the research evidence and presents Norwegian data on family conflict resolution and ego development in late adolescent girls.

In Chapter 3 ("A narrative approach to the study of moral orientation in the family: tales of kindness and care") Michael W. Pratt, Mary Louise Arnold, and Susan M. Hilbers discuss Carol Gilligan's concept of the care voice and the role the family may play in its socialization, in particular highlighting recent narrative approaches to moral development. A longitudinal family study is then described which focuses on parents' stories about family socialization, and explores gender differences in these family narratives. The care voice of mothers appears closely linked to adolescents' own moral self-concepts. Pratt, Arnold, and Hilbers then provide some suggestions for future research, focusing on the complexity of usage of various moral voices within the family and across different contexts.

The next three chapters focus mainly on empirical data and on the influence of culture and social change. Torild Hammer (Chapter 4: "Social parameters in adolescent development: challenges to psychological research") argues that in psychological research on adolescence it is important to consider how a changing society affects the social conditions and opportunities for development during the adolescent years. Hammer describes and analyzes some important aspects of social change in the adolescent situation and living conditions during the last decade in Norway. An especially noteworthy change was increased differentiation in female career choice.

Lars Wichstrøm (Chapter 5: "Self-concept development during adolescence: do American truths hold for Norwegians?") considers the issue of self-perception and presents a study which surveyed a nationwide sample of more than 10,000 Norwegian adolescents (aged 13–19 years) using Susan Harter's Self-Perception Profile for Adolescents. Five topics related to self-concept development in adolescence were addressed: gender differences, age trends, differentiation of the self-concept during adolescence, the relative importance of self-concept domains for overall self-esteem, and finally, the effect of pubertal development. The results revealed gender differences in self-concept according to prevailing sex-role stereotypes. The gender difference in perceived physical appearance was particularly strong, with boys scoring much higher than girls. No gender differences were observed with respect to the impact of pubertal development. Adolescents who were particularly late in their pubertal development scored lower on all self-concept domains as compared to those who were on time or early. Wichstrøm notes that several of the findings are in conflict with results obtained in the USA and discusses the role of culture and context.

Within the area of developmental psychology, there is increasing interest in ethnic issues. In Chapter 6 ("Language and ethnic identity in indigenous adolescents"), Siv Kvernmo points out that language is salient to several aspects of ethnic group membership and ethnic identity. For indigenous people like the Sami, the contact with majority groups has been dominated by assimilation, a process which often leads to language shift and language death. Kvernmo presents a study examining the relationship between language and ethnic identity, a topic crucial to all aboriginal groups across the world. A significant relationship between ethnic identity (self-defined and ascribed) and mother tongue among Sami and Norwegian monolinguals and bilinguals was found. The results showed, however, that ethnic identity in these three linguistic groups of Sami adolescents is clearly associated with contexts which linguistically and culturally transfer and support Sami values, both at the family and community level. Another main finding indicated that language contexts which are supportive of Sami culture can provide ethnic identity to Sami adolescents without Sami language competence. Further investigations are needed to explore ethnic factors other than language and context which may provide a strong sense of ethnic group membership to aboriginal adolescents.

The final three chapters include life span perspectives with different, but closely related topics as main themes. Eva E. Aspaas Skoe (Chapter 7: "The ethic of care: issues in moral development") reviews Carol Gilligan's theory of the care ethic and recent research aimed at elucidating one of the most heated debates in psychology: gender differences in moral development. This chapter describes Skoe's increasingly used moral reasoning measure, the Ethic of Care Interview (ECI), which is based on Gilligan's (1982) theory, and provides an overview of studies with the ECI across the life span. The findings point to the importance of care-based morality for general human development, especially personality development. Skoe concludes that several variables, such as generational differences, cultural and family background, historical context, and stage or period in life, must be considered in addition to gender in understanding differences in moral development. Directions for future research are also outlined.

Jane Kroger (Chapter 8, "Adolescence as a second separation–individuation process: critical review of an object relations approach") provides a review and appraisal of contemporary theoretical and empirical efforts to elucidate intrapsychic and interpersonal dimensions of the adolescent separation–individuation process initially described by Blos (1967). Kroger also provides suggestions for conceptual refinements in theory and future research directions.

The last chapter is a most unique and creative piece of work by James E. Marcia (Chapter 9: "Peer Gynt's life cycle"). Using the literary figure of Peer Gynt (Henrik Ibsen's stage play), Erik Erikson's psychosocial stage theory of personality, and the research which has issued from it, are applied to analyze the life cycle. A special focus is on identity formation and part identities as they interweave with earlier and later developmental stages. Marcia introduces the verb "adolescing" to allow for continued identity reformulation throughout development. Peer is seen as a man who is ill-prepared by all earlier psychosocial stage resolutions to meet the next, except that he has achieved the first stage of basic trust, which gives him energy and charm. Ibsen has shown relentlessly in his play how each chance of redemption at significant turning points of development is wasted, leaving a person with only roles and appearances, with self absorption and despair. Yet, the play, and Marcia's chapter, end with a faint glimmer of hope.

The unifying theme in this book is that all of the chapters deal in various ways with the self–other relationship. Also, a common thread is the importance of examining the relevance of various contextual factors. Personality development involves a "sequential process that follows certain emotional, cognitive, social, and contextual changes, phases, and stages over time" (L'Abate, 1994, p. 55). The challenges to researchers in personality development include providing a more precise and differentiated specification of this sequential process and the factors that influence it across a variety of cultures, not least to identify factors that have transcultural significance. This book presents empirical data from several different nations, and comparisons made among countries show that it is vital to consider the wider context of culture. Only by pursuing such work will we come to understand the role of culture in personality formation.

ACKNOWLEDGMENTS

We thank the many individuals and organizations who helped making this volume become a reality. The University of Tromsø, the Norwegian Research Council's Program for Youth Research, and the Norwegian Research Council, Humanities and Social Sciences, all contributed generously with financial grants, providing researchers and students in Norway with opportunities for interchange with international scholars. The preparation for this book was also assisted by a Fulbright Fellowship and a Norwegian Research Council grant to Eva Skoe. Finally, we express our appreciation to the editors at Routledge who have assisted greatly in all phases of the production process.

BIBLIOGRAPHY

Block, J. (1971) *Lives Through Time*, Berkeley: Bancroft Books.
Blos, P. (1967) The second individuation process of adolescence, *Psychoanalytic Study of the Child*, 22: 162–6.
Eisenberg, N. (1995) Editor's introduction, in N. Eisenberg (ed.), *Social Development. Review of Personality and Social Psychology*, vol. 15, p. vii, Thousand Oaks: Sage.
Gilligan, C. (1982) *In a Different Voice: Psychological Theory and Women's Development*, Cambridge: Harvard University Press.
L'Abate, L. (1994) *A Theory of Personality Development*, New York: Wiley.

Part I
Family context

1 Individuality and connectedness in adolescent development[1]
Review and prospects for research on identity, relationships, and context

Harold D. Grotevant and Catherine R. Cooper

The overarching purpose of our program of research has been to understand the role of adolescents' experiences of individuality and connectedness in close relationships; the family experiences that facilitate children's, adolescents', and young adults' development of these qualities and other valued goals in their cultural communities; and the reciprocal linkages between such individual "outcomes," experiences in family and other relationships, and cultural and economic context. We view development across the life span as closely connected to culture and economic opportunities. In this chapter, we review our original theory and empirical work, then present three focal themes of our continuing work: identity, relationships, and cultural and economic context. In doing so we highlight conceptual, empirical, and methodological advances.

INDIVIDUALITY AND CONNECTEDNESS: THE CORE THEORY

Our work has focused on the interplay between individuality and connectedness in the ongoing mutual regulation involved in relationships. Rather than framing individuality and connectedness as mutually exclusive qualities, such as is common in discussions of individualism and collectivism, our model proposes that such transactions influence both individual and relational development, shaping attitudes, expectations, and skills in self and relational functioning within and beyond the family (Cooper, Grotevant, and Condon, 1983; Grotevant and Cooper, 1985, 1986).

Individuality refers to processes that reflect the distinctiveness of the self. Specifically, individuality is comprised of two dimensions: self-assertion, displaying one's own point of view and taking responsibility for communicating it clearly; and separateness, expression of the distinctiveness of oneself from others. Connectedness involves processes that link the self to others. It is comprised of two dimensions: permeability, expressing responsiveness to the views of others; and mutuality, expressing sensitivity and respect for others' views, especially in taking into account the other's viewpoint when expressing one's own. We view individuation as a property of a relationship that exhibits this interplay of individuality and connectedness, whereas others have used the term individuation to refer to an intrapsychic (Barnhill, 1979) or family systems quality (Beavers, 1976). (As we will discuss in this chapter, individuality and connectedness have been conceptualized and measured both in terms of face-to-face conversations as well as self-reported attitudes, for example, feelings of conflict and closeness.)

In our early research, analyses of the conversations of families of middle-income European American adolescents revealed that family communication reflecting the interplay of both individuality and connectedness was associated with adolescent identity development and role taking skill. These findings supported the model's first proposition, which hypothesized links between family processes and specific forms of adolescent competence. A second proposition of the model, known as the *continuity hypothesis*, is that children's and adolescents' experiences in family relationships regarding the interplay of individuality and connectedness are linked to attitudes and behavior beyond the family context.

Before we began our investigations, the research literature on family relationships was not organized in a way that directly helped us answer our questions. Sociological studies of families did not attend to the interior functioning or dynamics of families or to families' effects on children, but more typically focused on issues such as social class or the development of the family as a unit across time, as seen in the concept of the family life cycle. Although socialization models in psychology did address issues of parent–child relationships, these models were also limited. Most studies made assumptions that the direction of influence was unidirectional, from parent to child, and focused on attitudes (such as restrictiveness) or global qualities (such as warmth) rather than actual interaction. Many studies drew causal inferences from correlational data collected at one point in time, and many focused on limited child "outcomes," often cognitive outcomes such as IQ.

The longitudinal research of Diana Baumrind (for example, 1975, 1991) was pivotal in the development of our model. Her work shares elements of the "parenting styles" work described above but also sheds light on the interactive nature of parent–child relationships. In her longitudinal study of the development of instrumental competence (defined to include agency and social responsibility), she identified three now well-known styles of parenting: authoritarian, authoritative, and permissive. Although these qualities may appear to fit with the unidirectional approach to socialization, they contain an important difference. In both authoritarian and permissive parenting, control in relationships moves primarily in one direction. In the case of authoritarian parenting, it flows from parents to children; in the case of permissive parenting, it flows from children to parents. Both styles differ from authoritative parenting, which involves give-and-take between parents and children. Although the parents are assumed to be the primary socializing agents, authoritative parents listen to their children, recognize their individual and developmental characteristics, and see parenting as a two-way process. Within this style of parenting, then, are contained the important elements of assertiveness and responsiveness, both of which will be discussed in the context of individuality and connectedness in this chapter.

Several goals and related domains of previous research guided the development of our model and the empirical work to test it. First, we sought to develop a model that would draw clear theoretical linkages between family process and adolescent competence. Second, we wanted to observe family interaction, because the research literature had demonstrated that parental attitudes do not necessarily correspond to parental behaviors. Third, we were interested in the emerging literature on family process, especially in studies linking family communication patterns to outcomes of schizophrenia or other forms of psychopathology (for example, Mishler and Waxler, 1968). Fourth, we were influenced by sociolinguistic models of language and discourse, which focused on the interpersonal function of language and the ways in which participants collaborate in conversation (for example, Coulthard, 1977). Finally, we were influenced by the developmental work of James Youniss (1980; Youniss and Smollar, 1985), whose synthesis of the views of Piaget and Sullivan described how adolescence is a time marked by the renegotiation of parent–child relationships, at least in part because of the newly emerging cognitive abilities of adolescents.

Our work parallels research and theory on parent–infant attachment (for example, Hazen and Durrett, 1982; Sroufe, 1979), which has demonstrated that relationships with caregivers that offer infants secure attachments in the first year of life predict their abilities as toddlers to explore the physical and social environment away from these relationships and as older children to establish friendships with peers (Elicker *et al.*, 1992). Analogously, our model is based on the premise that security in adolescents' relationships with their parents will be most predictive of adolescents' abilities to explore their sense of self, identity, and the future. We did not intend our model to be viewed as an omnibus model that would apply to all aspects of family processes or adolescent developmental "outcomes." Rather, we have focused our attention on those processes in family interaction predicted to relate to adolescents' emerging sense of self, identity, and relationships.

Identity

Identity has traditionally referred to one's sense of coherence of personality and continuity over time; it is the meshing of personality with historical and situational context. Thus, the construct of identity stands at the interface of individual personality, social relationships, and external context, and has major implications for optimal adolescent development. Development of identity is a life-long process, characterized by cycles of exploration and consolidation as well as experiences of competence and vulnerability. Although this task has its roots in childhood, it takes on new dimensions in adolescence because of the confluence of physical, cognitive, and relational changes during this period. Identity development during adolescence is also important because it provides a foundation for adult psychosocial development and interpersonal relationships, and because difficulties in identity development have been associated with problematic behavior, such as substance use (Jones and Hartmann, 1988; Jones *et al.*, 1989) and sexual intercourse unprotected against the possibility of HIV infection (Hernandez and DiClemente, 1992).

Including the processes of exploration and commitment in the construct of identity necessitates an interactional perspective because these processes refer to a dynamic attunement of individual, relationships, and context. The possibility for reformulation of identity exists across the life span, because individual, relationship, and contextual changes occur (Graafsma *et al.*, 1994). Factors internal and external to individuals can facilitate or impede such reformulation, and such factors are the focus of our current and future work.

Although the relational nature of identity was not highlighted in early discussions of the concept, much has been written about this perspective in the past decade. Josselson expressed its importance well: "Although identity is, in part, distinct, differentiated selfhood, it is also an integration of relational contexts which profoundly shape, bound and limit, but also create opportunities for the emergent identity" (1994, p. 166).

In most discussions, occupational choice has been stressed as a fundamental component of identity exploration and commitment (Archer, 1994) and emblematic of the general sense of economic opportunity, free exploration of alternatives, and rational choice on which democratic ideologies rest (Bellah *et al.*, 1985). However, even when occupational opportunities are constrained by economic, political, cultural, racial, or gender issues, identity development is still important because it embodies a person's central values, definition of relationships with others, and conceptualization of one's connection with his or her community and social institutions.

In our recent work, we have expanded our consideration of the interplay between individual, relational and contextual forces in adolescent identity development. Grotevant (1987, 1992, 1993) has examined the process through which identity develops, and distinguished between those aspects of identity that are chosen (for example, one's occupation) and those that are assigned or involve less choice (for example, gender, ethnicity, adoptive status). The assigned components of identity contextualize those aspects over which adolescents and young adults have greater personal choice. Observable characteristics (such as gender or race) might place constraints (either real or perceived) on the array of opportunities available for an adolescent's exploration, for example, through racial discrimination or gender stereotyping (Grotevant and Cooper, 1988). Or less observable attributes (such as being an adopted person) might impose psychological constraints on choice. For example, adopted persons might feel they are "missing a crucial piece of the puzzle" because of lack of knowledge about their birthparents, and might find the process of identity development longer and more complex because of this additional set of issues to deal with. Grotevant (1992) proposed that linkages between assigned and chosen aspects of identity might be most intertwined developmentally when there is a direct interface between specific aspects of the two (for example, adoptive status might have little to do with religious or political values, but might have much to do with views about relationships); when the individual's assigned characteristics are undervalued by society; or when the adolescent's parents do not effectively match their communication about the assigned domain with what the adolescent is seeking to understand.

During late adolescence, exploration of possibilities for one's sense of identity is typical, at least in social niches that provide requisite opportunities. Cooper's research has complemented Grotevant's by investigating the roles of culture, ethnicity, immigration, schooling, and economic opportunity in adolescents' identity development and relationships (1988, 1994; Cooper and Cooper, 1992; Grotevant and Cooper, 1988). With a series of studies involving adolescents from African, Filipino, Chinese, Japanese, Mexican, Central American, Vietnamese, and European American descent as well as multiple-heritage youth, she has been examining both occupation and ethnic identity (Cooper, in preparation).

Linking identity development and family processes/relationships

In the first phase of our work (Grotevant and Cooper, 1985, 1986), we were especially interested in the links between family processes and adolescent identity exploration during the last year of secondary school in the USA, when such exploration is particularly important for those adolescents who anticipate educational and career opportunities. A sample of 121 two-parent, middle-class, European American families living in a mid-size city in Texas, each with a high school senior (average age 17.6 years), participated in the study. Each family was visited once in their home, and the adolescent also came for one visit to our lab for additional assessment. (Although the demographic homogeneity of this sample clarifies the interpretation of our findings by limiting the degree to which ethnic or social class differences might be operating, this homogeneity also limits generalization of the findings to other populations.)

Identity exploration was assessed in an individual interview with the target adolescent (Grotevant and Cooper, 1981). Questions were asked in the domains of occupational choice, religion, politics, friendships, dating, and gender roles; the degree of identity exploration in each domain was rated on a 4-point scale by trained coders; and the exploration ratings were summed across the six domains. This study focused on identity exploration rather than commitment or status, because commitments during late high school years are relatively transient and exploration is the theoretically more significant indicator of identity development at that time.

For this project, we devised a family interaction task (based on the work of Watzlawick, 1966) in which we asked family members (both parents, the target adolescent, and one sibling, if present) to talk together for 20 minutes in order to plan a two-week family vacation for which they had unlimited funds. Their task was to decide where they would go and what they would do on each of the 14 days. By designing the task in this way, we insured that there were multiple opportunities for decisions, that activating pre-existing family roles about particular kinds of expertise (for example, about cars) or money would be minimized; and that the adolescent's opportunity to participate would be maximized. This contrasts with the tasks involving a single decision that are often used to study family conflict (for more extensive discussion of these issues, see Grotevant and Cooper, 1986). The audiotape of the family interaction was transcribed verbatim, and the first 300 utterances of the transcript were coded according to the family discourse code (Condon, Cooper, and Grotevant, 1984). The frequency of each of 14 communication behaviors, tallied for the person speaking and the person spoken to, were computed. Although we attempted to characterize individuality and connectedness at the family level, we found significant variability in the expression of these qualities for specific dyads within the family; thus, most analyses focused on specific dyads.

In general, we found that adolescents rated higher in identity exploration came from families in which they had opportunities to express and develop their own points of view in a supportive environment. (These results controlled statistically for adolescents' levels of verbal ability and sociability.) Some gender differences also emerged, in that different patterns of parent–adolescent interaction were predictive of identity exploration for adolescent males and females. Sons higher in identity exploration showed assertiveness and separateness that was supported by their fathers' acknowledgment and willingness to let them step forward in the conversation. Daughters higher in identity exploration experienced more challenging from their parents. These patterns suggest that European American middle-income parents used different strategies to encourage agency in their children (although not necessarily consciously). Perhaps for sons, simple encouragement was all that was needed to support the assertiveness that they had associated with their masculine gender role expectations since childhood. Perhaps for daughters, some challenging or even abrasiveness on the part of their parents served to counteract the traditional feminine gender role pressures for them to express nurturance and connection but not assertiveness or conflict (Cooper and Grotevant, 1987).

However, adolescents scoring highest in exploration came from families in which they participated with at least one parent in interactions in which *both* individuality and connectedness exceeded the mean for the sample (Grotevant and Cooper, 1983). Negotiations in such families were marked by a sustained focus on identifying different viewpoints, disagreeing and arguing, as well as developing satisfactory resolution to disagreements. Negotiations in families of adolescents rated lower in identity exploration more typically involved individual suggestions chained together without coordination, and those in which one family member (usually a parent) elicited suggestions and imposed a solution unilaterally. From this study we now provide two examples of the link between family communication patterns and adolescent identity development, the first exemplifying individuation (that is, both individuality and connectedness), the second, a lack of such individuation.

Interactions in the family of the first adolescent, whom we shall call Carol, illustrate the relationship property of individuation in which both members of the relationship contribute individuality and connectedness. Her father's opening statement in the Family Interaction Task set the tone for the discussion: "I think probably what we all ought to do is decide the things that we want to do, each one of us individually. And, then maybe we'll be able to reconcile from that point . . . . Let's go ahead and take a few minutes to decide where we'd like to go and what we would like to do. And maybe we'll be able to work everything everybody wants to do in these fourteen days. Okay?" All three family members were active and involved; humor, candor, spontaneity, and vulnerability were all displayed. For example, Carol's mother commented: "I think we all have good imaginations." During her identity interview, Carol said, "I have a say but not a deciding vote in family decisions." A distinctive quality of her identity exploration was that she experienced her parents as providing room for her to explore beyond their own experiences. For example, she reported that both parents felt that religion had been forced on them as children, so they decided not to force it on her. Consequently, she had been able to explore several religions with her friends as possible alternatives for herself.

In contrast, Janet's family reflected non-individuated marital and parent–child relationships, marked by few disagreements, self-assertions that largely coincided with the family's point of view, and frequent expressions of connectedness. Janet disagreed with her father only once, and he never disagreed with her, whereas she was responsive to him 29 times, and he was responsive to her 10 times. Janet's low rating on identity exploration may reflect a lack of exploration of issues outside the consensual family beliefs. With regard to her career choice, Janet commented, "I'm having a hard time deciding what to do. It would be easier if they would tell me what to do, but of course I don't want that."

Issues of context and opportunity structure, institutions, culture

The first phase of our work left us with important unsettled questions. For example, we became increasingly aware of the limitations inherent in defining identity development in terms of exploration and choice within unlimited opportunity structures in which "a subjective sense of an invigorating sameness and continuity" results (Erikson, 1968, p. 19). In an overview of the issues of individual, relationship, and contextual interplay in identity development, we considered ways that "significant numbers of American children are growing up in contexts ascribed or at least seriously constrained as a function of their ethnicity, socioeconomic status (SES), or gender" and that these factors "may function as stimulus variables that act as elicitors of how others treat children and may thus override the impact of their distinctive individual characteristics such as ability, motivation, or potential" (Grotevant and Cooper, 1988, p. 247). Furthermore, we also believe it is essential to look not only at the stabilities in human development and developmental contexts, but also at instabilities in family life and economic status in order to understand adolescence. We now turn to these issues of identity, relationships, and opportunity structures. For each issue, we describe our more recent conceptual, methodological, and empirical work that has resulted in a revision of our original model and means of assessing both adolescents and their families.

NEW QUESTIONS OF IDENTITY, RELATIONSHIPS, AND CONTEXT

Identity and narrative coherence

Conceptual advances

The early identity status work, conducted in the late 1960s and 1970s, examined identity in the domains of occupation, religion, and political ideology, in keeping with Erikson's (1950) emphasis on the importance of work and ideology for human identity. Subsequent approaches to the empirical investigation of identity expanded the number of domains being investigated, in particular adding domains tapping interpersonal relationships (for example, Grotevant *et al.*, 1982); ethnicity (for example, Phinney, 1990; Phinney and Rosenthal, 1992), and potential conflict between domains, such as between work and family (for example, Archer, 1985). Several researchers also called for examining domains separately, since research had shown that one could have differing degrees of exploration and commitment in different domains. The result was that the conceptual and empirical work on identity became fragmented and the compelling issues of organization, integration, continuity, and consistency described by Erikson tended to be overlooked. Most domains of identity examined in the research literature were those over which individuals have at least some degree of control, such as occupation, ideologies, values, and relationships. However, there are others over which they exercise less choice, such as gender, race or ethnicity, sexual orientation, and adoptive status. The importance of each of these domains for understanding of the self is documented in extensive, yet largely separate, literatures. Grotevant's current work focuses on family processes and identity in adoptive families. A key question raised from prior research is how the experience of adoption is integrated into adolescents' overall identity: in what way is a coherent whole formed? To the degree that one accepts Erikson's argument that an important aspect of identity is continuity across past, present, and future, coming to terms with one's identity as an adopted person would play an important role in overall identity development. To quote one personal account: "I seem to have a compelling need to know my own story. It is a story that I should not be excluded from since it is at least partly mine, and it seems vaguely tragic and somehow unjust that it remains unknown to me" (Andersen, 1988, p. 18).

To understand how different domains of identity are linked to one another, particularly how those that are assigned, such as adoptive status, are related to those that are more freely chosen, Grotevant has turned to a narrative approach. This approach is receiving increasing attention within psychology, although its theoretical and methodological roots cross into other disciplines, especially linguistics, discourse analysis, and comparative literature. Narrative psychology currently focuses on such phenomena as identity formation (for example, Grotevant, 1992; McAdams, 1988), in which coherence of a person's life story is viewed as the benchmark for evaluating how well meaning and a sense of integrity are maintained over time (for example, Polkinghorne, 1991). McAdams was one of the first to link the narrative approach to identity: "The problem of identity is the problem of arriving at a life story that makes sense—provides unity and purpose—within a sociohistorical matrix that embodies a much larger story" (1988, p. 19).

The narrative approach is also being used by developmentalists who view reconstructed stories as keys to understanding current functioning. A central figure in this area is Mary Main, whose Adult

Attachment Interview (Main and Goldwyn, 1985) is used to assess adults' internal working models of their relationships with their parents. Another example of the narrative approach made newspaper headlines in the USA when John Gottman and his collaborators published findings showing that variables coded from an "Oral History Interview" conducted with married couples strongly predicted which couples would be divorced or still married 3 years later (Buehlman *et al.*, 1992).

One important criterion for evaluating the quality of a narrative is *coherence*, which describes how well the story "hangs together." More specifically, coherence addresses the issue of integration and provides a window for investigating how the different domains of identity are connected to one another. In a longitudinal follow-up study of 190 adoptive families with adolescents by Grotevant and McRoy (in progress), a narrative approach is being used to assess identity development in adopted adolescents. Two aspects of identity are of particular interest: how adolescents have made sense of their status of being adopted, and the interplay between adoptive status and other aspects of identity.

Methodological advances

A new approach to identity assessment has been sought because of limitations of the traditional identity status paradigm and the desire to examine integration of identity across domains. This approach stems from Grotevant's participation in the Family Story Collaborative Project (FSCP), with Barbara Fiese, Susan Dickstein, Deborah Fravel, Arnold Sameroff, and Fred Wamboldt, in which participants have developed the conceptual framework and methodological tools to address the issue of narrative coherence. Each participant has conducted research using interviews with family members or groups.

The purpose of the FSCP has been to examine processes by which both risk and resilience are transmitted across generations, particularly focusing on married adults, their families of origin, and their children. The FSCP is especially interested in "meaning-making," how individuals and couples construct meanings about events in their lives. The meanings embody interpretations of events and interactions and reflect their expectations about the future and about relationships in which they do or might participate. A primary goal is to illuminate how those constructed meanings shape subsequent interaction and outcomes, and how narratives about one's family (hereafter called *family narratives*) contribute to reduction of risks or enhancement of strengths passed from one generation to the next. Intergenerational continuity is viewed as a constructed transactional process rather than as a blueprint passed from one generation to the next. This constructive process involves how families come to interpret other family members' behavior, how individuals interpret their own experiences in the family, and how adults in committed relationships bring forth processes from their families of origin.

Project members have developed a series of rating scales to assess 4 aspects of narrative coherence: internal consistency, organization, congruence between affect and content, and flexibility. The *internal consistency* of the narrative reflects its completeness and may range from a "theory" that is well developed and integrated to one that has little rationale and is full of holes. The components of internally consistent narratives fit together in a sensible way, and specific examples are given to support the "theory." Narratives lower in internal consistency may include contradictions that are neither recognized nor explained. *Organization* refers to the respondent's management of the narrative, with particular attention to statements that convey information and how points are made. An organized narrative provides the listener with a sense of orientation or context, and referents (who, what, where); such narratives flow smoothly with completed thoughts and are direct and to the point. Poorly organized narratives may be full of starts and stops and may get off track without self-correcting. *Congruence between affect and content* assesses the "fit" between actions or thoughts described and the emotion expressed with regard to them. Narratives scored high in this dimension show a good match between descriptions of events or actions and corresponding emotions, both in the type of affect expressed and the level of intensity. *Flexibility* refers to the respondent's ability to explore new ideas and alternatives, their ability to view issues as they might be seen by others, and their recognizing more than one side to a story.

Trained raters evaluate an interview on each scale, assigning ratings from 1 to 5. To date, the rating scales have been applied to interviews conducted in four different projects, including Grotevant and McRoy's study on relationships in adoptive families. In that project, the four components of coherence were rated from the interviews individually administered to adoptive fathers and mothers. Although the interviews were not intended to assess identity, they did tap adoptive parents' philosophies about adoption, as questions focused on their experiences with adoption, their choices and decisions about the type of adoption they had, their relationships with their children and their children's birth family members, and their projections into the future.

The interviews conducted with adoptive parents of more open adoptions demonstrated greater narrative coherence in both individual and couple contexts and for both husbands and wives than the interviews of adoptive parents in confidential or mediated adoptions (Grotevant *et al.*, 1995). Furthermore, for both wives and husbands, coherence ratings made from their individual and couple interviews were moderately and positively correlated. However, spousal correlations on the coherence scales were generally higher for the couple interviews than for the individual interviews. It appears that the "jointness" of the couple interview contributed to greater spousal similarity in that setting. This was expected, given the volunteer nature of this non-clinical sample. Coherence ratings made from the conjoint couple interviews were highly correlated with ratings of the interaction itself. More coherence displayed by each partner in the conjoint narrative was related positively and significantly to the marital partners' greater confirmation of one another in the interview, greater collaborative style in their account, and more warm and inviting interaction with the interviewer. On the other hand, coherence ratings made from the individual interviews were moderately related to ratings of the interaction for wives, but not for husbands. This points to the stronger role that wives might play in setting the tone for the dyadic conversation, or at least to the stronger continuity that might exist between wives' behavior in individual and couple interviews. Differences between an individual's narrative coherence in the individual and couple interview contexts were examined as an aspect of the interaction. We assumed that greater coherence rated in the individual than in the couple interview indicated that the individual was being "pulled down" by the spouse when they were together and that such a situation would predict greater dissatisfaction with the marriage. This hypothesis was upheld for wives, but not for husbands. Finally, we predicted that spousal asymmetries in coherence within the couple interview would indicate that one partner was carrying the other partner conversationally or scaffolding his or her participation. Larger asymmetries were related behaviorally to lower couple co-construction, less confirmation of one spouse by the other, and greater marital dissatisfaction of the partner doing the carrying.

New questions

Now that these four components of narrative coherence in the adoptive parents have been defined and successfully assessed, the rating scales will be applied to the interviews of adopted adolescents to understand how they integrate their adoptive status into their broader sense of identity. We will be especially sensitive to developmental differences in coherence within adolescence because of the cognitive demands present in constructing narratives. Research questions in this program of work will probe the degree to which adoption affects other life decisions; whether there are gender differences in the role adoption plays in identity; whether assigned and chosen components of identity are interdependent; to what degree adolescents' ability to integrate adoption into their sense of identity is related to how well their adoptive parents have accepted the adoptive parenting role as part of their own identities; and whether adolescent adjustment and mental health are positively related to adolescents' ability to come to terms with being adopted, perhaps as indexed by degree of coherence of the interviews.

Issues of individuality and connectedness in relationships

As summarized above, a central finding of our early work on family communication and adolescent identity development was that family members' expressions of their points of view, as well as their disagreements, appeared predictive of adaptive identity exploration and relational skills in high school adolescents. In such interactions, adolescents could consider and integrate differing points of view, and family decisions were made through negotiation rather than by parents unilaterally imposing their solutions (Cooper, 1988). Cooper, together with Cindy Carlson and their students, extended this approach with families (like Grotevant and Cooper's earlier sample) living in central Texas, with early adolescents, including both one- and two-parent families (Carlson *et al.*, 1991; McDonough *et al.*, 1994). Several key findings emerged that enrich our understanding of developmental realignments during adolescence, particularly with regard to three key issues: the negotiation of individuality and connectedness within the family system, linkages between family and peer relationships, and developmental changes in individuality and connectedness from early to later adolescence.

Negotiation of individuality and connectedness in the family system

Does family members' communication play a role in their influence on family decisions? Guillot (1993) examined negotiation and power in the families of early adolescents by mapping the links between communication reflecting individuality and connectedness and the number of ideas in their planning of the vacation that were accepted by the family. Fathers wielded more power than either mothers or adolescents, and mothers more than adolescents. Fathers were also more efficient than either mothers or adolescents: that is, it required fewer suggestions for them to have an idea accepted by the family. Adolescents' power was positively associated with their assertiveness with fathers and with their mothers' connectedness to them, but negatively associated with mothers' disagreements.

How do alliances function in families of early adolescents? St. John *et al.* (1993) examined the disagreements between these early adolescents and their parents for patterns of alliances, or taking sides in disputes. Unlike the descriptions of coalitions in the literature on family structural therapy, the non-clinical families in this sample did not exhibit rigid alignments. Instead, they typified well-functioning families, whose members can shift alignments flexibly depending on the issue (Aponte, 1981). Alliances occurred in over half of the disagreements. Alliances between mothers and fathers were the most frequent. Family members took sides by supporting ideas more often than by opposing them. Fathers supported mothers' ideas more often in families with boys compared to families with girls. In families with sons, mothers were more likely than fathers to create a parental alliance by negating their son's ideas. Contrary to predictions, adolescents aligned themselves equally with mothers and fathers.

Links between family and peer relationships

What is the nature and extent of continuities and discontinuities between family and peer relationships? Models of linkages between adolescents' relationships with parents and peers once centered exclusively on their differences—how the two relational systems operate to compensate for one another's deficits, compete with one another for adolescents' loyalty, or contrast in the way power is distributed, with parent–adolescent relationships seen as asymmetrical and peers as egalitarian chums (Cooper and Cooper, 1992). Based on the core model of individuality and connectedness, Cooper and Carlson tested the proposition that adolescents' experiences of individuality and connectedness in the family affect both their individual and interpersonal competence. The model is based on a premise that psychological well-being is defined not simply in terms of autonomy or self reliance but on the capacity to differentiate a distinctive self while maintaining closeness with others.

For this reason, Cooper and Carlson assessed how family experiences might offer adolescents the capacities to express distinctive viewpoints while being able to sustain cohesion in peer relationships. Their research team conducted open-ended interviews in which adolescents gave descriptions of actual conflicts with their friends, their ratings of self and relational competence, and their responses to an analogue of Selman's Interpersonal Negotiation Strategies interview (Spradling *et al.*, 1989, cited in Cooper and Cooper, 1992). Adolescents who saw themselves as competent appeared able to integrate individuality and connectedness in a hypothetical dilemma with a peer by using negotiation strategies involving collaboration. For example, they were more likely to approach negotiating with a peer who wanted them to drink by declining the drink while offering face-saving remarks that retained connectedness with the friend, rather than using the popularized strategy of "just saying no". Those who evaluated themselves in less favorable terms said they would use unilateral strategies involving either submission or dominance with the peer. These findings provide evidence that linkages between self esteem and relational competence are expressed in the ability to coordinate self and other in collaborative conflict resolution.

Besides observing these adolescents in the vacation planning task with their parents, Cooper and Carlson also observed each of these adolescents in an analogous task with their closest friend, in which they planned a weekend together (with unlimited funds and full parental permission). With their friends, early adolescent boys and girls disagreed more openly than with parents, with whom they expressed more connectedness. These patterns are consistent with Piaget and Sullivan's portraits of the egalitarian nature of adolescents' relationships with their peers compared to parents (Cooper and Cooper, 1992). Despite these average differences between peer and family patterns, individual differences among adolescents in their negotiations with friends could be predicted by their family negotiation patterns. Those who coordinated individuality and connectedness with their peers could be seen as experiencing similar patterns in negotiations with their parents, particularly their fathers. Adolescents whose fathers provided more scaffolding showed fewer disagreements and more agreements with their friends than did adolescents whose fathers provided less scaffolding. These fathers were also more likely to agree with their daughters' suggestions and less likely to disagree with their daughters' suggestions than were fathers who provided less scaffolding. So connectedness in the family was associated with adolescents' connectedness with their peers, and inversely with their disagreements. These findings suggest that the origins of key qualities of peer relationships can be traced to family experience in adolescence.

Shifts in individuality and connectedness between early and later adolescence

Change and continuity at the level of relationships in the family can be seen in the interplay of individuality and connectedness in family negotiation from early to later adolescence (Cooper *et al.*, 1990). When we compared the families of sixth and twelfth grade European American adolescents who had all participated in the vacation planning task, we found that, compared with younger adolescents, parents negotiated with older adolescents, both males and females, in a more egalitarian manner, as seen in their expressions of compromises and agreements. In contrast, fathers typically prompted early adolescents' ideas with questions while mothers provided both task-oriented directives and acknowledgments. Older adolescent girls, compared to younger girls, expressed both more disagreements and more compromises with their fathers, indicating their greater ability to negotiate disagreements by coordinating and integrating perspectives.

Houchins (1991) looked more closely at developmental changes and continuities in the way that guidance was provided by the parents of older and younger adolescents in this task. She found that fathers of younger adolescents elicited their children's suggestions more often than fathers of older adolescents, stated more reasons for their decisions, offered more compromises incorporating their adolescents' suggestions, and rejected their adolescents' suggestions less often than did fathers of older adolescents. Older adolescents were likely to bring greater knowledge and more skills in making their views clear, which prepared them for more independent participation. Mothers' levels of elicitation of their adolescents' ideas were equal at the two age levels. This work demonstrates that change and continuities can both occur within the family system in guidance and negotiation.

Methodological advances

Just as our conceptual advances inspired methodological ones in the area of identity development, the same has happened with regard to assessment of individuality and connectedness. One limitation of frequency-based coding of family discourse is that higher scores on variables are achieved when specific utterances occur frequently; the importance of salient but rare events is not captured using this method, and we found it to be a limitation of relying solely on frequency data. To register both the frequency and salience of communication patterns, Bengtson and Grotevant (forthcoming) developed a

Q-sort for assessing individuality and connectedness in dyadic relationships. The measure includes 35 items selected on the basis of Cooper and Grotevant's conceptual and methodological work with individuation. Criterion Q-sorts for individuality and connectedness were developed from responses of eight expert raters; interrater reliability ranged from 0.73 to 0.93 for individuality and from 0.83 to 0.93 for connectedness. Evidence for construct validity has been obtained by linking Q-sort assessments of individuality and connectedness with the results of the microanalytic coding from families seen in Grotevant and Cooper's Family Process Project (Cooper *et al.*, 1983; Grotevant and Cooper, 1985).

Issues of context: culture and economic opportunity structure

American psychologists and educators have long considered autonomy and emancipation from parents as signs of adolescent maturity. They have also seen adolescent identity formation and career development as a process of exploration among relatively unrestricted opportunities. More recently, scholars have been critical of this failure to address issues of gender, ethnicity, and restrictions in opportunities, including those in schooling and work (Cooper *et al.*, 1995; Grotevant and Cooper, 1988).

Stability and change in cultural values of individuality and connectedness

Although adolescent maturity has often been defined in terms of individualistic qualities such as autonomy, independence, and initiative, many cultural traditions accord a central role to *familism*—norms of collective support, allegiance, and obligation. In such traditions, adolescents are expected to show support, respect, and reticence in the family, especially towards their fathers. Adolescents' academic or occupational achievement or failure brings pride or shame to the family as a whole rather than signifying autonomy or independence of the individual adolescent. Familistic values have been considered adaptive for ethnic minority families, especially under conditions of racism, immigration, or poverty. One key question concerns how such values continue or change within families as they immigrate to the USA, and across generations.

Cooper, Baker, Polichar, and Welsh (1994) assessed three issues involving familistic values and communication. First, they investigated whether adolescents with recent immigration experiences would endorse familistic values more than European American adolescents whose families had been in the USA for multiple generations (indicating continuity), yet less than their parents (indicating change). Cooper *et al.* also assessed whether immigrant youth were more likely to endorse norms of respect towards their parents, as compared to European descent adolescents, thereby making direct expression of assertions, disagreements, and disclosures less valued. Third, given these norms, the role of siblings as links to adolescents' peer relationships was examined.

Two distinctive methodological approaches were developed. Throughout the study, *focus group interviews* with adolescents from each participating cultural group were held to make instrument development, data analysis, and interpretations consistent with their experiences (Stewart and Shamdasani, 1990). To understand the expression of individuality and connectedness where norms of respect might make direct expressions of individuality rare, self-report methods were used rather than observations of face-to-face family conversations as in our earlier studies.

On the survey, the college students in the northern California sample described themselves with more than 30 ethnic terms. Findings presented here involve students in five cultural groups: those describing themselves as of Mexican, Vietnamese, Filipino, Chinese, and European descent. (The remaining adolescents included approximately 10 percent multiple-heritage youth.) Many were immigrants to the USA, including 27 percent of Mexican, 52 percent of Chinese, 50 percent of Filipino, and 84 percent of Vietnamese descent youth; 5 percent of European descent adolescents were immigrants.

Adolescents rated the degree to which they viewed a list of familistic values as held by themselves, their mothers, fathers, and maternal and paternal grandparents. This list, adapted from those used in studies of acculturation, assesses the extent to which families are seen as sources of support and obligation and as a reference group for decision-making (Sabogal *et al.*, 1987).

Adolescents from all five cultural groups strongly endorsed the statement, "Family members should make sacrifices to guarantee a good education for their children." However, Mexican, Chinese, Vietnamese, and Filipino descent adolescents endorsed values of mutual support among siblings as well as turning to parents and other relatives in making important decisions.

Intergenerational differences suggested both continuity and change, with some indication of distinctive patterns across the cultural groups. For example, in response to the statement, "Older siblings should help directly support other family members economically," Vietnamese and

Chinese descent adolescents reported sharing their parents' *strong* endorsements, European American adolescents reported sharing their parents' *weak* endorsements, and Filipino and Mexican descent adolescents endorsed this value *less* than their parents. Adolescents in all five groups saw their parents as holding stronger expectations for them to consider the family as a frame of reference in making decisions than they did.

Adolescents also characterized their communication of individuality and connectedness with parents, siblings, and friends, including how comfortable they felt discussing school, careers, cultural and ethnic heritage, and sexuality, dating, and marriage with each person. Within each cultural group, students reported more formal communication with fathers in contrast to more open communication and more negotiation with their mothers, siblings, and friends. For example, students in all five groups rated the statements "This person communicates openly with me about their feelings" and "I discuss my problems with this person" as less true with respect to their fathers than their mothers, siblings, or friends. They reported that their fathers "make most of the decisions in our relationship," particularly among Chinese, Filipino, and Vietnamese descent students.

We held focus groups with students from each cultural group to discuss these findings. Immigrant youth confirmed holding familistic values that they should turn to their families for advice on important decisions and that their relationships with their parents were marked by respect, formality, and reticence. Students elaborated that they might discuss topics involving school with their fathers but might withhold facts such as having changed their undergraduate major from pre-med to humanities or social science. For these more sensitive issues, peers played a special role in supporting identity exploration and the continuing development of family relationships.

The continuity and change in familistic values and the mutual interplay between adolescents' identity development, their relationships with family and friends, and the cultural and economic context of immigration is illustrated by this narrative of a Filipina college student we call Lourdes:

> I was with a single mother and I have one sister and it was really harsh . . . we basically did whatever she said, to keep the family alive . . . . We went through a lot of rough times in our childhood . . . . But in terms of family values (my mother) would encourage family first—since this is the family that is giving you support, you need to be loyal to it and respect authority . . . I grew

up with a lot of conflict with her, especially in my junior high and high school years . . . she wanted me to do really well in school but she didn't understand that those extra-curricular things you have to do to get into college mean taking you out of the home . . . I think because she was so much on her own, she knew what it took to survive and she wanted to make sure that I survived too . . . . There was a lot of pressure on us to make sure we do well. We are like representatives of this family. Right now my mom and I are really good friends and I think the reason is my awareness of her life . . . . She started listening to the things that I was agreeing with and I said, 'a lot of the things that I do is because of the values that you taught me . . . loyalty and respect for people, to be caring and giving.' So it's funny, . . . I've kind of impacted her now.

(Cooper, in preparation)

In our focus groups, students remarked that their informal conversations with peers involve the same topics as those addressed by our study. Lourdes observed, "My friends and I have these same conversations about what are we going to do about our lives. That's why we are involved with student groups. They really function as a way to talk about what is on young Asian and Pacific Islanders' minds and our future . . . I can talk to (my mother) about my career goals a little bit more now, but it definitely started with these people here because I don't think I could figure that out all by myself."

In sum, these findings regarding values and communication in adolescents' relationships with families and peers challenge traditional definitions of adolescent maturity in terms of autonomy from parents. College students of Chinese, Filipino, Mexican, and Vietnamese descent saw themselves and their parents as holding norms of reliance on family members for both support and guidance in decision making. Communication appeared more formal with fathers than mothers in all cultural groups, with hierarchical patterns especially evident within Asian American families, with change over time and generations towards more egalitarian patterns evident. Findings also indicate support for the hypothesis that when norms of respect render adolescents' relationships with parents more formal, sibling and peer relationships may play especially important roles in adolescents' lives.

Economic opportunity structure issues

It could be anticipated that constricting economic opportunities would have deleterious effects on identity exploration. For example, in New

Zealand between 1984 and 1990, Kroger (1993b) found increasing numbers of female college students whose identity development appeared foreclosed, showing low levels of exploration but high levels of commitment, and decreasing numbers of students rated as identity achievers, showing high levels of exploration followed by high levels of commitment. This difference, primarily marked by decreased exploration of choices, was observed for females only. Using evidence from intensive case studies, Kroger (1993a) also found that foreclosed individuals sometimes limit their own life contexts, that identity achievers stabilize their life contexts following exploration, and that those showing extensive exploration while delaying commitment (moratorium) expand their life contexts. Kroger's two studies demonstrate that opportunity structures clearly place limits on identity development, but also that individuals can create "personal contexts within their larger sociohistorical milieu that differ quite markedly" (Kroger, 1993a, p. 159). There may be an ongoing process in which decreased opportunities suppress exploration, even beyond the time when opportunities become more open.

On the other hand, Fordham and Ogbu (1986; Fordham, 1988) have argued that black adolescents, like members of other ethnic minority groups with histories of restricted access to educational and occupational institutional opportunities, may feel that success in such institutions requires them to develop a "raceless" persona that masks their ethnic identity. As Fordham and Ogbu write: "many of the successful students find themselves juggling their school and community personae in order to minimize the conflicts and anxieties generated by the need to interact with the various competing constituencies represented in the school context" (p. 80). Fordham and Ogbu also point to the tension of school success being defined in terms of integrity of the existing fictive kinship system in the black community.

Conditions that lead ethnic minority youth to define doing well in school as "acting white," or like a "banana," "Oreo cookie," "coconut," or "apple" (derogatory terms which connote appearing Asian, Black, Latino, or Native American, respectively, but having a "white" core identity) can stigmatize ethnic minority adolescents' exploration of their potential opportunities in school and work. Are these experiences inevitable? In the following sections we examine how adolescents, their relationships, and the institutional contexts in which they live can all play a part in reframing the meaning of challenges as resources.

Linking identity, relationships, culture, and opportunity structure: the multiple selves, multiple worlds framework

Our recent work supports a view of identity and opportunity structures in interaction, particularly as mediated by close relationships. One key feature of the economic opportunity structure studied in the USA and other nations is the "academic pipeline" through school to work, which has often been idealized as a smooth developmental pathway. Such a model may be particularly inappropriate for adolescents who encounter racial, economic, or political barriers to schooling and occupational choice. Educators are increasingly concerned that with each advancing cohort of students, the percentage of ethnic minority adolescents shrinks. Ironically, parents often have high educational and professional aspirations for their children, but those with little formal education may lack specific knowledge about schools and the resources available through them. Families with histories of immigration or minority status may lose confidence that schooling is accessible or even beneficial to their children. For these reasons youth and their families often benefit from others who can offer a bridge from the family to educational, occupational, and personal goals and resources. We now discuss three studies that exemplify our recent efforts to link identity with opportunity structures through the multiple selves, multiple worlds perspective and one study recently completed by a colleague that fits well with this perspective.

Multiple selves and multiple worlds of Latino and African American adolescents

Cooper *et al.* (1995) built on Phelan *et al.*'s (1991) concept of multiple worlds to explore the experiences of Latino and African American junior high school, high school, and college students in northern California who participate in university programs designed to link students' worlds of families, peers, school, college, and work. Seeking to learn about the experiences of these youth, we adapted anthropological research methods to develop a new assessment instrument that did not make assumptions about the nature of family relationships, social contexts or their interrelationships.

To learn about adolescents' worlds, the research team conducted focus group interviews with each age group. They asked such questions as: What are your main worlds? What things do you usually do in each world? Who are the main people in each of your worlds? What kind of person do people in each world expect you to be? What kind of person do you want to be? How do these people help you become what they want you to be? How do these worlds fit together for you? Which feel separate? Which feel as though they overlap? How does being your ethnicity and your gender affect your experiences in these worlds? As students sat around a table and ate snacks, they discussed each question and then drew and wrote about their worlds. On the basis of their answers, a questionnaire was developed to assess similarities and differences across age, gender, and ethnic groups as well as individual differences within groups. The following responses of junior high school students illustrate how focus groups were useful in formulating questions for the questionnaire.

Students discussed and drew the worlds in their lives, including families, countries of origin, friends' homes, churches, mosques, academic outreach programs, shopping malls, video arcades, clubs, and sports. Over half described more than one family world. They discussed and drew how some worlds fit together and others were in conflict or far apart, and how the academic outreach programs served as bridges across worlds. A number saw their schools and neighborhoods as worlds where people expected them to fail, become pregnant and leave school, or engage in delinquent activities. The outreach programs provided students with high academic expectations and moral goals to do "something good for your people," such as working in their communities and helping their siblings attend college.

In discussions related both to moving across worlds and through the "academic pipeline" from high school to college, two patterns stood out. First, students felt *gatekeeping* when teachers and counselors discouraged them from taking classes required for university admission or attempted to enroll them in non-college tracks. Students also described *brokering* across these barriers when families, program staff, teachers, siblings, and friends provided refuge from such experiences or spoke up for them at school. Staff in programs helped when parents were unable to persuade school officials, and conveyed their role as bridges between families and school as they told parents, "you can trust us with your kids."

In the context of these experiences, students developed a sense of their future by drawing on positive and negative role models and reflecting on their own role in helping themselves and causing themselves difficulties. They cited family and academically involved friends, the dropouts and arrests of peers and friends, and their own negative experiences as strengthening their determination to study hard to "prove the gatekeeper wrong." In addition, they anticipated working on behalf of their families and communities. As one Mexican

American male high school student recounted: "The most important experience for me did not even happen to me. It happened to my mother. She wanted to go to college and become a professional. She did not accomplish her dream because back then, women were born to be housewives, not professionals. Her parents did not pay for her education because of this" (Cooper, in preparation).

Multiple selves and multiple worlds of Japanese, Japanese American, and European American adolescents

A USA-Japan collaborative team of developmental psychologists adapted the multiple selves, multiple worlds framework and assessment to examine how Japanese, Japanese American, and European American adolescents differentiate and coordinate their sense of identity across their multiple worlds, particularly with regard to restrictions in opportunities related to gender and ethnicity (Cooper, Gjerde *et al.*, 1994; Gjerde and Cooper, 1992). For example, young women in Japan face dilemmas in their careers: although opportunities are mandated by an equal opportunity law, women are excluded from the professional tracks of many Japanese corporations. In the USA, Japanese American youth, like other children and grandchildren of immigrants, face challenges in defining their sense of identity in the face of conflicting expectations across the worlds of their more traditional parents and those of "mainstream" schools and peers, where they may encounter stereotyping. Although the "model minority" stereotype exists in the USA, whereby Asian American students are expected to excel in mathematics and science, discrimination also continues in employment opportunities (Takanishi, 1994). Multiple-heritage youth may face special difficulties in developing their sense of ethnic identity.

The research team adapted questions from both qualitative and quantitative versions of the multiple worlds survey of Cooper, Jackson *et al.* (1994). Student responses indicated similarities across the three cultural communities, with adolescents in all three groups emphasizing the importance of friendships and student organizations in helping them establish their sense of identity. Variability within cultures was found: females in each group saw their career opportunities as restricted because of gender more than males.

Evidence of differences across cultural groups was also found. Japanese Americans were most likely to report both restrictions of opportunity and advantages related to ethnicity, such as when "model minority" stereotypes motivated them to work hard. Some reported two separate worlds, one involving Japanese friends, family, and church, and the other, "American;" these students were angry that "people don't know the Japanese community exists." They felt frustration at the lack of role models and information about their cultural background, or reported not "feeling Japanese," yet others saw their worlds as connected and felt strong and stable Japanese American identities. They grew up in communities with Japanese schools and families involved in Japanese traditions and strengthened their sense of identity through friendships in Japanese college student organizations.

Multiple selves and multiple worlds of adopted adolescents

The multiple selves, multiple worlds framework is also being used to understand the experiences of adopted adolescents. Like young people from ethnic minority groups, adopted adolescents (of all ethnicities) have an "assigned" aspect of identity that ultimately must be woven into their sense of self. However, unlike adolescents of color, the adoptive background of an adolescent may or may not be known to others. The multiple selves multiple worlds framework perspective is worthwhile both for the study of adolescents of color and for adopted adolescents because it addresses issues of identity development in context. In what ways are adolescents' explorations of self supported or hindered by significant individuals or relationships in their lives?

In their longitudinal follow-up of these adopted adolescents, Grotevant and McRoy are using the revised identity interview of Grotevant and Cooper (1995). This protocol is based on Grotevant and Cooper's (1981) earlier modification of Marcia's original instrument and also incorporates the work by Cooper on multiple selves and multiple worlds (for example, Cooper, Jackson, Azmitia, Lopez, and Dunbar, 1994). Adopted adolescents are asked questions concerning occupational choices, religious or spiritual values, ideas about relationships, and how they have thought about adoption. They are also asked how adoption may or may not relate to each identity domain about which we inquire: to what degree do they "fit" or conflict with one another? In addition to probing adolescents' self-definition, the investigators ask about adolescents' self-defined social worlds, with whom they talk about being adopted, to what degree they feel positively or negatively about the way being adopted is connected to each of their worlds, and the role that such interactions play in their identity. These interviews will give us important new insights into the integration of the fact of one's being adopted into an overall sense of identity. The identity dilemma faced by adopted persons was clearly described by an adoptive father in the first wave of data collection in our study, who remarked:

> I keep thinking ever since the miniseries "Roots" was on that a lot of people are interested in their backgrounds and who they are. Especially adopted children, because people have a sense of who they are by who's around them. "If I'm not part of you, who am I part of? Where did I come from? What heritage do I have?" There's a lot of searching that way to normal people and normal children, natural children . . . . But in that way [having some information about themselves] the child will get to, will have something to tell them who they are. Not so much where they come from, but who they are.

Social networks of lesbian and bisexual young women in the coming-out process

In a recent investigation, Oswald (1994) interviewed six college-age young women who self-identified as lesbian or bisexual, as well as 25 of the family members and friends in their social networks. The study concerned how the primary subject's coming-out affected the relationships within their social network. The author concluded "that lesbian or bisexual identity is negotiated within the context of network and other relationships" (p. 180). Because her study included multiple members of each social network and multiple types of relationships, she was able to document the role of both supportive and rejecting relationships in identity development. A key conclusion from this research provides an important touchstone for our work and that of others on identity development: "Given what I have learned from this research, I am no longer willing to view coming-out as something that individuals do and then tell their families. Declaring and maintaining a bisexual or lesbian identity is an ongoing negotiation that is embedded within the events and relationships of every day life" (p. 181).

CONCLUSIONS

In this chapter, we have shown how our initial goal of understanding the link between the transactive interplay of individuality and connectedness in relationships and development of identity endures, but that our conceptual model and research methods have both undergone transformation. Our conceptual model has been expanded in order to take cultural context, particularly around issues of opportunity structures, into account. Likewise, our research methods have been elaborated in order to probe the nuances of identity, relationships, and cultural contexts more fully. In closing, we would like to emphasize three general points. First, our findings are consistent with the general view that identity develops over the life span as a process of active individual and social construction of meaning, linking the construction of individual narrative with relational negotiation. It does not involve a linear progression from exploration to commitment; rather, this negotiation is an ongoing process that involves significant complexity, particularly for adolescents who have "assigned" aspects of identity (such as ethnicity, adoptive status, sexual orientation) that are not seen as "mainstream." Future research needs to explore further the tensions between the quest for personal coherence and the inherent dialectic within the multiple selves and multiple identities of these young people.

A second theme is how relationships, including those within the family system and those involving peers, teachers, and other significant persons develop as children move through adolescence. Researchers have seldom tracked developmental change in relationships other than in the family. However, because the roles of friends, teachers, and others outside the family are so important in navigating opportunity structures over the years, understanding developmental changes in these relationships is important as well. Early work on adolescent development and the family was conducted with middle-class European American groups in a way that isolated the study of relationships and adolescent development from broader contexts. The insights generated by these studies and the continuing research focus on the family itself contributed to the oversimplified view that families alone determine the development course of their children's lives. Recent work, including our own, looks more centrally at what Bronfenbrenner (1979) called the *mesosystem*, the interface between family relationships and other contexts. For example, the issue of openness in adoption requires such a view, because the adopted child links two interacting microsystems: the family of rearing and the birth family.

The third theme is how opportunity structures in schooling, work and other politically—and economically—influenced institutions affect the experiences of identity development, inevitably involving complex interplays of challenges and resources, and the need to "make meaning" of them in a way that fosters a sense of resiliency. Examples include the availability of schooling, financial resources, or jobs; access to bridging institutions with specific missions (such as PFLAG

[Parents and Friends of Lesbians and Gays], or Korean Culture Camp, for children of Korean ancestry adopted into European American families); and legal issues such as immigration policy. A recurring issue in our own work and that of others concerns the barriers and bridges across family, peer, school, and other social worlds that must be navigated and negotiated by adolescents.

We have shown that the capacity to coordinate self and other in relationships is learned in the context of the family and appears to be carried into worlds beyond it. This can be seen in the roles of strong ties, including those involving parents, siblings and other kinship relationships, as well as those involving weaker ties with friends of a range of ethnic backgrounds and institutional agents such as teachers or counselors (Stanton-Salazar and Dornbusch, 1995). Future work will focus on the linkages across such strong and weak ties as adolescents navigate their pathways through opportunity structures and on how the process of making meaning helps adolescents and others in their lives reframe difficulties and foster their resiliency. In doing so, we join colleagues in the USA and other nations (for example, Abraham, 1986; Kashiwagi, 1992; Nurmi, 1994; Nurmi *et al.*, 1995; von der Lippe, Chapter 2) in our views of the importance of understanding these issues for the well-being of youth.

NOTE

1 An earlier version of this paper was presented at a conference on "Adolescence: Developmental Paths," held at the University of Tromsø, Norway, May 9–11, 1994. We gratefully acknowledge the sponsors whose funding has supported the various projects discussed in this paper: National Institute of Child Health and Human Development, the Hogg Foundation for Mental Health, the University Research Institute of the University of Texas at Austin, the William T. Grant Foundation, the Minnesota Agricultural Experiment Station, the Spencer Foundation, the Linguistic Minority Research Institute and the Pacific Rim Foundation of the University of California, the National Center for Research in Cultural Diversity and Second Language Learning of the US Office of Educational Research and Improvement, and the John D. and Catherine T. MacArthur Foundation. We thank Paul C. Rosenblatt for particularly insightful and helpful comments on an earlier draft of this chapter. Correspondence can be directed to either author: Harold D. Grotevant, Department of Family Social Science, University of Minnesota, 1985 Buford Avenue, St. Paul, MN 55108 USA [e-mail: HGROTEVANT@CHE2.CHE.UMN.EDU] or Catherine R. Cooper, Department of Psychology, University of California at Santa Cruz, Santa Cruz, CA 95064 USA [e-mail: CCOOPER@CATS.UCSC.EDU].

BIBLIOGRAPHY

Abraham, K.G. (1986) Ego-identity differences among Anglo-American and Mexican-American adolescents, *Journal of Adolescence*, 9: 151–66.

Andersen, R.S. (1988) Why adoptees search: motives and more, *Child Welfare*, 67: 15–19.

Aponte, H.J. (1981) Structural family therapy, in A.S. Gurman, and D.P. Kniskern (eds.), *Handbook of Family Therapy*, pp. 310–60, New York: Brunner/Mazel.

Archer, S.L. (1985) Identity and the choice of social roles, in A.S. Waterman (ed.), *Identity in Adolescence: Processes and Contents*, pp. 79–99, San Francisco: Jossey-Bass.

—— (1992) A feminist's approach to identity research, in G.R. Adams, T.P. Gullotta, and R. Montemayor (eds.), *Advances in Adolescent Development*, vol. 4, *Adolescent Identity Formation*, pp. 25–49, Newbury Park, CA: Sage.

Archer, S.L. (ed.) (1994) *Interventions for Adolescent Identity Development*, Thousand Oaks, CA: Sage.

Barnhill, L.R. (1979) Healthy family systems, *Family Coordinator*, 28: 94–100.

Baumrind, D. (1975) The contributions of the family to the development of competence in children, *Schizophrenia Bulletin*, 14: 12–37.

—— (1991) Effective parenting during the early adolescent transition, in P.E. Cowan, and E.M. Hetherington (eds.), *Family Transitions: Advances in Family Research*, vol. 2, pp. 111–63, Hillsdale: Erlbaum.

Beavers, W.R. (1976) A theoretical basis for family evaluation, in J.M. Lewis, W.R. Beavers, J.T. Gossett, and V.A. Phillips, *No Single Thread: Psychological Health in Family Systems*, pp. 46–82, New York: Brunner/Mazel.

Bellah, R.N., Madsen, R., Sullivan, W.M., Swidler, A., and Tipton, S.M. (1985) *Habits of the Heart: Individualism and Commitment in American Life*, Berkeley: University of California Press.

Bengtson, P., and Grotevant, H.D. (forthcoming) The Dyadic Relationship Q-Sort: A Measure for Assessing Individuality and Connectedness in Dyadic Relationships, *Personal Relationships*.

Bronfenbrenner, U. (1979) *The Ecology of Human Development,* Cambridge: Harvard University Press.

Buehlman, K.T., Gottman, J.M., and Katz, L.F. (1992) How a couple views their past predicts their future: predicting divorce from an oral history interview, *Journal of Family Psychology*, 5: 295–318.

Carlson, C.I., Cooper, C.R., and Spradling, V. (1991) Developmental implications of shared vs. distinct perceptions of the family in early adolescence, in R. Paikoff (ed.), *Shared Perspectives on the Family: New Directions for Child Development*, 51, pp. 13–31, San Francisco: Jossey-Bass.

Condon, S.L., Cooper, C.R., and Grotevant, H.D. (1984) Manual for the analysis of family discourse, *Psychological Documents*, 14, 2616.

Cooper, C.R. (1988) The analysis of conflict in adolescent-parent relationships, in M.R. Gunnar and W.A. Collins (eds.), *21st Minnesota Symposium on Child Psychology: Development During the Transition to Adolescence*, pp. 181–7, Hillsdale: Erlbaum.

—— (1994) Cultural perspectives on continuity and change in adolescents' relationships, in R. Montemayor, G.R. Adams, and T.P. Gullotta (eds.),

Advances in Adolescent Development, vol. 6, *Personal Relationships during Adolescence*, pp. 78–100, Newbury Park, CA: Sage.

——— (forthcoming) Cultural perspectives on individuality and connectedness in adolescent development, in C. Nelson and A. Masten (eds.), *Minnesota Symposium on Child Psychology: Culture and Development*, Hillsdale: Erlbaum.

Cooper, C.R., Baker, H., Polichar, D., and Welsh, M. (1994) Values and communication of Chinese, European, Filipino, Mexican, and Vietnamese American adolescents with their families and friends, in S. Shulman, and W.A. Collins (eds.), *The Role of Fathers in Adolescent Development: New Directions in Child Development*, pp. 73–89, San Francisco: Jossey-Bass.

Cooper, C.R., Carlson, C.I., Grotevant, H.D., Guillot, S., and Keller, J. (1990) *Shifts in Family Discourse from Early to Late Adolescence: Age and Gender Patterns*, paper presented at National Institute of Mental Health Family Research Consortium Summer Institute, Monterrey.

Cooper, C.R., and Cooper, R.G. (1992). Links between adolescents' relationships with their parents and peers: models, evidence, and mechanisms, in R.D. Parke and G.W. Ladd (eds.), *Family-Peer Relationships: Modes of Linkages*, pp. 135–58, Hillsdale: Erlbaum.

Cooper, C.R., Gjerde, P.F., Teranishi, C., Onishi, M., Kosawa, Y, Shimizu, H., and Suzuki, O. (1994) *Multiple Worlds of Adolescent Competence in Japan and the U.S.: Between- and Within-Cultural Analyses*, paper presented at Western Psychological Association, Kona.

Cooper, C.R., and Grotevant, H.D. (1987) Gender issues in the interface of family experience and adolescent peer relational identity, *Journal of Youth and Adolescence*, 16, 247–64.

Cooper, C.R., Grotevant, H.D., and Condon, S.L. (1983) Individuality and connectedness in the family as a context for adolescent identity formation and role-taking skill, in H.D. Grotevant, and C.R. Cooper (eds.), *Adolescent Development in the Family: New Directions in Child Development*, no. 22., pp. 43–59, San Francisco: Jossey-Bass.

Cooper, C.R., Jackson, J.F., Azmitia, M., and Lopez, E.M. (forthcoming) Multiple selves, multiple worlds: ethnically sensitive research on identity, relationships, and opportunity structures in adolescence, in V. McLoyd, and L. Steinberg (eds.), *Conceptual and Methodological Issues in the Study of Minority Adolescents and their Families*, Hillsdale: Erlbaum.

Cooper, C.R., Jackson, J.F., Azmitia, M., Lopez, E.M., and Dunbar, N. (1994) *Multiple Selves, Multiple Worlds Survey: Qualitative and Quantitative Versions*, Santa Cruz: University of California at Santa Cruz.

——— (1995) Bridging students' multiple worlds: African American and Latino youth in academic outreach programs, in R.F. Macias, and R.G. Garcia Ramos (eds.), *Changing Schools for Changing Students: An Anthology of Research on Language Minorities*, pp. 211–34, Santa Barbara: University of California Linguistic Minority Research Institute.

Cooper, C.R., Teranishi, C., Gjerde, P.F., and Onishi, M. (1994, April) *Antecedents of Competence in Early and Late Adolescence: An Ecocultural Analysis of Japanese, Japanese American, and European American Adolescents*, paper presented at the meeting of the Western Psychological Association, Kona.

Coulthard, M. (1977) *An Introduction to Discourse Analysis*, Essex: Longman House.

Elicker, J., Englund, M., and Sroufe, L.A. (1992) Predicting peer competence and peer relationships in childhood from early parent–child relationships, in R.D. Parke, and G.W. Ladd (eds.), *Family-Peer Relationships: Models of Linkages*, pp. 77–106, Hillsdale: Erlbaum.

Erikson, E.H. (1950) *Childhood and Society*, New York: Norton.

—— (1968) *Identity: Youth and Crisis*, New York: Norton.

Fordham, S. (1988) Racelessness as a factor in Black students' school success: pragmatic strategy or Pyrrhic victory?, *Harvard Educational Review*, 58: 54–84.

Fordham, S., and Ogbu, J.U. (1986) Black students' school success: coping with the "burden of acting White," *The Urban Review*, 18: 176–206.

Gjerde, P.F., and Cooper, C.R. (1992) *Family Influences on Adolescent Competence in Japan and the U.S.: Between- and Within-Cultural Analyses of Ecocultural Niches*, University of California Pacific Rim Research Program.

Graafsma, T.L.G., Bosma, H.A., Grotevant, H.D., and deLevita, D.J. (1994) Identity and development: an interdisciplinary view, in H.A. Bosma, T.L.G. Graafsma, H.D. Grotevant, and D.J. deLevita (eds.), *Identity and Development: An Interdisciplinary Approach*, pp. 159–74, Thousand Oaks: Sage.

Grotevant, H.D. (1987) Toward a process model of identity formation, *Journal of Adolescent Research*, 2: 203–22.

—— (1992) Assigned and chosen identity components: A process perspective on their integration, in G.R. Adams, T.P. Gullotta, and R. Montemayor (eds.), *Advances in Adolescent Development*, vol. 4, *Adolescent Identity Formation*, pp. 73–90, Newbury Park: Sage.

—— (1993) The integrative nature of identity: bringing the soloists to sing in the choir, in J. Kroger (ed.), *Discussions on Ego Identity*, pp. 121–46, Hillsdale: Erlbaum.

Grotevant, H.D., and Cooper, C.R. (1981) Assessing adolescent identity in the areas of occupation, religion, politics, friendships, dating, and sex roles: manual for administration and coding of the interview, *JSAS Catalog of Selected Documents in Psychology*, 11, 52, ms. no. 2295.

—— (1983, April) *The Role of Family Communication Patterns in Adolescent Identity and Role Taking*, paper presented at the meeting of the Society for Research in Child Development, Detroit.

—— (1985) Patterns of interaction in family relationships and the development of identity exploration, *Child Development*, 56: 415–28.

—— (1986) Individuation in family relationships: a perspective on individual differences in the development of identity and role-taking skill in adolescence, *Human Development*, 29: 82–100.

—— (1988) The role of family experience in career exploration during adolescence, in P.B. Baltes, D.L. Featherman, and R.M. Lerner (eds.), *Life-Span Development and Behavior*, vol. 8, pp. 231–58, Hillsdale: Erlbaum.

—— (1995) *Interview for Adopted Adolescents*, unpublished manuscript, University of Minnesota.

Grotevant, H.D., Fravel, D.L., Gorall, D., and Piper, J. (1995, April) *Narrative Coherence in Interviews of Adoptive Parents: Couple and Individual*

Perspectives, in B.H. Fiese (organizer), *A Multidimensional View of Family Narratives: Coherence, Interaction Style, and Beliefs*, Symposium presented at the meeting of the Society for Research in Child Development, Indianapolis.

Grotevant, H.D., and McRoy, R.G. (1995) *Adoptive Families: Longitudinal Outcomes for Adolescents*, unpublished grant application, funded by the William T. Grant Foundation, University of Minnesota.

Grotevant, H.D., Thorbecke, W.L., and Meyer, M.L. (1982) An extension of Marcia's identity status interview into the interpersonal domain, *Journal of Youth and Adolescence*, 11: 33–47.

Guillot, S. (1993) *Patterns of Power Negotiation in the Families of Early Adolescents*, unpublished doctoral dissertation, University of Texas at Austin.

Hazen, N.L., and Durrett, M.E. (1982) Relationship of security of attachment to exploration and cognitive mapping abilities in 2-year-olds, *Developmental Psychology*, 18: 751–59.

Hernandez, J.T., and DiClemente, R.J. (1992) Self control and ego identity development as predictors of unprotected sex in late adolescent males, *Journal of Adolescence*, 15: 437–47.

Houchins, S.C. (1991) *Parental Scaffolding of Early Adolescents' Interpersonal Negotiation Skills*, unpublished dissertation, University of Texas at Austin.

Jones, R.M., and Hartmann, B.R. (1988) Ego identity: developmental differences and experimental substance use among adolescents, *Journal of Adolescence*, 11: 347–60.

Jones, R.M., Hartmann, B.R., Grochowski, C.O., and Glider, P. (1989) Ego identity and substance abuse: a comparison of adolescents in residential treatment with adolescents in school, *Personality and Individual Differences*, 10: 625–31.

Josselson, R. (1994) Identity and relatedness in the life cycle, in H.A. Bosma, T.L.G. Graafsma, H.D. Grotevant, and D.J. deLevita (eds.), *Identity and Development: An Interdisciplinary Approach*, pp. 81–102, Thousand Oaks: Sage.

Kashiwagi, K. (1992) *The Developmental Psychology of Fathers*, unpublished manuscript, University of California at Santa Cruz.

Kroger, J. (1993a) Identity and context: how the identity statuses choose their match, in R. Josselson, and A. Lieblich (eds.), *The Narrative Study of Lives*, vol. 1, pp. 130–62, Newbury Park: Sage.

—— (1993b) The role of historical context in the adolescent identity formation process, *Youth and Society*, 24: 363–76.

Main, M., and Goldwyn, R. (1985) *An Adult Attachment Classification and Rating System*, unpublished manuscript, University of California at Berkeley.

McAdams, D.P. (1988) *Power, Intimacy, and the Life Story: Personological Inquiries into Identity*, New York: Guilford.

McDonough, M., Carlson, C., and Cooper, C.R. (1994) Individuated marital relationships and the regulation of affect in families of early adolescents, *Journal of Adolescent Research*, 9: 67–87.

Mishler, E,G., and Waxler, N.E. (1968) *Interaction in Families: An Experimental Study of Family Processes and Schizophrenia*, New York: Wiley.

Nurmi, J.-E. (1994) Development and self-definition in age-graded sociocultural environments, in J.J.F. ter Laak, P.G. Heymans, and A. I. Padol'skij (eds.), *Developmental Tasks: Towards a Cultural Analysis of Human Development*, Dordrecht and Boston: Kluwer Academic.

Nurmi, J.-E., Poole, M.E., and Seginer, R. (1995) Tracks and transitions: a comparison of adolescent future-oriented goals, explorations, and commitments in Australia, Israel, and Finland, *International Journal of Psychology*, 30: 355–75.

Oswald, R.F. (1994) *Young Bisexual and Lesbian Women Coming-Out: A Qualitative Investigation of Social Networks*, unpublished master's thesis, Department of Family Social Science, University of Minnesota.

Phelan, P., Davidson, A.L., and Cao, H.T. (1991) Students' multiple worlds: navigating the borders of family, peer, and school cultures, in P. Phelan, P., and A.L. Davidson (eds.) *Cultural Diversity: Implications for Education*, New York: Teachers College Press.

Phinney, J. (1990) Ethnic Identity in Adolescents and Adults: A Review of Research, *Psychological Bulletin*, 180: 499–514.

Phinney, J., and Rosenthal, D.A. (1992) Ethnic identity in adolescence: process, context, and outcome, in G.R. Adams, T.P. Gullotta, and R. Montemayor (eds.), *Advances in Adolescent Development*, vol. 4, *Adolescent Identity Formation*, pp. 145–72, Newbury Park: Sage.

Phinney, J.S. (1993) Multiple group identities: differentiation, conflict, and integration, in J. Kroger (ed.), *Discussions on Ego Identity*, Hillsdale: Erlbaum.

Polkinghorne, D.E. (1991) Narrative and self-concept, *Journal of Narrative and Life History*, 1 (2 and 3): 135–53.

Sabogal, F., Marin, G., Otero-Sabogal, R., Marin, B.V., and Perez-Stable, E.J. (1987) Hispanic familism and acculturation: what changes and what doesn't? *Hispanic Journal of Behavioral Sciences*, 9: 397–412.

St. John, L., Koch, P., and Carlson, C.I., (1993, March) *Alliance Patterns among Early Adolescents and their Parents*, paper presented at the meeting of the Society for Research in Child Development, New Orleans.

Sroufe, L.A. (1979) The coherence of individual development, *American Psychologist*, 34: 834–41.

Stanton-Salazar, R.D., and Dornbusch, S.M. (1995) Social capital and the reproduction of inequality: information networks among Mexican-origin high school students, *Sociology of Education*, 68: 116–135.

Stewart, E.W., and Shamdasani, P.N. (1990) *Focus Groups: Theory and Practice.* Newbury Park: Sage.

Takanishi, R. (1994) Continuities and discontinuities in the cognitive socialization of Asian-originated children, in P. Greenfield and R.R. Cocking (eds.), *Cross-Cultural Roots of Minority Child Development*, pp. 351–62, Hillsdale: Erlbaum.

Trueba, H.T. (1991) Linkages of macro-micro analytical levels, *The Journal of Psychohistory*, 18: 457–68.

Watzlawick, P. (1966) A structured family interview, *Family Process*, 5: 256–71.

Werrbach, G.B., Grotevant, H.D., and Cooper, C.R. (1990) Gender differences in adolescents' identity development in the domain of sex role concepts, *Sex Roles*, 23: 349–62.

—— (1992) Patterns of family interaction and adolescent sex role concepts, *Journal of Youth and Adolescence*, 21: 609–23.

Youniss, J. (1980) *Parents and Peers in Social Development: A Sullivan-Piaget perspective*, Chicago: University of Chicago Press.

Youniss, J., and Smollar, J. (1985) *Adolescent Relations with Mothers, Fathers, and Friends*, Chicago: University of Chicago Press.

2 Are conflict and challenge sourc~ of personality development?

Ego development and family communic~

Anna Louise von der Lippe

The family as an arena for development of ego functions in the offspring is widely accepted. Several studies seem to confirm that the way parents interact with their offspring and how they handle conflict have important consequences for the internalization of ego structures in the offspring (Bell and Bell, 1983; Grotevant and Cooper, 1985; Lamborn *et al.*, 1991; Hauser *et al.*, 1984; Hauser *et al.*, 1987; White *et al.*, 1983). The family also continues to exert influence on the young throughout the adolescent period (Smollar and Youniss, 1989).

Conflict and conflict resolution within the family is of daily concern to clinicians, because pathological families are characterized by unsuccessful problem-solving strategies such as denial or displacement of conflicts, withdrawal, rigidity of solutions, repetitive fighting or more severe forms of communication deviance (Bateson, 1985; Singer and Wynne, 1963). The relationship between severe psychopathology and communication deviance has been empirically demonstrated (Goldstein, 1988; Riskin and Faunce, 1970). Absence of family conflict, on the other hand, does not seem to characterize families who foster mature development in their children, especially in girls. A positive relationship between personality development and interpersonal conflict in girls has been noted earlier (for example, Gilligan, 1993). In a longitudinal study of social and cognitive development, Block *et al.* (1986) found that the genders reacted differently to parental divorce and amount of change in the family. Girls at the inception of puberty (11 years) who had experienced large amounts of negative change were resourceful, social in orientation and well functioning. Boys who had experienced object loss, on the other hand, showed numerous neurotic traits not shown by girls. Werner and Smith (1982) concluded from their Hawaiian study of risk and protective factors that girls coped better with risk factors during childhood than boys. These observed relationships contrast with some findings that ego-functions in offspring, like interpersonal incompetence, are associated with observed marital conflict in the parents (Gottman and Katz, 1989; Long *et al.*, 1987). Different levels of conflict may have been observed in the two studies, having different impact on the children.

The findings from the studies cited may be viewed within an optimal challenge–optimal growth hypothesis forwarded by Garmecy, Masten and Tellegen (1984) and Baumrind (1991), and echoed in the "optimal frustration" hypothesis of ego psychology (Blanck and Blanck, 1974). Presence of conflicts may be a challenge to development, the effects of which will depend on their magnitude, their resolution, and particularly on the emotional context in which they are resolved. A similar optimalization hypothesis has been followed up by Allen *et al.* (1994) in the Harvard longitudinal study on family communication and ego development. Hauser and collaborators have related family communication and ego development over a two-year period in young adolescents (Hauser *et al.*, 1984, 1991).

Stierlin (1969), in his works on conflict and reconciliation in interpersonal relationships, described the dialogical relationship as characterized by mutuality, the ability to see the other person as subject *and* the possibility of confrontation. Conflict confrontation may be an aspect of a mature relationship, and its constructive handling presupposes affiliation and a regard for the right of the other to remain a subject in the dialogue. Similarly, disqualifying cognitive communications may be disruptive to self definitions within a downgrading relationship, but not within an essentially affiliative relationship (Dodge and Murphy, 1984; Wickstrøm *et al.*, 1993). Walker and Taylor (1991) have suggested a similar parental interaction pattern for the development of moral reasoning. They found that high levels of conflict between parents and offspring predicted advances in the development of moral reasoning, but only in the context of supportive interactions.

Dyadic relationships in the family also appear to have different meanings depending on the participants (Gjerde, 1986; Youniss and Ketterlinus, 1987). Steinberg (1987) found that negotiation of role relationships with the mother was especially salient for the pubertal boy's development. In light of the literature, recent Norwegian studies (von der Lippe and Amundsen, 1997; von der Lippe and Møller, 1997; Ringdal and Stenberg, 1997) raised the question whether adolescent girls who have reached higher levels of ego development also have families who negotiate conflicts in identifiable ways that set them apart from girls at lower levels of development. Furthermore, these studies sought to identify some of the characteristics of dyadic family communications associated with different levels of conflict negotiation.

EGO DEVELOPMENT AND INFLUENCING FACTORS

Ego development as conceptualized by Jane Loevinger (1976) is one of the more comprehensive constructs in developmental theories of personality. In her theory, the ego is a cognitively based structure of meanings (Noam, 1993), and ego development is thought to be characterized by increasing degrees of differentiation, complexity and integration in several domains of personality. The ego is considered by Loevinger a "master trait" of personality and includes interpersonal and cognitive development as they are also represented in the preoccupations of consciousness. The construct has not grown out of and indeed has an ambiguous relationship to psychodynamic theory (Blasi, 1989). Nevertheless, it has some of the same properties as the analytic construct of the ego's synthesizing ability. This is considered the meta-function that seeks and creates meaning by integrating experience at different levels of developmental maturity, according to the maturity of other functions. Hauser (1976) defined the ego as: "the *framework* of meaning that the individual imposes on his or her experience." Loevinger said about her concept:

> I am convinced that the self, I or me is in some sense real, not created by our definition. My purpose is to comprehend the way the person navigates through life, not to create artificially demarcated entities (self, ego, I, me) . . . . What I have called ego development is I believe, the closest we can come at present to tracing the developmental sequences of the self, or major aspects of it.
>
> (Loevinger, 1984, p. 50)

Loevinger's conceptualization draws on several theories that deal with the developments of self, morality and cognition. Common to them all is that they focus on the meaning aspect in development and see development as hierarchic, stepwise, qualitative, and passing through invariant stages, each stage organizing personality in recognizable ways. It is related to age, but not defined by age. The rate of development can vary and after 14 years of age, large variations in ego level will be found in age-cohorts (Redmore and Loevinger, 1979).

The construct of ego development is theoretically unrelated to psychopathology, although different forms of psychopathology are expected to accrue from the different stages of development (McCrae and Costa, 1980, 1983). Particular aspects of ego development will surface in salience during certain periods of development, and then recede in importance. An example is impulse control, which shows a curvilinear relationship to development. Ego development is both a developmental sequence and a dimension of individual differences within an age-group (Loevinger, 1976). Although this is a stage theory, development is still conceptualized as continuous with regard to increasing differentiation and complexity in the structure of meaning and the structure of character.

Loevinger measures ego development through the Washington University Sentence Completion Test (WUSCT) from which maturity in meaning interpretations are coded (Loevinger and Wessler, 1970). There are seven stage sequences and three transitional stages. In later works, one transitional stage has been dropped and the two remaining are now defined as real stages. One transitional stage between conformity and conscientiousness (the self-aware stage) has been shown to be the modal level in the adult population in a number of studies, both in the USA and in Norway (for example, Holt, 1980; Lee and Snarey, 1988; von der Lippe, 1986; Redmore and Loevinger, 1979). In its current form the stages are called the *presocial* (not measurable); the *impulsive* (E2); the *self-protective* (E3); the *conformist* (E4); the *self-aware* (E5); the *conscientious* (E6); the *individualistic* (E7); the *autonomous* (E8); and the *integrated* (E9) levels.

Empirically, ego level as measured by WUSCT has been found to be positively related to psychosocial maturity, defined by Erikson's stages of identity, intimacy, and generativity (Vaillant and McCulloch, 1987), and to openness to experience, an aspect of creativity (McCrae and Costa, 1980); it was not related to mental health, psychopathology or maturity of defenses in normal samples (Helson and Wink, 1987; McCrae and Costa, 1983; Vaillant and McCulloch, 1987). Westenburg and Block (1993), in a study of the relationship between ego development and broad personality variables, showed that for 14-year-olds, and later when they were 23 years of age, ego resilience (psychological mindedness, intellectualism, and resilience) and interpersonal integrity (morality, and interpersonal intimacy) increased with increasing ego development. Lee and Snarey (1988) found in a meta-analysis support for a positive relationship between ethic of justice and ego development, whereas Skoe and von der Lippe (1997) found support for a strong positive relationship between ethic of care and ego development.

Ego development has been found to be positively related to active resourcefulness in the parents (von der Lippe, 1986). The mother's child-rearing emphases on independence and conflict tolerance predicted higher ego levels, whereas moderate responsiveness to the child was more predictive than strong responsiveness. The mothers of high ego-level girls seemed to foster autonomy and avoid oversocialization of the child, thereby avoiding the danger of repressive enmeshment and mutual oversensitivity which are seen to characterize a number of mother–daughter relationships (Hoffman, 1977).

Cognitive complexity in high ego-level women may play a role in the way they describe individuals close to them. Complex individuals describe themselves and their relatives in more conflicted, paradoxical, unconventional, and less flattering terms than those with a cognitive organization which seeks singular perspectives and external criteria of a believed objective truth (Vaillant and McCulloch, 1987). These authors maintain that the cognitively more complex accept ambiguity, paradoxes, and nuances. Their cognitive organization rests on inner meaning and psychological dynamics, on principles and on integrated and transcended dualism—all aspects of ego development.

Several studies underscore the complexity dimension in ego development. Helson, Mitchell and Hart (1985) found that women with advanced ego development had lived lives neither orthodox nor easy, and that verbal aptitude in high school, psychological mindedness in college and stimulation of life paths in ensuing years predicted later ego development (Helson and Roberts, 1994). Hauser and Safyer (1994) demonstrated that diversity of emotional communication and conflict within communication occurred more often in the speeches of adolescent at higher stages of ego development.

Higher ego development seems to allow for better coping with hardships. Defenses become more internalized (Levit, 1993) and more mature (Noam *et al.*, 1991), and high ego level individuals can meet crises with less disturbance. Rierdan and Koff (1993) found that high ego-level girls met early maturing (menarching) with less depression than low ego-level girls. Fuller and Swensen (1992) in their study of elderly couples found that cancer patients with high ego development reported a strengthening of the marital relationship over the course of their illness. Noam *et al.* (1991) found that psychiatrically hospitalized adolescents who progressed in ego development after nine months also decreased in psychiatric symptoms and changed their coping and defense mechanisms. In another study they found that ego development and symptom severity scores were negatively related in psychiatric outpatients (Noam and Dill, 1991). They interpret their findings to mean that psychiatric symptoms are better tolerated and coped with at higher ego development and therefore are experienced with less intense distress.

The question still remains whether external hardship is just better dealt with at higher levels of ego development or whether ego development also is enhanced by external hardship. Bursik (1991), in a study of 104 women in the process of separation or divorce, found that women who had experienced the divorce as a disequilibrating life change at the time, but who had made a successful adaptation one year later, also showed a significant increase in ego development. Those women whose adaptation had deteriorated also showed a decrease in ego development scores. Bursik made the point that ego development occurs when individuals meet the challenge to accommodate unpleasant life experiences to new schemata for understanding. Oz, Tari and Fine (1992) found that teen-age mothers, who had previously been found to have experienced more traumatic childhoods, showed more advanced ego development than non-mothers. Whether the difficult childhoods or the experience of early motherhood were the more salient for ego development is unclear.

Hardships in themselves do not necessarily predict advance in development, however. For example, Silver *et al.* (1990) found no relationship between chronic illness, severity or onset, and ego development. Most likely, the individual must have reached a certain level of ego maturity to be able to cope successfully with the hardship, which in turn may instigate further ego development.

Growing from crises may be more characteristic of girls and women, than of boys and men. Girls tend to be presented with overly protective childhood environment both inside and outside the home (Block, 1984). Block argues that girls are presented with environments and prefer environments conducive to assimilation of experience, whereas boys are presented with environments which challenge them to accommodate to new schema.

Girls may therefore profit from more challenging family environments. Parents, particularly mothers, who create more demanding, complex and tension-producing milieus may also be those who raise daughters to higher ego levels. Grotevant and Cooper (1986) have studied identity-exploration rather than ego development in late adolescence. They also found differences in the patterns of parent–adolescent interactions which predicted identity-exploration in sons and daughters. High exploring daughters experienced more challenging from their mothers (Cooper and Grotevant, 1987).

Conflict and conflict tolerance may in addition be a particular mother–daughter issue which cannot be generalized to other significant relationships, neither to father–daughter relationships nor to relationships involving sons. The extensive study by Hauser and collaborators (Hauser *et al*., 1984) on ego development and family communications corroborates that the reciprocal enabling interaction between the mother and the adolescent had a larger influence on the children's ego development than the parallel interaction between father and adolescent. Hauser and collaborators have, however, not corroborated the view that the mother–daughter relationship may be different from the mother–son relationship. Enabling or facilitative communicative behavior in their study seemed to be positively predicted and constraining or impeding communicative behavior negatively predicted by ego levels in the family regardless of the adolescent gender.

EGO DEVELOPMENT AND INDIVIDUATION

As a developmental personality concept, individuation is related to ego development. The development of individuation is thought to take place during interaction with other people, where the balance between the need for individuality or autonomy, and the need for interconnectedness or inter-dependence are negotiated (for example, Grotevant and Cooper, 1985; Stierlin, 1974). There has been a tendency in Western psychology to value autonomy as the goal of development (Beavers and Voeller, 1983; Blos, 1967; Kohlberg, 1978) at the expense of interconnectedness. The focus on separation as mandatory for growth of autonomy has been criticized by feministic psychologists who state that development to autonomy may follow different paths: through separation or through identification and relationships (for example, Chodorow, 1989; Gilligan, 1993; Miller, 1984). These writers argue that women value the continuance of relationships with others in a different way than men and that women may reach autonomy through differentiation *in* relationships. Stierlin (1974) views individuality alone as isolation and connectedness alone as fusion and maintains that it is in the interface of the two that related individuation unfolds.

It is regarded as important for adolescent growth to be able to continue a close, but evolvingly different relationship with the parents (Baumrind, 1991; Bell and Bell, 1983; Feldman and Gehring, 1988; Hauser *et al*., 1984). This relationship serves as a base from which the adolescent can explore the world (Cooper *et al*., 1983). For the latter authors the challenge for the adolescent and the family is to enhance the youngster's individuality, while remaining connected. Anderson and Sabatelli (1990) stated that the family's tolerance for its members' age-adequate individuation is critical for psychological growth.

Blos (1967) used the second individuation process as a term to describe adolescence and saw the process toward autonomy as internal and as a movement toward increasing self–other differentiation (see Kroger, Chapter 8). The cultural shift from a focus on individuality to a focus on the tension between individuality and belonging is noted by many (for example, Mahler, Pine and Bergman, 1975; Josselson, 1988; Chodorow, 1978). Karpel (1976) used the concept "individuated dialogue," a mature position where the opposition between "I" and "we" is transcended.

Carlson and Grotevant (1987) made individuation a property of relationships, not individuals. The individuation concept contains three theoretical levels according to Grotevant, where the first and general one is the individuation concept itself. The next level is the differentiation between individuality and connectedness in individuation, and the third level is the further differentiation of individuality into self-assertion and separateness and connectedness into mutuality and permeability. Self-assertion means to be aware of and to communicate clearly one's point of view. Separateness has to do with knowing that one is different from others. Self-assertion and separateness reflect individuality. Mutuality means sensitivity to and respect for others, and permeability means flexibility or openness to the point of view of others. The latter two concepts reflect the connectedness part of individuation. The four dimensions were supported by a factor analysis of micro-coding of family communication (Cooper *et al.*, 1983). According to the model, an individuated relationship will be moderate to high on both individuality and connectedness.

In this chapter, some findings from a Norwegian research group (von der Lippe, 1986; von der Lippe and Møller, 1997; von der Lippe and Amundsen, 1997; Ringdal and Stenberg, 1997) will be summarized which bear on the issue of the "optimal growth" hypothesis. The effect of family communication and conflict resolution on character development and on individuation are addressed and compared with American studies on similar issues. The effect of interpersonal conflict in normal personality development has received relatively little attention in personology and has mostly been left to clinical and to social psychology, and findings are still fragmentary. It is felt that a broadening of the field to study both the context of conflict and how conflict is mastered is important also for the study of personality.

EGO DEVELOPMENT AND EXPOSURE TO CONFLICT

In a study of the relationship between 39 middle-aged mothers and their primi-parae pregnant daughters (von der Lippe, 1986), a positive relationship was found between ego development and exposure to interpersonal conflict, assessed through interview and several standard questionnaires. Not only were high ego-level daughters taught tolerance of conflict, they were also more exposed to interpersonally created conflict during their developmental history. They had been subjected to more parental conflict including divorce, daughters and mothers described more conflicts with each other, and daughters described more conflict with their spouses and fathers. The relationship to the father was overinvolved in high ego-level women and patterns of conflict with the father were repeated with the husband. Those relationship factors that predicted ego development in the daughters were individuation from the mother (in Stierlin's (1980) sense of a non-fused and dialogical relationship) and maturity of conflict solutions with the father.

Looking further into the developmental challenge of negative life events, Ringdal and Stenberg (1997) in a recent study of 60 adults, age 15–67, investigated the relationship between life events in three developmental time periods and adult ego development. They found that adult negative life events and ego development, controlled for age, were positively related regardless of whether the life event was brought about by the individual themselves or by external circumstances. Life events in childhood or adolescence were unrelated to ego development. How the individual had coped with the life events throughout their lives was also related to their ego development. High ego development individuals were more able to see potentialities in the events and went from experiencing the event negatively to later experiencing its positive consequences. These results replicated Bursik's (1991) findings that disequilibratingly experienced life experiences when later mastered led to increase in ego development. The findings suggested that negative life events may further psychological development if they happen to an individual who has already developed some self-efficacy or more mature coping strategies. The effects of negative life events on the immature person were indeterminate in the studies cited of normally functioning individuals.

EGO DEVELOPMENT AND INDIVIDUATION

Individuation was assessed in a study of 39 Norwegian families with adolescent daughters, aged 16–18 years old (von der Lippe and Amundsen, 1997). Condon, Cooper and Grotevant's (1984) scoring of individuality and connectedness in family discussions was used. The instructions to the family were not to "plan a vacation" as for Condon *et al.*, but were discussions about family disagreements on ethical and personal issues. A principal component analysis of the resulting scores gave four independent factors, two related to individuality (self-assertion/separation and dominance) and two related to connectedness (clarification and acceptance).

The hypothesis that the personality concepts of individuality and connectedness, alone or in concert as individuation, would be related to ego development was only partly supported. Connectedness between parents and daughters proved to be that aspect of interactional individuation which was related to ego development. The data suggested that the two variables, individuality and connectedness, do not form a coherent concept of individuation in the way suggested by Grotevant and colleagues. As individuality is operationalized by Condon *et al.*, it does not have relational properties, but is scored when the individual asserts or separates him/herself by creating distance from the other. The interpretation made here is that connectedness presupposes differentiation between self and other to form interdependence, while self-assertion and separation often express pseudo-independence in the adolescent. Connectedness without separation of self and other does not mark interpersonal closeness but fusion of identities.

It is my belief that autonomy is better understood as an internal process of self–other differentiation, the behavioral manifestations of which may be many and not necessarily be self-assertion. Self-assertion and separateness may often be expressions of opposition rather than of autonomy, especially in adolescence. At least in the Norwegian study, individuality operationalized as self-assertion and separation did not co-vary with positive indices of development. The results replicate previous finding (von der Lippe, 1986) that individuation from mother, coded as related dialogue (as opposed to fusion or isolation) predicted ego development in young women. For women, it may be suggested that the development of individuation needs no other explanational concept than connectedness interpreted as interdependence which combines autonomy and relatedness. Allen *et al.* (1994) studied the two concepts, autonomy and relatedness, in observed parent–adolescent interactions in their longitudinal study of ego development. Here autonomy and relatedness were coded from the family discussions of disagreements over ethical dilemmas on which is based the Constraining and Enabling Coding System (CECS) (Hauser *et al.*, 1985); they also are the same family discussions from which individuality and connectedness were coded in the von der Lippe and Amundsen study. Allen *et al.* found that autonomous relatedness were strongly related to current ego development in the adolescent, contrary to the Norwegian finding that only connectedness was thus related, and they found that fathers' display of autonomous relatedness toward the adolescent predicted increase in both indices over two years. The authors stated that their operationalization of autonomy and relatedness resemble Grotevant and Carlson's (1987) coding system, but with some differences, like combining molecular speech by speech codings with molar codings based on the entire dyadic interaction. Three scales were constructed on a priori grounds, one scale for exhibiting autonomous-relatedness, including codes for "expressing and discussing reasons behind disagreements, confidence in stating one's positions, validation and agreement with another's position, and attending to the other person's statements" (Allen *et al.*, 1994, p. 183). In addition, they included a scale of inhibiting autonomy and one of inhibiting relatedness. In their study then, the relationship of autonomy by itself to ego development was not investigated, only autonomy and relatedness combined in one score. The comparison of autonomy in their study and individuality in the Norwegian study cannot therefore be directly made. In the American study, the father's behaviors seemed to be the more predictive, while in the Norwegian study the mother's behaviors toward the adolescent daughter showed the closest relationships to the daughter's ego development.

EGO DEVELOPMENT AND FAMILY COMMUNICATION

The link between conflict exposure and ego development was followed up in the above sample of Norwegian families (von der Lippe and Møller, 1997). In a revealed difference design (Strodtbeck, 1958), the families discussed ethical and personal issues on which they disagreed. Moral dilemmas (constructed either by Hauser *et al.* (1984, 1985) for their longitudinal ego development study or by the Norwegian researchers) were presented individually to the family members. The dilemmas were, for example, conflicts about stealing medicine for a seriously ill wife; who should try to repair a space ship from the outside: the captain or a crew; a breach of promise to an adolescent because of a family *force majeure*; or reading a daughter's diary which discloses narcotics use. Moos' (1974) Family Environment Scale was also included for more personal family disagreements (Bell and Bell, 1983). Stories or items on which the family members suggested different solutions were then presented for discussion and video and audio taped and coded according to CECS (Hauser *et al.*, 1985). The enabling variables consist of four cognitively enabling categories (explaining, problem solving, focusing, and curiosity) and two affectively enabling categories (accepting and empathy). The constraining variables consist of three cognitively constraining categories (distracting, withholding, and judgmental) and three affectively constraining categories (devaluing, indifference, and gratifying).

In the Norwegian sample, the ego level of parents were unrelated, and the ego level of the daughter was only related to the ego level of the father. In the analyses of relationship between ego development and family communication, only the daughters' ego level showed reliable connections. This finding is at variance with Hauser *et al.*'s (1984) results which demonstrated significant relationships also between parental ego levels and communication style. Restriction in the range of ego development scores in the Norwegian parent sample may account for those results.

Enabling indices were constructed consisting of all enabling scores minus all constraining scores directed at a person (expressed as a proportion of their total statements addressed to that person). An index named "challenge" was also constructed, consisting of cognitive constraining categories (distracting, withholding, and judgmental statements) and affective enabling categories (accepting, and active understanding). The latter score was constructed to test the hypothesis that parental challenge within an accepting relationship would be conducive to ego development. Of special interest was to investigate whether this was a mother–daughter issue as suggested by earlier research (von der Lippe, 1986) and by Grotevant and Cooper (Chapter 1).

The daughter's ego development was positively and significantly correlated with the parents' enabling index (or constraining/enabling balance as the index is called by Hauser) and also with the parents' challenging communications. These results supported Hauser *et al.*'s (1984) results that enabling communications from parents go together with advanced ego development in adolescent children. In addition, the results suggested that daughters were positively affected by being challenged by affectionate parents, at least during that period of life. Subjecting the data to a more rigorous regression analysis, controlling for more variables, only the mother's challenging behaviors predicted ego development in the daughters (von der Lippe and Møller, 1997). Allen *et al.* (1994) found on the other hand that fathers', but not mothers' challenging behaviors toward either son or daughter predicted increases in ego development in adolescent offspring over time, that is, challenge in the context of support. Lesser and Snarey (1989) also pointed to the salient effect of fathers for autonomous functioning in the adolescent girl as perceived by the adolescent. Grotevant and Cooper (this issue), on the other hand, comment on the abrasive quality of some mother-to-daughter communications. It is evident that more research is needed to clarify the differential impact of parents on ego development of girls. It may be that the mother–daughter relationship is especially salient for the development of emotional and interpersonal competence (such as conflict negotiation), while fathers may show their influence on their daughters' development of instrumental skills.

In the analysis of communication and ego level in the daughter in the Norwegian study, it was unexpectedly found that problem solving in the father, that is, reminding the others or suggesting solutions to the family dilemmas, was negatively related to ego level, both in the daughter and in the fathers themselves. Qualitative analyses revealed that this tended to be an effort on the part of the father to impose unilateral leadership on the family. This seems to reflect a similar communication style which has been termed "relationship controlling" or "disqualifying" communications by Holte and Wickstrøm (1991). Interestingly, such problem solving efforts on the part of the women were positively related to other enabling communications on their part as suggested by Hauser et al. (1984). Similar behaviors on the part of the two parents may therefore have quite different implications.

EGO DEVELOPMENT AND FAMILY NEGOTIATION OF CONFLICT

In a further effort to analyze the maturity with which Norwegian families solve conflicts among themselves, a conflict negotiation scale was constructed on the basis of extensive analyses of the family discussions (von der Lippe and Møller, 1997). There were altogether 320 family discussions. A tentative scale was constructed guided by Stierlin's (1969) theory of related dialogue and conflict reconciliation in the development of interpersonal relationships. Seven levels of negotiation were constructed with several solutions at each level. At the lower levels, the subcategories represented either solutions characteristic of enmeshed or pseudo-mutual families where the task has to be distorted to avoid conflict confrontation or solutions characteristic of isolated or pseudo-hostile families where no negotiation is possible because disagreement is final. Middle negotiation level families were characterized by static disagreements, pretended solutions, or superficial solutions. Characteristic for higher levels of negotiating capacity was increasing tolerance of conflict and confrontation, making the family increasingly able to listen to the arguments of others without defensiveness and with mutual respect. At the highest level the family was able to transcend individual differences to reach a solution which acknowledged all individual viewpoints in a more inclusive understanding.

The scoring included both an evaluation of the process of negotiation leading to the final solution and the final solution itself. The scale was tried out and revised in several steps until discussions could be meaningfully and reliably coded from videotapes (von der Lippe and Møller, 1997). The modal level of negotiation was used, that is, each family was scored for each of ten different discussions, making a distribution of negotiation scores for that family. The most frequent score was called the modal negotiation level. If there was a tie, the higher score was chosen. Whereas the scale could be seen as dimensional with respect to maturity of solution, each level was different in their pattern of solution from the next. The modal level was therefore felt to be most representative for the family negotiation climate. The mean level was, however, also noted as was the highest score achieved in any one discussion. The three scores were significantly correlated, but not equivalent ($r = 0.71–0.88$).

In the regression analyses of family negotiation solutions and the variables predicting negotiation, the predictor variables were entered after other remaining variables to maximize independence of variables. As anticipated, the daughter's ego level was significantly related to the maturity with which the family negotiated conflict. The parents' ego level was not. Whether the narrow range of ego levels in the parents masked a relationship cannot be determined from this study. In the analyses of the daughter's communications it was found that the daughter's attention to and facilitative behavior toward the mother were those most saliently related to the maturity of the negotiation climate in the family. Her cognitively enabling communications to the father, on the other hand, predicted negotiation level negatively, indicating that attention to the father interfered with the mother–daughter communications.

Turning to the analysis of parental dyadic communications to the daughter, the results showed that the mother's affectively enabling and challenging communications contributed positively, while her cognitively enabling communications contributed negatively to the maturity of the family's negotiation climate. The father's contributions to the conflict negotiation climate was the reverse. His positive influence was seen to be his cognitively enabling behaviors.

The parental contributions to family negotiation skills therefore seemed to be in some ways complementary. The mother's role was to be affectively supportive, but also challenging, while the father's role was to be cognitively helpful, but not to interfere with the mother–daughter relationship if the conflict negotiation climate should reach higher levels of maturity. Lesser and Snarey (1989) also noted that the mother–daughter relationship is qualitatively different from the father–daughter relationship by being more affectively involved and ambivalent and that it is nested within the mother–father–daughter triangle.

Oz, Tari and Fine's (1992) findings that high ego level teen-age daughters had highly involved relationships with their mothers and negative relationships with their fathers, seem in agreement with the Norwegian findings. The mother–daughter relationship seemed to be the most important and complex, and daughters seemed to be wary of their relationship to the father lest it interfered with their attention to the mother. In families with ego-enhancing negotiation climate, the fathers seemingly had to be enabling and not challenging.

INDIVIDUATION AND FAMILY NEGOTIATION

It was anticipated that the connectedness aspect of individuation which related to ego development also would be related to the family's negotiation climate. This anticipation was confirmed. Connectedness between mother and daughter[1] positively predicted negotiation capacity. Individuality between father and daughter[2] on the other hand predicted negotiation negatively in the regression analysis. Once again, the mother–daughter relationship seemed to be the more predictive one, especially their mutual bonding. The father–daughter relationship was mostly predictive in what they should avoid in order to contribute to conflict resolution. In the Norwegian results, the father and daughter were not self-assertive and did not flag separateness toward each other when conflict negotiation was at higher levels in the family triad.

CONCLUSIONS

In this chapter the attempt has been to support the argument that crises in a supportive, but challenging and tension-producing parental environment are conducive to character development. This optimal challenge–optimal growth thesis has received low keyed and dispersed support in the literature, but the evidence is fairly consistent. The argument made has been that challenge is especially important to girls who tend to grow up in more protected milieus than boys, but the thesis may by true for boys as well and could have some transcultural validity. Some findings linking family communication and ways of dealing with conflict to character development in adolescent have been pointed to, some of which are affirmative of recent personality research and some which are at variance with American research.

One main finding in the Norwegian studies was that ego development in late adolescent girls was related to families' facilitative and inhibitory communication patterns in general and to the maturity with which they solve conflicts in particular. When the daughter had reached more complex ego levels, the family negotiated disagreements in ways which come closer to dialogical relationships, as defined by Stierlin (1974). Each individual is respected and acknowledged for his or her arguments, and the family utilizes the contribution of each person to reach more inclusive and complex solutions at higher levels. Disagreements are met with curiosity and not with defense. Daughters with lower ego development, on the other hand, lived in families where disagreements were more poorly tolerated, leading to avoidance of conflict, static conflict or pseudoresolutions.

The positive relationship between ego development and family negotiation parallels the findings by Grotevant and Cooper (Chapter 1) that high identity exploration in adolescents was predicted by family negotiation marked by a sustained focus on identifying disagreements to reach satisfactory resolutions. Low-exploring adolescents came from families where one parent imposed unilateral solutions. A positive relationship between identity status (patterns of identity exploration and commitments) and ego development has been found in earlier studies (for example, Adams and Shea, 1979).

The other major finding was that negotiation skill was related to complementarity rather than symmetry in the mother–daughter and in the father–daughter relationship.

Negotiation skill was high when the mother was affectively facilitating, but cognitively non-facilitating, toward the daughter and was met with facilitating communications by the daughter; negotiation skill was high when the daughter was affectively facilitating, but cognitively non-facilitating, toward the father and was met with enabling communications from the father.

Communication patterns in conflict resolution seem to require a systemic understanding. The specific role relationships should be considered both separately and in concert. In the Norwegian research, it seemed important for the family negotiation climate that the daughter was most facilitative and attentive to the mother. The sensitivity, sometimes brittleness of the mother–daughter relationship observed by many (for example, Chodorow, 1978; Chasseguet-Smirgel, 1964), seems to require much careful handling by the daughter. With regard to the father's role, it was important that he was facilitative and not intrusive or dominating, that is, he seemed to be careful not to detract from the mother–daughter focus. It also seemed important that the cooperation between adolescent and parent while complementary in the cognitive domain, was symmetrical in the affective domain. Also, good conflict resolution required complementarity in the parental relationship pattern to the daughter. The most productive pattern was when the father was cognitively enabling, while the mother was affectively enabling. It also seemed productive for the conflict negotiation climate that the father was supportive and avoided unilateral solutions, while the mother could be abrasive toward the daughter. In fact, challenging behavior in the mother was also positively related to the mother's own ego development. A more inclusive understanding may be needed, that the family functions as a system, that is, that an adolescent girl's relationship to the parents in conflict negotiation depends on complex complementarity in all relationships for its success.

A third focus of the discussion has been the relationship between the concept of individuation and ego development. The argument is that individuation is a result of firm self–other differentiation and cognitive and emotional connectedness, and that the concepts of individuality and connectedness should not be separated and not be seen as internally warring phenomena. Individuality without connectedness is not autonomy, but isolation, and connectedness without self–other differentiation is not interdependence, but fusion. Ego development and cognitive and emotional connectedness, especially as manifested in the mother–daughter relationship seemed to characterize the late teenage girl.

The findings regarding the interplay between individuation, ego development and the complex balance of the mother–father–daughter communication matrix need further refinement and more validation. The importance of being optimally challenged in order to develop is beginning to receive some cross-national evidence. The Norwegian research discussed in this chapter indicated that mature girls have received this challenge primarily from the mother, and in the context of a supportive, affectionate maternal relationship. The research evidence from studies of ego development generally point to the complexity and often tension producing and confrontative relationships created by high ego level women, where the mother–daughter relationship may be the most salient and the prime model for later relationships. Questions of the trajectories of female personality development, the salience of the mother–daughter dyad and the family's functioning as a complex system are in need of much further research. Studies from different societies are important in order to approach the issue of societal variation and trans-societal invariance, but small sample studies like those reported in this chapter certainly need replication. The family, although an important unit to study, is also but one influence on the personality development of the adolescent youth; we need to expand our studies of personality to the larger systems of siblings, peers, adult models, the educational and work systems, and the availability of potential meaningful goals in the adult world.

NOTES

1 The sum of connectedness factors for mother and daughter directed at each other.
2 The sum of individuality factors for father and daughter directed at each other.

BIBLIOGRAPHY

Adams, G.R., and Shea, J.A. (1979) The relationship between identity status, locus of control and ego development, *Journal of Youth and Adolescence*, 8: 81–9.

Allen, J.P., Hauser, S.T., Bell, K.L., and O'Connor, T.C. (1994) Longitudinal assessment of autonomy and relatedness in adolescent-family interactions as predictors of adolescent ego development and self-esteem, *Child Development*, 65: 179–94.

Anderson, S A., and Sabatelli, R.M. (1990) Differentiating differentiation and individuation: conceptual and operational challenges, special issue, Marital and family measurements, *American Journal of Family Therapy*, 18: 32–50.

Bateson, G. (1985) *Mind and Nature*, London: Santana.

Baumrind, D. (1991) Effective parenting during the early adolescent transition, in: P.A. Cowan and A.M. Hetherington (eds.), *Family Transitions. Advances in Family Research Series,* Hillsdale: Erlbaum.

Beavers, W.R., and Voeller, M.N. (1983) Family models: comparing and contrasting the Olson Circumplex model with the Beavers Systems Model, *Family Process*, 22: 85–98.

Bell, D.C., and Bell, L.G. (1983) Parental validation and support in the development of adolescent daughters, in H.D. Grotevant, and C.R. Cooper (eds.), *Adolescent Development in the Family: New Directions for Child Development*, San Francisco: Jossey-Bass.

Blanck, G., and Blanck, R. (1974) *Ego Psychology: Theory and Practice*, New York: Columbia University Press.

Blasi, A. (1989) *The Place of Loevinger's Theory of Ego Development within the Cognitive-Developmental Approach*, paper presented at the meeting of the American Psychological Association, New Orleans.

Block, J.H. (1984) Differential premises arising from differential socialization of the sexes: some conjectures, *Child Development*, 54: 1335–54.

Block, J.H., Block, J., and Gjerde, P. (1986) The personality of children prior to divorce: a prospective study, *Child Development*, 57: 827–40.

Blos, P. (1967) The second individuation process of adolescence, *Psychoanalytic Study of the Child*, 22: 162–86.

Bursik, K. (1991) Adaptation to divorce and ego development in adult women, *Journal of Personality and Social Psychology*, 60: 300–6.

Carlson, C.I., and Grotevant, H.D. (1987) A comparative review of family rating scales: guidelines for clinicians and researchers, *Journal of Family Psychology*, 1: 23–47.

Chasseguet-Smirgel, J. (1964) Feminine guilt and the Oedipus complex, in J. Chasseguet-Smirgel (ed.), *Female Sexuality*, Ann Arbor: University of Michigan Press

Chodorow, N.J. (1978) *The Reproduction of Mothering. Psychoanalysis and the Sociology of Gender*, Berkeley: California University Press.

—— (1989) *Feminism and Psychoanalytic Theory*, Cambridge: Polity Press.

Condon, S.L., Cooper, C.R., and Grotevant, H.D. (1984) Manual for the analysis of family discourse, *Psychological Documents*, 14, 8; ms. no. 2616.

Cooper, C.R., and Grotevant, H.D. (1987) Gender issues in the interface of family experience and adolescent peer relational identity, *Journal of Youth and Adolescence*, 16: 247–64.

Cooper, C.R., Grotevant, H.D., and Condon, S.L. (1983) Individuality and connectedness in the family as a context for adolescent identity formation and role-taking skill, in H.D. Grotevant and C.R. Cooper (eds.), *Adolescent Development in the Family: New Directions in Child Development*, no. 22, pp. 43–59, San Francisco: Jossey-Bass.

Dodge, K.A., and Murphy, R.R. (1984) The assessment of social competence of adolescents, in P. Karoly and J.J. Steffen (eds.), *Adolescent behavior disorders: Foundations and contemporary concerns*, pp. 61–96, Lexington, MA: Lexington.

Feldman, S.S., and Gehring, T.M. (1988) Changing perceptions of family cohesion and power across adolescence, *Child Development* 59: 1034–45.

Fuller, S., and Swensen, C.H. (1992) Marital quality and quality of life among cancer patients and their spouses, *Journal of Psychosocial Oncology*, 10: 41–56.

Garmecy, N., Masten, A.S., and Tellegen, A. (1984) The study of stress and competence in children: a building block for developmental psychopathology, *Child Development* 55: 97–111.

Gilligan, C. (1993) *In a Different Voice. Psychological Theory and Women's Development*, 2nd edn, Cambridge: Harvard University Press.

Gjerde, P. (1986) The interpersonal structure of family interaction settings: parent–adolescent relations in dyads and triads, *Developmental Psychology*, 22: 297–304

Goldstein, M.J. (1988) The family and psychopathology, *Annual Review of Psychology, 39* : 283–99.

Gottman, J.M., and Katz, L.F. (1989) Effects of marital discord on young children's peer interaction and health, *Developmental Psychology* 256, 3: 373–81.

Grotevant, H.D., and Carlson, C.I. (1987) Family interaction coding systems: a descriptive review, *Family Process*, 26: 49–74.

Grotevant, H.D., and Cooper, R.C. (1985) Patterns of interaction in family relationships and the development of identity exploration, *Child Development*, 56: 415–28.

—— (1986) Individuation in family relationships: a perspective on individual differences in the development of identity and role-taking skill in adolescence, *Human Development*, 29: 82–100.

Hauser, S.T. (1976) Loevinger's model and measure of ego development: a critical review, *Psychological Bulletin*, 83: 928–55.

Hauser, S.T., Book, B.K., Houlihan, J., Powers, S., Weiss-Perry, B., Follansbee, D., Jacobsen, A.M., and Noam, G.G. (1987) Sex differences within the family: studies of adolescent and parent interaction, *Journal of Youth and Adolescence*, 16: 199–220.

Hauser, S.T., Houlihan, J., Powers, S.I., Jacobsen, A.M., Noam, G.G., Weiss-Perry, B., Follansbee, D., and Book, B.K. (1991) Adolescent ego development within the family: family styles and family sequences, *International Journal of Behavioral Development*, 14, 2: 165–93.

Hauser, S.T., Powers, S., Noam, G., Jacobsen, R., Weiss-Perry, B., and Follansbee, D. (1984) Familial contexts of adolescent ego development, *Child Development*, 55, 1: 195–213.

Hauser, S.T., Powers, S., Weiss-Perry, B., Follansbee, D., Rajapark, D., and Green, W.M. (1985) *The Constraining and Enabling Coding System Manual*, unpublished manuscript.

Hauser, S.T., and Safyer, A.W. (1994) Ego development and adolescent emotions, special issue, Affective processes in adolescence, *Journal of Research on Adolescence*, 4: 487–502.

Helson, R., Mitchell, V., and Hart, B. (1985) Lives of women who become autonomous, special issue, Conceptualizing gender in personality theory and research, *Journal of Personality*, 53: 257–85.

Helson, R., and Roberts, B.W. (1994) Ego development and personality change in adulthood, *Journal of Personality and Social Psychology*, 66: 911–20.

Helson, R., and Wink, P. (1987) Two conceptions of maturity examined in the findings of a longitudinal study, *Journal of Personality and Social Psychology*, 53, 3: 531–41.

Hoffman, L.W. (1977) Changes in family roles, socialization and sex differences, *American Psychologist*, 32: 644–57.

Holt, R.R.(1980) Loevinger's measure of ego development: reliability and national norms for male and female short forms, *Journal of Personality and Social Psychology*, 39: 909–20.

Holte, A., and Wickstrøm, L. (1991) Disconfirmatory feedback in families of schizophrenics, *Scandinavian Journal of Psychology*, 31: 198–211.

Josselson, R. (1988) The embedded self: I and though revisited, in D.K. Lapsley and F.C. Power (eds.), *Self, Ego, and Identity: Integrative Approaches,* New York: Springer-Verlag.

Karpel, M. (1976) Individuation: from fusion to dialogue, *Family Process*, 15: 65–82.

Kohlberg, L. (1978) Revisions in the theory and practice of moral development, in W. Damon (ed.), *New Directions in Child Development*, vol. 2, *Moral Development*, San Francisco: Jossey-Bass.

Lamborn, S.D., Mounts, N.S., Steinberg, L., and Dornbush, S.M. (1991) Patterns of competence and adjustment among adolescents from authoritative, authoritarian, indulgent, and neglectful families, *Child Development*, 62, 5: 1049–65.

Lee, L., and Snarey, J. (1988) The relationship between ego and moral development: a theoretical review and empirical analysis, in D.K. Lapsley and F. Clark Power (eds.), *Self, Ego and Identity*, pp. 151–208, New York: Springer-Verlag.

Lesser, V., and Snarey, J. (1989) Ego development and perceptions of parents behavior in adolescent girls: a qualitative study of the transition from high school to college, *Journal of Adolescent Research*, 4: 319–55.

Levit, D.B. (1993) The development of ego defenses in adolescence, *Journal of Youth and Adolescence*, 22 5: 493–512.

Loevinger, J. (1976) *Ego Development: Conceptions and Theories*, San Francisco: Jossey-Bass.

—— (1984) On the self and predicting behavior, in R.A. Zucker, J. Aronoff, and A.I. Rabin (eds.), *Personality and the Prediction of Behavior*, pp. 43–68, Orlando: Academic.

Loevinger, J., and Wessler, R. (1970) *Measuring Ego Development*, vol. 1. *Construction and Use of a Sentence Completion Test*, San Francisco: Jossey-Bass

Long, N., Forehand, R., Fauber, R., and Brody, G.H. (1987) Self-perceived and independently observed competence of young adolescents as a function of parental marital conflict and recent divorce, *Journal of Abnormal Child Psychology*, 15: 15–27.

Mahler, M.S., Pine, F., and Bergman, A. (1975) *The Psychological Birth of the Human Infant*, New York: Basic Books.

McCrae, R.R., and Costa, P.T. (1980) Openness to experience and ego level in Loevinger's Sentence Completion Test: dispositional contributions to developmental models of personality, *Journal of Personality*, 39, 1–6: 1179–90.

—— (1983) Psychological maturity and subjective well-being: toward a new synthesis, *Developmental Psychology*, 19, 2: 243–8.

Miller, J. (1984) *The development of women's sense*, Wellesley: Stone Center Working Papers Series.

Moos, R.H. (1974) *Manual for the Family Environment Scale*, Palo Alto: Consulting Psychologist Press.

Noam, G.G. (1993) Ego development: true or false? *Psychological review*, 4: 43–9.

Noam, G.G., and Dill, D.L. (1991) Adult development and symptomatology, *Psychiatry*, 54: 208–16.

Noam, G.G., Recklitis, C.J., and Papet, K.F. (1991) Pathways of ego development: contributions to maladaptation and adjustment, *Development and Psychopathology*, 3: 311–28.

Oz, S., Tari, A., and Fine, M. (1992) A comparison of the psychological profiles of teen-age mothers and their non-mother peers, *Adolescence*, 27: 193–202.

Redmore, C.D., and Loevinger, J. (1979) Ego development in adolescence: longitudinal studies, *Journal of Youth and Adolescence*, 81: 1–20.

Rierdan, J., and Koff, E. (1993) Developmental variables in relation to depressive symptoms in adolescent girls, *Development and Psychopathology*, 53: 485–96.

Ringdal, C., and Stenberg, N. (1997) *Å vokse på en krise* (Growing from a crisis: A study of the relationships between life events, coping and ego development), dissertation, University of Oslo.

Riskin, J., and Faunce, F.E. (1970) Family interaction scales. I. Theoretical framework and method, *Archives of General Psychiatry*, 22: 504–12.

Silver, E.J., Bauman, L.J., Coupey, S.M., Doctors, S.R., and Shelley, R. (1990) Ego development and chronic illness in adolescence, *Journal of Personality and Social Psychology*, 59: 305–10.

Singer, M.T., and Wynne, L. (1963) Differentiating characteristics of parents of childhood schizophrenics, childhood neurotics and adult schizophrenics, *American Journal of Psychiatry*, 120: 234–43.

Skoe, E.E., and von der Lippe, A.L. (1997) *Do Moral and Ego Developments Follow Different Paths? The Relations among Care, Justice and Ego Development*, manuscript in preparation, University of Tromsø, Tromsø.

Smollar, J., and Youniss, J. (1989) Transformations in adolescents' perceptions of parents, *International Journal of Behavioral Development*, 12: 71–84.

Steinberg, L. (1987) The impact of puberty on family relations: effects of pubertal status and pubertal timing, *Developmental Psychology*, 23: 451–60.

Stierlin, H. (1969) *Conflict and Reconciliation*, New York: Doubleday-Anchor and Science House.

—— (1974) *Separating Parents and Adolescents. A Perspective on Running Away, Schizophrenia, and Waywardness*, New York: Quadrangle.

—— (1980) *The First Interview with the Family*, New York: Brunner/Mazel.

Strodtbeck, F.L. (1958) Husband–wife interaction and revealed differences, *American Sociological Review*, 16: 468–73.

Vaillant, G.E., and McCulloch, L. (1987) The Washington University Sentence Completion Test compared with other measures of adult ego development, *American Journal of Psychiatry*, 144 9: 1189–94.

von der Lippe, A.L. (1986) Ego development in women without higher education, *Scandinavian Journal of Psychology*, 27: 150–62.

von der Lippe, A.L., and Amundsen, E. (forthcoming) Individuation, Ego Development and Conflict Resolution in the Family of Adolescent Girls, in *Scandinavian Journal of Psychology*.

von der Lippe, A.L., and Møller, I.U. (1997) *The Relationship between Negotiation of Conflict in the Family and Ego Level of the Adolescent Daughter*, manuscript submitted for publication, University of Oslo.

Walker, L.J., and Taylor, J.H. (1991) Family interactions and the development of moral reasoning, *Developmental psychology*, 27: 330–7.

Werner, E.E., and Smith, R.S. (1982) *Vulnerable but invincible. a longitudinal study of resilient children and youth*, New York: McGraw Hill.

Westenburg, P.M., and Block, J. (1993) Ego development and individual differences in personality, *Journal of Personality and Social Psychology*, 65, 4: 792–800.

White, K.M., Speisman, J.C., and Costos, D. (1983) Young adults and their parents: individuation to mutuality, *New Directions for Child Development*, 22: 61–76.

Wickstrøm, L., Holte, A., Husby, R., and Wynne, L.C. (1993) Disqualifying family communication as a predictor of changes in offspring competence: a 3-year longitudinal study of sons of psychiatric patients, *Journal of Family Psychology*, 8: 104–8.

Youniss, J., and Ketterlinus, R.D. (1987) Communication and connectedness in mother– and father–adolescent relationships, special issue, Sex differences in family relations at adolescence, *Journal of Youth and Adolescence*, 16: 265–80.

3 A narrative approach to the study of moral orientation in the family[1]
Tales of kindness and care

Michael W. Pratt, Mary Louise Arnold and Susan M. Hilbers

Twenty years ago, Carol Gilligan posed the question of whether moral thinking was distinctively gendered in North American society, and whether the field of developmental psychology had recognized this appropriately in its traditional theorizing and research (Gilligan, 1977, 1982). Gilligan argued that women think about morality in ways distinct from men, focusing their concerns around considerations of "care," relationships, and the needs of others and the self. In contrast, men's reasoning on this subject centers more around considerations of "justice" and the rights of self and others (as elucidated by Piaget and Kohlberg in the traditional developmental research in this area; for example, Kohlberg, 1976). Gilligan's central claim, then, was that the "voice" of women had been largely ignored in previous theory and research on this topic.

Undeniably, Gilligan's initial critique has had a profound impact on the field and has led to many studies of the role of gender in moral development. Moreover, despite persistent (and often heated) controversy over the legitimacy of many of her original claims (for example, Walker, 1995), Gilligan's central thesis, that males and females often do orient differently to real-life moral situations, has continued to have a strong intuitive appeal. Thus far, however, little empirical research has been addressed to the possible explanations for any such gender differences in moral development as may exist. In the present chapter, we explore some possible accounts of the family's role in these matters in adolescence, focusing particularly on some recent narrative evidence of our own regarding processes of moral socialization.

To date, research efforts to evaluate Gilligan's (1982) ideas have produced somewhat mixed results, depending on varying interpretations of her claims. The suggestion that women's thinking may be devalued as a result of scoring biases within the traditional moral developmental scoring systems (such as the Moral Judgment Interview of Kohlberg or the Defining Issues Test of Rest) has been quite consistently refuted. Numerous studies have shown that there are few systematic differences between the sexes in terms of stage levels of moral reasoning, once background factors have been controlled (for example, Thoma, 1986; Walker, 1995). However, to the extent that these traditional stage systems were designed with a focus on justice reasoning development, in effect they do preclude clear consideration of alternative orientations in moral thinking, such as the focus on "care" (for example, Brown *et al.*, 1995).

An accurate evaluation of Gilligan's broader claim of sex differences in the orientation of moral reasoning is complicated. However, here the evidence regarding differences in at least some types of moral problem solving is considerably more promising (for example, Brown *et al.*, 1995; Gilligan and Attanucci, 1988). For example, Walker (1989) has found some indications of such differences among adults in real-life reasoning about personal problems, although not in hypothetical dilemmas. Similarly, we have also observed moral orientation differences in men's and women's real-life reasoning, but primarily among mid-life adults and particularly among those currently parenting children (Pratt *et al.*, 1988). Specifically, a sample of married adults with children were more likely to show this gender-based differentiation in moral orientation than were a sample of married adults without children (Pratt *et al.*, 1988, study 2).

Moreover, the salience of gender differences in use of the "care" and "justice" orientations seems to depend heavily on contextual factors. Dilemmas that involve close personal relationships seem particularly likely to elicit "care"-oriented thinking, whereas those of a more institutional, impersonal nature are more likely to be addressed by "justice" considerations, for both men and women (Pratt *et al.*, 1991; Walker, 1989; Wark and Krebs, 1996). The gender difference in real-life moral orientations reported by several investigators has seemed primarily a function of women's greater tendency to think about and report more relationship-focused dilemmas from their personal lives (Walker, 1995). Given these patterns of findings, it is now generally agreed that both sexes have both types of reasoning available, and differences in usage are primarily the result of differential accessing of the two modes within different contexts (for example, Clopton and Sorrell, 1993; Gilligan and Attanucci, 1988; Turiel, 1998; Walker, 1995).

Whatever the contextual factors here, findings of adult variations in moral orientation associated with gender obviously raise important questions about socialization. When do such differences between males and females develop, and what might account for them? A few studies have examined moral orientation differences specifically in adolescence, with limited success in clarifying the evidence. Differences in orientation in children's and adolescents' responses to the dilemmas posed in Aesop's fables have been mixed (Garrod *et al.*, 1990; Johnston, 1988). In the context of self-generated real-life problems, girls have sometimes shown a tendency to relate more personal dilemmas and boys more impersonal problems, and thus to differ in orientation usage (for example, Johnston *et al.*, 1990). However, other studies of adolescents' moral reasoning in varying contexts have reported no gender differences in orientation (for example, Kahn, 1992; Smetana, 1995; Walker, 1989). Some research specifically on the development of care thinking has suggested that adolescent gender differences may be quite age-specific, with girls differing from boys only in very early adolescence (Eisenberg *et al.*, 1991; Skoe and Gooden, 1993).

In the rest of this chapter, we concentrate on explanatory frameworks and some empirical evidence for the potential role of the family in the socialization of possible gender differences in moral orientation among adolescents. We begin with a review of how traditional theories of moral and gender socialization might apply here (for example, Beall and Sternberg, 1993; Maccoby, 1992; Serbin *et al.*, 1993), and then turn to a discussion of our own research on narrative processes in the family in relation to this question.

CLASSIC THEORIES IN MORAL AND SEX-ROLE SOCIALIZATION

Freud's psychoanalytic framework for discussing moral socialization centered on the powerful role of the family and *emotional* conflict (for example, Miller, 1969). Freud's model focused on same-sex identification processes during the late preschool (or oedipal) period. More recently, neoanalytic models have stressed the importance of the even earlier-established attachment relationship to the mother for both sexes in these developments. In particular, basing her argument on the work of Chodorow (for example, 1978) and others, Gilligan has argued that women's and men's differences in their orientations to relationships are derivative from very early experience in the mother–child dyad (for example, Gilligan and Wiggins, 1987). Mothers are said to experience female and male infants differently, as "similar to" and "different from" themselves, respectively. Due to this difference in experience, young children are socialized in distinctive ways by mothers. Girls experience a focus on maintaining the closeness and similarity of the maternal relationship, whereas boys are oriented toward individuation and separation from the mother (Gilligan, 1982). These early differences in the maternal attachment relationship lead to the establishment of quite distinctly gendered moral and social orientations in children and later in adults according to this model. Females are said to see the self in "relational" terms, whereas males view the self in "individuated" fashion. However, despite the intuitive appeal of these claims about gender and early socialization differences, no systematic research in early childhood has explored these issues with respect to moral orientation, and this account remains speculative (Walker, 1995).

Social learning theory, with its emphasis on the roles of both reinforcement processes and modeling, has been extremely popular as an explanatory approach, both in the development of moral behavior generally (for example, Burton and Kunce, 1995) and in the area of gender socialization (for example, Serbin *et al.*, 1993). There is substantial evidence that many agents of socialization (for example, parents, peers, the media) provide gender-differentiated models of attitudes and behaviors for the child (Huston, 1983). Furthermore, both observational and experimental studies indicate that changing such models can have an impact on gender-differentiation in children's own behavior (Lott and Maluso, 1993). Although there is considerable evidence that parents as models can provide some types of moral guidance to children, there has been little research to date on this socialization process with respect to moral orientation. A recent study by Lollis, Ross and Leroux (1996), however, suggests that mothers and fathers interact differently in the ways in which they intervene in 2- to 4-year-old siblings' property disputes. These investigators found that mothers were more likely than fathers to intervene with care-oriented comments in these situations (about two-thirds of the time overall). Intervention by the father were slightly more likely to comment on "rights" than "needs" (Lollis *et al.*, 1996).

This overall difference by parent gender held regardless of the genders of the children involved. Given this pattern, it is difficult to understand how the feedback differences themselves can operate to socialize differences in children's own moral orientations by gender. However, as noted by the investigators, these differences in the styles of intervention by mothers and fathers could certainly be observed and imitated in a gender-differentiated way by children (Lollis *et al.*, 1996).

Cognitive-developmental researchers have also investigated moral socialization in the family, specifically the development of moral thinking (for example, Boyes and Allen, 1993; Walker and Taylor, 1991). The central focus of these studies has been on the Piagetian notion that development in moral reasoning is stimulated by challenging and open parent–child discussion, which in turn produces "disequilibration" of the child's current reasoning by encounters with somewhat more advanced levels of thinking about issues. The acquisition of gender concepts themselves within the cognitive-developmental framework has been viewed as a natural, universal developmental process which proceeds from the young child's labeling of the self as "male" or "female," and then coming to understand that gender as a category is permanent and irreversible (Kohlberg, 1966). Given this theoretical framework of universality in early development, this approach has shown little interest in the study of individual differences in socialization, however.

A related cognitive model of gender socialization, gender-schema theory, has been more attentive to such individual differences in the gender schemata established by different children (for example, Martin and Halverson, 1981; Serbin *et al.*, 1993). Differences between children with more and less salient gender-related schemata for thinking about the self and others are viewed as accounting for some of the individual variations in the development of gender roles (for example, Bem, 1981). However, this framework has apparently not been applied to moral orientation development to date.

One recent cognitively-focused program of research has been directed to aspects of moral orientation. Skoe (Skoe, Chapter 7; Skoe and Marcia, 1991; Skoe and Diessner, 1994) has sought to explore Gilligan's (1982) suggestion of developmental trends in the growth of care reasoning, through the formulation of a three-stage model. In a series of studies, Skoe has established that balanced consideration of the needs of both self and other appears to develop gradually across childhood into young adulthood, somewhat paralleling the developmental trends in justice-based reasoning (for example, Skoe and Diessner, 1994). However, Skoe has not yet investigated family influences on such development in her work, although she acknowledges their likely role (Skoe, Chapter 7).

Each of the traditional models of gender socialization reviewed has potential to contribute to an account of the development of moral orientation within the family, although this potential has been little explored. In our view, what is missing in all of these traditional approaches is a focus on the person's construction of his or her own particular and unique life experiences and self. Recent work on narrative and the self in psychology offers considerable promise in this regard (for example, Gergen, 1991; McAdams, 1993).

SOCIALIZATION IN THE NARRATIVE MODE

In a recent paper, Day and Tappan (1996) invite cognitive developmental researchers of morality to "take the narrative turn." They suggest that Gilligan's work and that of her colleagues (Brown *et al.*, 1995) has been central in the development of a narrative approach to morality for two important reasons. First, focusing on people's real-life moral problems and their consideration has highlighted the critical role that the narrative mode of discourse plays in this domain, as in so much of everyday human interaction and thought (for example, Bruner, 1986). Moral thinking and activity are determinedly "storied," and it behooves researchers to attend to this in both their methods and theorizing (Pratt and Arnold, 1995; Vitz, 1990).

Second, Gilligan's work has suggested the existence of multiple "voices"—specifically in this case those of justice and care—in people's narratives about their personal moral lives. Irrespective of the possible gendered aspects of these voices, the fact that people can and do speak, think, and engage in dialogue using both modes is widely acknowledged (Day and Tappan, 1996). This point leads to an appreciation of everyday moral thinking and reasoning as composed of a polyphony of voices (of which justice and care are two exemplars), and of the moral self as fundamentally dialogical in nature (for example, Tappan, 1991). Drawing on the work of Bakhtin (1981), Tappan (1991) has contrasted the "epistemic" subject of Piaget's and Kohlberg's cognitive developmental tradition with the "dialogical" self of the sociocultural tradition. This fundamentally social dialogical self is constructed in ongoing interaction with others, and with their real or "appropriated" inner voices as covert audiences in the individual's everyday moral decision making and thinking (Day and Tappan, 1996).

What are the implications of this narrative approach to moral development for the study of the socialization of moral orientation in the family? First, of course, the role of narrative as a distinctive mode of discourse is strongly highlighted here. In the empirical work reported in this chapter, we have sought family members' own stories about moral learning and socialization, as one way of exploring such family processes.

Second, the importance of such a multiplicity of "voices of the mind" (to use Wertsch's 1991 term) in moral thinking within this sociocultural narrative model is obviously congruent with the potential role of parents as central socializers and guides for children's development. Although Piaget's traditional perspective on moral reasoning development has somewhat de-emphasized the role of parents, we believe that such an "internal" parental voice in decision making is generally a crucial component of the child's development. Furthermore, because the voices of justice and care in moral discourse may be distinctively gendered, we sought in this exploratory research to have both parents describe their experiences of family socialization separately, to investigate possible differences in the content and impact of mothers' and fathers' "voices."

While Gilligan and her colleagues have explored gender differences in adolescent and adult personal narratives of moral choice (for example, Gilligan and Attanucci, 1988; Lyons, 1983), is there empirical evidence for gender differences in the role of narrative in the direct transmission of values in the family (as suggested by Vitz, 1990)? Fiese *et al.* (1995) observed that mothers and fathers differed in the content of the narratives about their own childhood experiences that they described to their young children. Parents were asked to recount a story about a personal childhood experience that they would like to tell to their children about their own family of origin. The narratives were then scored for strength of affiliation and achievement themes. Results indicated that fathers told narratives with stronger achievement themes, whereas mothers told narratives with stronger affiliative themes. The gender of these young children itself did not seem to distinguish use of the two themes in the stories, however. Although not specifically focused on *moral* values, Fiese *et al.*'s (1995) findings certainly suggest that family stories may be informative regarding processes of differential gender socialization in the family.

STUDYING PARENT NARRATIVES ABOUT ADOLESCENT MORAL SOCIALIZATION

Our first investigation involved the elicitation of stories from mothers and fathers of adolescents regarding specific times when they attempted to socialize an important value for their teen-ager. This study involved a sample of 40 intact families with early adolescent children (age range 12–16, mean age = 14 years), participating in a larger study of moral socialization (for example, Pratt and Arnold, 1996). There were 21 daughters and 19 sons in the sample. Mothers and fathers were each interviewed separately in their homes about a number of issues, as well as observed in moral discussions with their children. As a part of the interview, each parent chose the three most important values or qualities that he or she most wished to see the adolescent exemplify from a list of ten (honest, ambitious, fair and just, kind and caring, trustworthy, independent, open and communicative, polite and courteous, sharing, careful and cautious).

An important component of this task involved the telling of a narrative; each parent was asked to describe an incident in which he or she had tried to teach the value chosen as most important for the child. An example narrative of a mother of a 15-year-old girl, focusing on "kind and caring" as a value, is provided below (it was scored as care-oriented):

> Jill was concerned for a friend who was in trouble and who thought she was pregnant, and who was very scared and was confiding in her. Jill came to me with the problem because she was worried for her friend. So I encouraged her to give certain advice to that friend, you know, and (Jill) felt that was really important so she did, and . . . her friend has made some good decisions in that area, so we thought that was good . . . . So Jill really wanted to help her friend and cared very much about the outcome of this whole thing. And we also encouraged her to carry on and then to, you know, be getting more involved.

Here is a parallel story told by a father about a 13-year-old boy, focusing on "fair and just" (and scored as justice-oriented):

> Last year there were some kids in the school who were quite poor and couldn't afford the newest clothes and going to extra activities that they had; and Jerry was in a situation where he was a little bit rough with one of them. So we went to talk to the vice principal and took Jerry with us and tried to teach him to treat everybody equally, no matter what their income or situation or color, to try to accept them and be fair. And we also try to tell him that there are things that people do that you don't necessarily accept what they do but you have to respect the person . . .

Finally, here is an example story by a mother about a daughter, focusing on "fair and just," which was scored as having "mixed justice and care" elements:

> Linda has a cousin who tends to irritate her, and because they're cousins of equal age, they see a lot of each other, and this cousin has poor hygiene and bad manners, and it just grosses Linda out. So we've been trying to work with her that that person is just that

person, you know, they have to deal with those problems and you just should try to see positive parts of the personality. If you look at the negative, you are going to be harder on some people and be more lenient on others and that's not fair . . . . And if this person irritates her a lot, you just cool off the relationship and get away from her for a while, and that way she'll keep a healthier relationship going there rather than getting too caught up in all her negatives . . .

This sample of families was re-interviewed approximately two years later (child mean age = 16 years); 36 of the original 40 families (90 percent) were retained for this follow-up (four families had moved and/or separated and did not want to participate again). The same value choice task was completed by each parent, and each parent again told a narrative regarding teaching one of their chosen values to the child.

Independent of the value chosen by the parent for discussion, the socialization narrative produced by each parent at each time of testing about this value was rated by two independent coders on a three-point scale, for an emphasis on "justice" (1) or "care" (3) considerations (or as showing "mixed justice and care" [score of 2]), following the general procedures of Lyons (1983). The coefficient of exact agreement for this coding was 84 percent across the total sample for time (t) 1, and 86 percent for $t2$. Interestingly, the levels of relative care orientation scores for each parent's narratives were only modestly positively inter-correlated over the 2-year follow-up period ($r = 0.37$ between $t1$ and $t2$ for mothers, $p<0.05$, and $r = 0.23$ for fathers, *n.s.*). This suggests that parents' moral orientation in child-rearing, as measured by our narrative index, did not remain particularly stable over these two years of mid-adolescent development in the families. Walker (1995) has previously pointed out that consistency of use of dominant moral orientations by the same individual has been a serious question; the present low positive correlations over two years for these parent social-ization story orientations are somewhat ambiguous, and this issue deserves further study.

A repeated measures analysis of variance, with gender of child as the between-participant factor, and parent (mother, father) and time of testing as the within-participant factors, revealed two significant main effects. Across *both* parents and over time, stories told to girls were significantly more likely to involve at least some "care" considerations (scores of 2 or 3 in our system) than were those for boys (51 percent vs. 20 percent, $p<0.01$), as shown in Figure 3.1. Second, mothers were more likely than fathers to express some level of "care" considerations (43 percent vs. 28 percent, $p<0.05$). There were no other significant effects in this analysis. Finally, it should be noted that, overall, there were more socialization stories told in the families that focused solely on justice considerations rather than including any care concerns (64 percent versus 36 percent, respectively).

Why did the parents in our sample tend to tell different types of stories to sons and daughters? An examination of the values selected by parents before telling these socialization stories revealed that the two prototypic values of "fair and just" versus "kind and caring" tended to be differentially chosen for sons and daughters. (Not surprisingly, these two different story types were more likely to be scored as "justice"- or "care"-oriented, respectively). There were 14 stories told about fairness in the sample across both times. Of these, 11 (79 percent) were told regarding sons. Twenty stories about kindness were told across both times of testing. Of these 20 stories, 14 were told about daughters (70 percent). Thus, parents were differentially inclined to remember and tell different types of stories regarding children of different genders for the two values of justice and kindness. Interestingly, however, none of the other eight values that could be chosen by parents showed significant differences based on child or parent gender. The most common stories for both mothers and fathers overall were told about being "honest" (38 percent of all stories told),

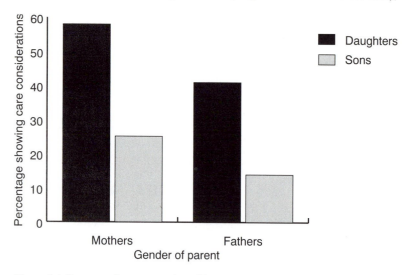

Figure 3.1 Percent of parent stories with some care considerations by gender group

although "kind and caring" was the next most common selection (14 percent), followed by "independent" (12 percent) and "fair and just" (10 percent of the total).

These findings for parents' socialization stories are reminiscent of the evidence reviewed above for adults, indicating that men and women tend to recall different types of specific moral problems in the standard Gilligan elicitation procedure, with women focusing more on "interpersonal" content regarding relationships (for example, Pratt *et al.*, 1988; Skoe *et al.*, 1996; Walker, 1995). It would appear that both parents, regardless of their own gender, recall prototypic examples of care versus justice values and concerns more commonly in association with daughters than sons, respectively, when asked to provide concrete examples of socialization processes and events that have occurred in their own families.

In addition, however, mothers' "voices" were somewhat more likely to focus on such care considerations in their stories about socialization than were those of fathers (see Figure 3.1). This gender of parent finding is of course consistent with women's tendency to tell interpersonal stories more often, and to consider care issues more readily in thinking about their own personal moral problems. As noted above, a gender difference in adult moral orientation usage has been particularly clear among samples of parents in our previous studies (Pratt *et al.*, 1988).

Was there any indication that the care orientation in parental socialization processes, as revealed by this narrative measure, was linked to children's actual development in our data? In this study, we collected a range of data on adolescent development, specifically including adolescent values, reasoning, and adjustment (including feelings of loneliness and self-esteem). We will discuss each of these three types of adolescent "outcome" measures in relation to parents' use of the care orientation in turn.

Because adolescents' own choices of three central values from the same list of ten completed by parents were also measured at each time of testing, we could assess how these were associated with patterns of parental narrative orientations. Adolescents' value choices were scored on a 4-point scale, from 0 to 3 at each time of testing, with 0 corresponding to a value not being selected at all, 1 to its selection as third most important, 2 to selection as second most important, and 3 to selection as most central for the self-ideal. Notably, only one of these ten value choices was differentiated by child gender over time; girls on average were more likely to value "kind and caring" for themselves compared with boys ($p<0.05$).

Table 3.1   Correlations between use of the care voice in parent narratives and measures of adolescent functioning

| | Correlation with care voice for: | |
Adolescent measure	Mothers	Fathers
Values kind and caring for self (Time 1)	.51*	.01
Values kind and caring for self (Time 2)	.39*	.28
Ethic of care reasoning level (Time 2)	.42*	.27
Loneliness score (Time 2):		
Girls	−.47*	−.05
Boys	.34	.03
Self-esteem score (Time 2)		
Girls	.40*	.37
Boys	−.53*	−.25

* p<.05, df=38 for combined sample,
Time 1 df=34 for combined sample,
Time 2 df=17 for girls alone, 15 for boys alone

Table 3.1 shows the data for the correlational analyses of relations between parent narratives and adolescent outcomes. As shown, mothers' emphasis on a care voice in their moral socialization narratives at each time of measurement was significantly positively linked to both girls' and boys' tendency to choose "kind and caring" in describing their ideals for themselves at that same time. Interestingly, fathers' emphasis on care in their narratives did not predict to adolescents' choices of "kind and caring" for themselves. None of the other nine value rankings by adolescents significantly associated with the moral orientation of stories told by parents across both testings, so this pattern of association with the value "kind and caring" was unique.

There was a further result of interest in terms of adolescents' socialization in the family. Both boys' and girls' level of reasoning about the ethic of care was assessed on Skoe's three-stage measure, using a standard dilemma drawn from her Ethic of Care Interview (Skoe and Marcia, 1991; Skoe, Chapter 7) at $t2$. Adolescents' level of care reasoning about this dilemma was significantly positively linked with mothers' emphasis on care in their socialization narratives at this same time (see Table 3.1). Thus, mothers who focus more on care issues in their families may encourage adolescents to think about such problems in more sophisticated terms. This pattern was not observed for fathers' story orientations and adolescents' care reasoning, however, as shown in the table.

Finally, we also collected some adjustment data on the adolescents in our sample at *t*2 which are relevant to these issues of gender and socialization. The adolescents filled out a standard 20-item self-report measure of loneliness (the UCLA Loneliness Scale). As well, they completed the standard 10-item Rosenberg Self-Esteem Scale. Consistent with the idea that these two measures are aspects of a general adjustment factor, they were found to be quite highly interrelated in our sample—$r = -0.66$, $p<0.01$—with greater reports of loneliness associated with lower levels of self-esteem in the adolescents, as might be expected.

While there were no overall gender differences in the levels of these two indices in the sample, less loneliness and higher self-esteem were consistently associated with a stronger "care" voice for mothers among girls in the sample, as shown in Table 3.1. For boys, surprisingly, these adjustment indices were actually inversely related to mothers' use of the care voice in narratives, as indicated in the table (this correlation was only significant for the self-esteem measure, as shown). Certainly this unpredicted finding that mothers' emphasis on care in their stories was negatively related to boys' feelings of self-esteem deserves to be followed up in future research. Finally, fathers' use of the care voice was again unrelated to either girls' or boys' adjustment scores.

The pattern of associations with adolescent development observed here was thus quite consistent across parent gender, as Table 3.1 indicates. Despite the fact that both mothers and fathers demonstrated usage of a care voice in their stories in our sample, particularly with girls, mothers' care emphasis in socialization was generally more consistently correlated in a positive way with adolescents' own development. While mothers' care voice thus seemed nurturing for adolescents, there was no evidence that fathers' use of a similar voice in socialization stories was linked to more positive adolescent development, as indicated in Table 3.1.

Such a possible difference between mothers' and fathers' apparent influence in socialization is not too remarkable, of course. Adolescents, both girls and boys, report feeling closer to mothers than fathers (for example, Larson and Richards, 1994), and many have argued for mothers' potentially stronger influence in the moral domain (for example, Gilligan, 1982). Obviously, these simple parent–child correlations can have little to say about actual processes, or about the earlier developmental history of these associations in the family. Further study of possible differences in the impact of mothers' and fathers' voices in moral orientation development is needed, particularly for children of different ages and over time.

A PRELIMINARY STUDY OF FAMILY MORAL NARRATIVES

In a second, exploratory study following the Fiese *et al.* (1995) procedure for eliciting family stories described above, we examined the use of narrative as a direct mode of moral socialization within a family analogue context. The purpose of this study was specifically to investigate the extent of any gender differences in the moral orientation of the personal narratives that adults tell about their own childhood experiences to their children. In this initial pilot study, a sample of 64 university students (32 males and 32 females; mean age 20) were each assigned to a condition in which they either imagined speaking to a future son or to a future daughter. Assignment of this "hypothetical" 10-year old child was counterbalanced across participants, so that 16 females and 16 males imagined having a son, and 16 females and 16 males imagined having a daughter.

After a brief encouragement to imagine this "future child," the participant was asked to think about two examples of times in her/his childhood when she/he learned a lesson about "right and wrong," and to recount the two stories about these times that she/he would tell to the child. The stories were then reliably scored for a focus on care orientation following similar procedures to those described above for socialization narratives. Results revealed only an effect for gender of child. "Future daughters" were more likely to be told care-focused stories than were "future sons" overall. Although female university students were somewhat more likely to tell care-oriented stories than were males, this gender of participant difference was not significant. Here is an example of a care-focused story, told by a woman to a "future daughter":

> My story took place in public school . . . . Some of my friends were making fun of and teasing someone who was less fortunate than we were. I didn't really start into that, I may have done it a few times, but then I just started seeing and realizing how badly this girl was feeling . . . I was the type of kid who was very emotional and took things to heart quite quickly. So just by realizing how hurt she was getting and seeing what my friends were doing, and just seeing that it doesn't feel good to make somebody else feel bad, especially when they're less fortunate than you, I guess I just learned to be friends with everybody because everybody's got that something special in them . . .

Although artificial in nature in some respects, this experimental storytelling study does suggest that girls and boys might tend to hear different types of family narratives. Obviously, follow-up work on family contexts with actual parents using the present story-telling technique would be desirable, and we are currently conducting such a study with parents of 5-year-olds. Interestingly, all participants in the present study were quite readily able to think of two stories that they would want to tell to a child, suggesting that this narrative mode of transmission of values is indeed easily accessed. This is consistent with the findings of Fiese *et al.* (1995), who showed that parents reported regularly telling such stories to their children and even to newborns and young infants. Note also that in this study, as well as the one on stories about socialization described above, more of the stories told were centered on justice rather than care considerations overall.

CONCLUSIONS

The results of these initial efforts to use narrative techniques as a way of understanding the socialization of moral orientation in the family appear promising. Consistent with some previous findings for descriptions of personal life problems, both parents used the care voice, but women were somewhat more likely to use it in socialization stories than were men overall (for example, Gilligan, 1982; Pratt *et al.*, 1988). Interestingly, observations on the relations between the care voice and children's own self-concepts and adaptation suggested that while both parents may tell more such stories about and to daughters than to sons, the care voice in the family context may be more influential from mothers than from fathers generally. Of course, these correlational observations on adolescent development and parent socialization orientation need to be followed up in a more systematic way over time, and the processes that underlie any such parent–child links need to be studied directly.

Nevertheless, in a more general sense, these results suggest the potential of the narrative approach, both as a research technique and a theoretical framework for addressing important questions of socialization in the moral domain. Despite considerable popular emphasis on the role of stories in moral development and "character education" (for example, Bennett, 1993), the studies reported here seem to be the first systematic observations of moral narratives in the family context in the research literature. All of us are inveterate story-tellers, and empirical description of such a fundamental category of experience in the moral domain is surely important. Furthermore, the results of the description presented here seem to shed light on the possible developmental history of moral orientation in adolescence and adulthood.

Finally, the relations between people's narrative accounts of their real-life moral experiences and the more traditional topics of moral feelings, actions, and reasoning (based in the historical approaches reviewed initially in this chapter) deserve serious research attention. Integrating the narrative focus with these more traditional approaches should ultimately be a fruitful strategy for utilizing this novel framework while anchoring it to previous research in the moral domain. Indeed, this has been the perspective with which we have undertaken the present research program (Pratt and Arnold, 1995).

In the present chapter, we have been concerned particularly with the role of the care voice in families of adolescents because it seemed to capture well the individual variability in our sample. But it was noteworthy that the justice voice was strong, and indeed, more widely used than care overall in both genders in the studies reported here. Such findings sharply highlight the multiplicity of moral voices with which people function in everyday life. In future research on moral orientation, we clearly need to develop a coherent understanding of how these two voices are both differentiated and perhaps ultimately integrated, across contexts, genders, and individuals, in the processes of personal decision making.

NOTE

1   This research was supported by a Social Sciences and Humanities Research Council of Canada grant to the authors Michael W. Pratt and Mary Louise Arnold, and to Joan E. Norris.

BIBLIOGRAPHY

Bakhtin, M. (1981) *The Dialogic Imagination*, Austin: University of Texas Press.
Beall, A., and Sternberg, R.J. (1993) *The Psychology of Gender*, New York: Guilford Press.
Bem, S. (1981). Gender schema theory: a cognitive account of sex typing, *Psychological Review*, 88: 354–64.
Bennett, W. (1993) *The Book of Virtues*, New York: Simon and Schuster.
Boyes, M., and Allen, S. (1993) Styles of parent–child interaction and moral reasoning in adolescence, *Merrill-Palmer Quarterly*, 39: 551–70.
Brown, L., Tappan, M., and Gilligan, C. (1995) Listening to different voices, in W. Kurtines and J. Gewirtz (eds.), *Moral Development: An Introduction*, pp. 311–35, Boston: Allyn and Bacon.
Bruner, J. (1986) *Actual Minds, Possible Worlds*, Cambridge: Harvard University Press.
Burton, R., and Kunce, L. (1995). Behavioral models of moral development: a

brief history and integration, in W. Kurtines and J. Gewirtz (eds.), *Moral Development: An Introduction*, pp. 141–71, Boston: Allyn and Bacon.

Chodorow, N. (1978) *The Reproduction of Mothering: Psychoanalysis and the Sociology of Gender*, Berkeley: University of California Press.

Clopton, N., and Sorrell, G. (1993) Gender differences in moral reasoning: stable or situational? *Psychology of Women Quarterly*, 17: 85–101.

Day, J., and Tappan, M. (1996) The narrative approach to moral development: from the epistemic subject to dialogical selves, *Human Development*, 39: 67–82.

Eisenberg, N., Miller, P., Shell, R., McNally, S., and Shea, C. (1991) Prosocial development in adolescence: a longitudinal study, *Developmental Psychology*, 27: 849–57.

Fiese, B., Hooker, K., Kutary, L., Schwagler, J., and Rimmie, M. (1995) Family stories: gender differences in thematic content, *Journal of Marriage and the Family*, 57: 63–70.

Garrod, A., Beal, C., and Shin, P. (1990) The development of moral orientation in elementary school children, *Sex Roles*, 22: 13–27.

Gergen, K. (1991) *The Saturated Self: Dilemmas of Identity in Contemporary Life*, New York: Basic Books.

Gilligan, C. (1977) In a different voice: women's conception of the self and of morality, *Harvard Educational Review* 47: 481–517.

—— (1982) *In a different voice: psychological theory and women's development*, Cambridge: Harvard University Press.

Gilligan, C., and Attanucci, J. (1988) Two moral orientations: gender differences and similarities, *Merrill-Palmer Quarterly*, 34: 223–37.

Gilligan, C., and Wiggins, G. (1987) The origins of morality in early childhood relationships, in J. Kagan and S. Lamb (eds.), *The Emergence of Morality in Young Children*, pp. 277–305, Chicago: University of Chicago Press.

Huston, A. (1983) Sex typing, in E.M. Hetherington (ed.), *Handbook of Child Psychology*, vol. 4., 4th edn, New York: Wiley.

Johnston, K. (1988) Adolescents' solutions to dilemmas in fables: two moral orientations–two problem-solving strategies, in C. Gilligan, J. Ward, and J. Taylor (eds.), *Mapping the Moral Domain*, pp. 49–71, Cambridge: Harvard University Press.

Johnston, D.K., Brown, L.M., and Christopherson, S.B. (1990) Adolescents' moral dilemmas: the context, *Journal of Youth and Adolescence*, 19: 615–22.

Kahn, P. (1992) Children's obligatory and discretionary moral judgments, *Child Development*, 63: 416–30.

Kohlberg, L. (1966) A cognitive-developmental analysis of children's sex-role concepts and attitudes, in E. Maccoby (ed.), *The Development of Sex Differences,* Stanford: Stanford.

—— (1976) Moral stages and moralization: the cognitive-developmental approach, in T. Lickona (ed.), *Moral Development and Behavior*, pp. 31–53, New York: Holt, Rinehart, and Winston.

Larson, R., and Richards, M. (1994) *Divergent Realities: The Emotional Lives of Mothers, Fathers, and Adolescents*, New York: Basic Books.

Lollis, S., Ross, H., and Leroux, L. (1996) An observational study of parents' socialization of moral orientation during sibling conflicts, *Merrill-Palmer Quarterly.*, 42: 475–95.

Lott, B., and Maluso, D. (1993) The social learning of gender, in A.E. Beall and R.J. Sternberg (eds.), *The Psychology of Gender*, pp. 99–126, New York: Guilford Press.

Lyons, N. (1983) Two perspectives: on self, relationships, and morality, *Harvard Educational Review*, 53: 125–45.

Maccoby, E. (1992) The role of parents in the socialization of children: an historical overview, *Developmental Psychology*, 28: 1006–17.

Martin, C., and Halverson, C. (1981) A schematic processing model of sex typing and stereotyping in children, *Child Development*, 52: 1119–34.

McAdams, D. (1993) *The stories we live by: Personal Myths and the Making of the Self*, New York: William Morrow.

Miller, D. (1969) The psychoanalytic theory of development: a re-evaluation, pp. 481–502, in D.A. Goslin (ed.), *Handbook of Socialization Theory and Research*, Chicago: Rand-McNally.

Pratt, M., and Arnold, M.L. (1995) Narrative approaches to moral socialization across the lifespan, *Moral Education Forum* 20: 13–22.

—— (1996, March) *Measuring the Climate of Moral Communication in Families of Adolescents using Narrative and Observational Techniques*, poster presented at the Meetings of the Society for Research on Adolescence, Boston.

Pratt, M., Diessner, R., Hunsberger, B., Pancer, S.M., and Savoy, K. (1991) Four pathways in the analysis of adult development and aging, *Psychology and Aging* 6: 666–75.

Pratt, M., Golding, G., Hunter, W., and Sampson, R. (1988) Sex differences in adult moral orientations, *Journal of Personality*, 56: 373–91.

Serbin, L., Powlishta, K., and Gulko, J. (1993) The development of sex typing in middle childhood, *Monographs of the Society for Research in Child Development*, 58, no. 2.

Skoe, E.E., and Diessner, R. (1994) Ethic of care, justice, identity and gender: an extension and replication, *Merrill-Palmer Quarterly*, 40: 102–19.

Skoe, E.E., and Gooden, A. (1993) Ethic of care and real-life moral dilemma content in male and female early adolescents, *Journal of Early Adolescence*, 13: 154–67.

Skoe, E.E., and Marcia, J. (1991) A care-based measure of morality and its relation to ego identity, *Merrill-Palmer Quarterly*, 37: 289–304.

Skoe, E.E., Pratt, M., Matthews, M., and Curror, S. (1996) The ethic of care: stability over time, gender differences and correlates in mid to late adulthood, *Psychology and Aging*, 11: 280–92.

Smetana, J. (1995) Context, conflict, and constraint in adolescent-parent authority relationships, in M. Killen and D. Hart (eds.), *Morality in Everyday Life: Developmental Perspectives*, pp. 225–55, New York: Cambridge University Press.

Tappan, M. (1991) Texts and contexts: language, culture, and the development of moral functioning, in L. Winegar and J. Valsiner (eds.), *Children's Development within Social Contexts*, pp. 93–117, Hillsdale: Erlbaum.

Thoma, S. (1986) Estimating gender differences in the comprehension and preference of moral issues, *Developmental Review* 6: 165–80.

Turiel, E. (1998) The development of morality, in W. Damon (ed.), *Handbook of Child Psychology*, 5th edn., vol. 3. New York: Wiley.

Vitz, P. (1990) The use of stories in moral development: new psychological reasons for an old educational method, *American Psychologist* 45: 709–20.

Walker, L.J. (1989) A longitudinal study of moral reasoning, *Child Development* 60: 157–66.

—— (1995) Sexism in Kohlberg's moral psychology?, in W. Kurtines and J. Gewirtz (eds.), *Moral Development: An Introduction*, pp. 83–107, Boston: Allyn and Bacon.

Walker, L.J., and Taylor, J. (1991) Family interactions and development of moral reasoning, *Child Development*, 62: 264–83.

Wark, J., and Krebs, D. (1996) Gender and dilemma differences in real-life moral judgment, *Developmental Psychology*, 32: 220–30.

Wertsch, J. (1991) *Voices of the Mind*, Cambridge: Harvard University Press.

Part II
Cultural context

4   Social parameters in adolescent development
Challenges to psychological research

Torild Hammer

In psychological research on adolescence it is important to consider how a changing society affects the social conditions and opportunities for development during adolescent years. In a sociological perspective the individual and the life course are culturally constructed (Meyer, 1988). Life course research has concentrated mainly on cohort analyses, how changes in social structure affect the life course of different cohorts (Elder, 1991; Sørensen *et al.*, 1986). The life course in modern society has been described as "consisting of institutionalized sequences of events, positions and roles which shape the individual's progression in time and space" (Buchmann, 1989, p. 43). Each stage of life is accompanied by the cultural definition of needs, competencies, tasks and behaviors thought to be appropriate for individuals belonging to a given age group. Such officially recognized attributes constitute the basic element of the individual's social identity. It is therefore important to understand the social context of identity formation in adolescence and how social change affect personal development. "The impact of changing historical epoch to adolescent identity formation process is an important and virtually untouched area of systematic research needing further investigation" (Kroger, 1993, p. 375).

The aim of this chapter is to describe and analyze some important aspects of social change in adolescent's situation and living conditions during the last decade in Norway and other Western European countries, and to call attention to possible implications for psychological research on adolescent development.

GROWING UP IN A NEW SETTING OF FAMILY LIFE

Most young people in Norway live at home with their parents during teen-age years. One of the main changes in their situation during the past ten to fifteen years is an increasing instability and dissolution of traditional family life, caused by an increasing divorce rate and single parent families. This development is the same in most Western European countries. Comparing different cohorts of teen-agers, the Central Bureau of Statistics (CBS) in Norway has calculated prognoses of the development (Jensen *et al.*, 1991). Figure 4.1 gives the proportion of 16-year-old children that will experience parents' divorce (or termination of cohabitation) during their childhood. These cohorts were born in 1972, 1978, and 1984.

Of the 1972 cohort 14 percent had experienced divorce compared to 31 percent of the 1984 cohort, according to prognoses. Oslo, the capital of Norway, has a much higher divorce rate than the rest of the country. Here, in 1993 one-third of the 16-year-olds had experienced divorce, and half of them now live in families with a new composition (Jensen, 1993). It is difficult to evaluate the impact of these changes for childhood and adolescent development. Some social consequences can be documented, however. First, divorce generates poverty implying economic problems in single parent families. Single mothers have an income 30 percent lower than two parent families (Jensen, 1993). Furthermore, British research indicates that adolescents from such families have a higher risk of drop out from schools, have a higher unemployment rate, and a higher risk of being without a place of residence when they leave home (Jeffs and Smith, 1990). Second, divorce increases the risk of loss of contact with biological father: a survey of

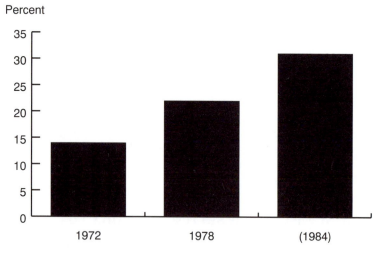

Figure 4.1 Proportion of 16-year-olds with divorced parents

3,000 16-year-old children in Norway showed that one-third of those from divorced families reported practically no contact with the biological father. This is in accordance with international research from the USA (Furstenberg *et al.*, 1983). Researchers talk about "femininization of childhood," and focus especially upon the female domination of mothers, child nursery personnel and teachers in children's social environment. "The missing fathers" contribute to this development, which generates several important questions such as the formation of identity among boys. The findings give some indications of the call for research on adolescent development in this area.

EDUCATION AND WORK

Today, most young people in Norway in the age group 16–19 years are in upper secondary education. According to a new school reform (Reform-94) all young people in this age group have the right to such education. In 1993, 95 percent of the 16-year-olds and 52 percent of the 19-year-olds were in school (CBS, 1993). According to the youth surveys carried out by the CBS, there has been a steady increase in education and consequently a dramatic decrease of adolescents participation in the workforce during the past ten to fifteen years (Moen, 1991). The same development takes place in nearly all European Union countries (European Commission, 1994a).

According to Figure 4.2, 30 percent of the age group 16–19 years was in the workforce in 1975 compared to 8 percent in 1990 in Norway. This development has several important consequences for adolescent socialization. So far, little research has addressed this question. Baethge (1992, p. 26) gives a theoretical analysis of socialization in work versus education as constituting factors of social identity:

- Prolonged education implies "a longer time spent with members of the same age group and later entry into a world of communication dominated by adults."
- A lengthening of the "psychosocial moratorium" with a greater tolerance of error and failure on the part of young people than is possible in serious business situations.
- A longer time spent in a situation conducive to the development of an individual rather than a "collective code of performance."

Baethge describes an increased individualism based on individual performance and competition in the educational system, as opposed to the collective code of working life. A collective code implies social relations based on work towards common goals, where young people

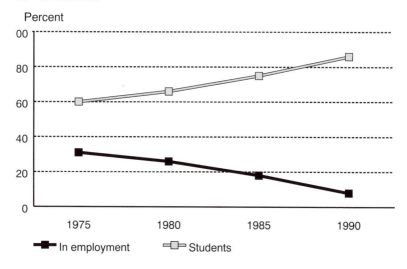

Figure 4.2 Proportion employed or in school, 17–19-years-olds, by year

participate in production and support themselves as adult members of society.

The development during the last fifteen years implies that the world of work has been closed for young people as an alternative arena for socialization and qualification. Consequently, working life has lost its integrative functions. Previously, a 15-year-old drop out from school could get a job, training in the work place and a secure future independent of school results. Learning in working life could compensate for school problems and low school performance. Today, the recruitment to work is mainly based on educational qualifications, and school drop out implies a very high risk of unemployment (Hammer, 1993a). The loss of working life's integrative functions have important social political implications, and contributes to the marginalization of young people. Such marginalization probably influences adolescent socialization, mental health and personal development. The rise of youth unemployment promotes this development.

Figure 4.3 shows the development of unemployment from 1980 to 1992 for the age group 16–19 years and 20–24 years (CBS, 1993). Essentially there has been a dramatic rise in unemployment since 1985.

Unemployment is primarily a youth problem: the unemployment rate is three times as high among young people under 25 years than among older age groups: 13 percent versus 4 percent calculated as a percentage of the workforce (CBS, 1994). Nearly 8 percent of the age

Percent

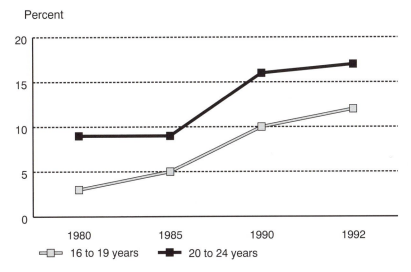

Figure 4.3 Unemployment as percent of the workforce, by age group and year

group 16–24 years old was unemployed in 1992. In the total group of unemployed about 40 percent are under 25 years old.

A lot of international research has been carried out that analyze causes and consequences of youth unemployment. It is well documented in many European studies that young unemployed people report more mental health problems than young people in education or work (for example, Banks and Ullah, 1988; Warr *et al.*, 1988; Hammer 1993b). This is to some degree caused by a selection effect implying that young people with mental health problems have a higher risk of unemployment. However, most studies have also found a weak but significant effect of unemployment in itself (Rosvold and Hammer, 1991). One of the main problems reported by young unemployed is hopelessness about the future. For young people especially, future plans about what career to choose and what to do in life are an important aspect of identity formation. Insecurity about plans for future work does not only concern the work itself, but will also affect future plans for establishing a family, having children, where and how to live, and so on.

Longitudinal studies of youth unemployment indicate different social processes of marginalization. First, previous unemployment seems to increase the risk of later unemployment (Hammer, 1997). Second, some studies have found that the length of the unemployment period affects the chance of getting a job. There is, however, a need for further research in this area. Such marginalization processes may lead to total exclusion of groups of young people from the labor market. Longitudinal research of labor market careers among young Norwegians in the last eight years, does not, however, confirm such a development. So far, young people have not been totally excluded. Their careers are characterized by periodic unemployment, moving about between work, education, unemployment and labor market programs (Hammer, 1996).

Unemployment is undoubtedly a significant youth problem in Norway. It is, however, important to stress that the unemployment rate still is much lower in Norway compared to other countries in western Europe (OECD, 1991). On the other hand, it is difficult to estimate the extent of unemployment. A lot of students both in upper secondary school and higher education would probably prefer employment if work was available. A survey conducted in 1990 found that 9 percent of the students in the age group 17–24 years old reported that the high unemployment rate among young people was their main motive for applying for their current education (Moen, 1991). The recruitment to higher education follows developments in the labor market over the past ten years, developments which have an increasing application in recession periods (Jørgensen, 1993). However, increasing educational activity may also signal higher motivation for education, implying that education is considered valuable in itself.

The increasing participation in upper secondary education has probably influenced competence and cognitive development among adolescents. Furthermore, the recruitment to higher education has increased dramatically over the last decade from 82,000 first registered students in 1980 to 160,000 in 1990 (Aamodt, 1992). The proportion of students in the age group 20–24 years old was 12 percent in 1980 versus 20 percent in 1990 (CBS, 1993), and it has increased even more over the last couple of years. A prolonged time spent in education probably leads to an expanding period as youth and a postponement of transition to adulthood. Accordingly, most young people are given the opportunity to experiment with different social roles which constitute social identity.

TRANSITION TO ADULTHOOD

In our society there are very few transition markers left that signal adulthood. Economic independence, leaving the parental home and the establishment of a family with children are the remaining crucial markers of an adult role. There has not been any significant changes over the last ten years with regard to the time when young people leave their parental home. According to the surveys on level of living (CBS, 1993), 36 percent in the age group 20–24 years were living in the parental home in 1980, compared to 34 percent in 1991.

Young women leave home much earlier than men. In 1991, 50 percent of men in this age group was still living with their parents compared to 19 percent among women (CBS, 1993). This is consistent with the development in other Western countries (Kerckhoff, 1990). However, more young people, both men and women, prefer to live alone. Figure 4.4 shows changes in marital status in the age group 16–19 and 20–24 years old from 1980 to 1991. The data are based on surveys of levels of living from the CBS from 1980, 1983, 1987, 1991, as analyzed by Fauske (1994). The figure gives the proportion of each age group married or cohabitating at each point of time.

There has been a dramatic decrease in marriages among young people during the past ten years. Cohabitation is much more prevalent than marriage. Figure 4.4 therefore shows the proportion of both marriage and cohabitation. According to the figure the proportion of marriage or cohabitation did not change much in the age group 16–19 years the past decade. However, in the age group 20–24 years there was a clear decrease, especially among women, from 60 percent in 1980 to 42 percent in 1991. It is reasonable to see this development in connection with increasing participation of women in higher education

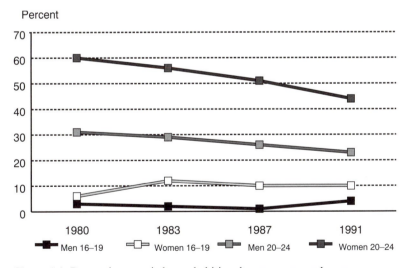

Figure 4.4 Proportion married or cohabiting, by age group and year

(Ellingsæter *et al.*, 1993). More young women leave their parents and live alone without a partner for a longer period in young adulthood, a social moratorium period implying no family obligations and post-ponement of family and childbirth.

Figure 4.5 shows birthrates from 1980–1991 among men and women in the age group 16–19 years and 20–24 years old (Fauske 1994). As can be seen from the figure, teen-age childbirth has practi-cally vanished during the last decade and represents no problem in Norway contrary to other Western countries. Among women aged 16–19 years old, the proportion with children was reduced from nearly 22 percent in 1980 to 2 percent in 1991. In the same age group the number of abortions in this age group increased from 1980 to 1986 (Kristiansen, 1989), but did not change greatly after this time (CBS, 1993).

Also in the age group 20–24 years, there was a clear reduction of parenthood during the last decade among both men and women. This is an interesting development which may express changes in transition to adulthood. Especially among young women who leave parental home at a young age, it may be fruitful to consider a concept of post-adolescence. A period, or life stage, where young women live alone without family responsibilities, may give them new opportunities and influence personal development, independence and identity formation. Further research should investigate whether this development is

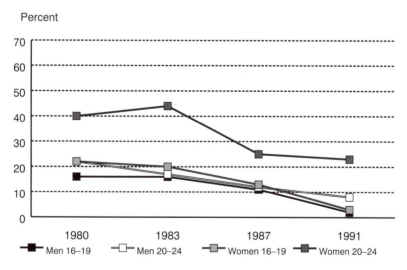

Figure 4.5 Proportion with children, age groups 16–19 and 20–24, by year

strongly related to participation in education or social class, or if this is a trend among all young women in our society.

Life course research that focuses upon the transition from youth to adulthood has found that the transition process is related to social class. A study from the Netherlands found that working class youth is characterized by a more traditional transition process, especially among young women, compared to the middle class (Bois-Reymond *et al.*, 1994). The traditional transition process is characterized by change of status in a defined order, such as from school to work, then marriage and children, while modernity involves a longer period of youth with more variation and individualization of careers. Unemployment, which primarily affects working class youth, seems to strengthen traditional gender roles (Hammer, 1996; Wallace, 1987).

Cohort analyses of the life courses of young women have also brought to light a more clear cut segregation between family and work-oriented life courses for women in the 1970s and 1980s than previously, referred to as an increased polarization or dualization of the female working career (Berger *et al.*, 1993). The results may indicate increased differences between women. This is in accordance with life course research that has documented a destandardization of transition to adult status, more diversified and individualized than previously (Buchman, 1989).

YOUTH AND MODERNITY

Modern societies provide increasing options for young people educationally, culturally and with regard to different lifestyles. They can make their own choices and are less bound by gender, religion, parental control or traditions. Ziehe and Stubenrauch (1983) describe this development as cultural emancipation, offering new possibilities for the young generation.

However, individual choices have to be legitimized. Young people are responsible for their own life course, a "choice biography" contrary to tradition (Bois-Reymond *et al.*, 1994). The dissolution of tradition, changing gender roles and family relations may imply a loosening of social network and social control. Accordingly, some researchers (Beck, 1992) talk about the risk society, cultural emancipation but at the same time increased risk of marginalization. (One example is increasing drug use and criminal activity among young women over the past twenty years.)

Analyses of adolescent transition to adulthood in the Netherlands (Bois-Reymond *et al.*, 1994), Great Britain (Banks *et al.*, 1992) and

USA (Buchman, 1989) have shown an extensive variation in career trajectories. However, gender and social class are still basic elements in social reproduction, influencing the individual's life chances and the outcome of individual choice. Accordingly, modernity involves new modes of social reproduction. Banks *et al.* found that although social class remained a powerful force " . . . it's immediate impact on the distribution of career opportunities operated largely through its link with educational achievement" (1992, p. 49). Bois Reymond *et al.* concluded that "also within a choice biography there appear to be gender and class related differences" (1994, p. 17). The biography of girls has changed more fundamentally than that of boys.

Developments in Norway during the last ten years seem to be congruent with this picture. Changes in transition to adulthood during this period indicate increased differentiation of the female career. To some extent this development, described as post-adolescence, may be explained by increased participation of women in higher education. However, the gender-related differences in higher education have not changed so dramatically during the last decade as to give a satisfying explanation for the development. The results may imply changed behavior among young women in higher education, or a general trend independent of educational career. Furthermore, previous research in the USA indicates that postponement of marriage and motherhood has a positive effect on women's attainments (Kerckhoff, 1990).

Changing gender roles probably influence the formation of gender-role identity in adolescence. A recent study of Norwegian adolescents found that girls showed a more androgynous profile than boys, as measured by Bem's inventory of sex-role identity (Bem, 1974). Girls had high scores on both femininity and masculinity, whereas boys had high scores only on the masculine dimension (Wichstrøm, 1994). Unfortunately, there has not been any comparable study previously in Norway, so we do not know if this is a new development. Further research should focus on this issue.

The results presented here make it possible to draw a picture of the Norwegian development also relevant for western Europe in general. Young middle class women seem to adjust very well to the new require-ments of the educational society. Girls do better in school than boys (Wichstrøm, 1993), they read more books, they are more engaged in global environmental problems, and they break with traditional gender roles without losing sight of traditional feminine values. On the other hand, working class boys report more problems at school with disci-pline and opposition towards both teachers and the school curriculum (Skogen and Wichstrøm, 1995), and they are more involved in a masculine culture where theoretical knowledge is associated with femininity (Willis, 1979). This is the group that probably is most affected by developments during the last decade; the exclusion of employment as an alternative arena for qualification and socialization in adolescence (Furlong and Cartmel, 1997). The remaining options are either several years in school or unemployment. The increase of unemployment, which is much higher among working class boys, contributes to the risk of marginalization.

Throughout the European Union, governments have been concerned with the increasing levels of youth unemployment. Rates of youth unemployment tend to be higher than among the general population, and there is a serious risk of marginalization and exclusion among young people. In May 1994 the rate of youth unemployment within the European Union was around 21 percent, more than twice the rate experienced by adults (9 percent). Indeed, in northern Europe, as in the other member states, about 35 percent of the unemployed population are under 25 years old, although this age group comprises only 20 percent of the total workforce. Over the last five years the rate of unemployment increase has been particularly sharp, especially among young men. Moreover, this increase has occurred despite a demographic decrease in the youth age range and despite an increased level of educational participation within most member states (European Commission, 1994a). A development with increased unemployment, family dissolution and growth in social assistance has created a political debate in the European Union about the increased risk of social exclusion of young people (European Commission, 1994b).

Unemployment among young men is associated with living in the parental home, contrary to young unemployed women, who move away from their parents independent of unemployment (Hammer, 1996). British studies confirm this development (Wallace, 1987). Parental dependency in unemployed young men prolongs the period of transition to adulthood. In most European countries young men leave home several years after young women, a result also independent of unemployment. According to a German study these "nest sitters," living in the equivalent of a hotel run by mummy, may generate a very different lifestyle than their female counterparts of the same age, (Zinnecker, 1994).

Young middle class women seem to have profited from increased requirements of theoretical education. In Scandinavia and several other European countries, such as Great Britain and Ireland, there are more females than males in upper secondary education which give access to the universities. Furthermore, women have been conquering new areas of university education previously dominated by men, such as medicine, law, economics, social sciences and so on. With regard to vocational education or skilled/unskilled work in the labor market, however, there has been practically no change during the past twenty years. Educational and occupational choice are as traditionally gender bound among working class women as ever (CBS, 1993). Young working class women hit by unemployment still have a cultural niche available: staying at home with the children and being supported by a husband (Hammer, 1996). But this is an increasingly insecure way to make a living. The dramatic rise in divorce rates or dissolution of cohabitation in most West European countries, combined with low wages for unskilled young women in the labor market, have led to increased poverty. A Danish study found that the combination of being female with small children, divorced and unemployed gave the highest risk of poverty in Denmark (Elm Larsen and Andersen, 1990). There is increasing international research into the femininization of poverty (for example, Daly, 1992; Pearce, 1985). The social system of the male breadwinner is still dominating the wage structure of the labor market (Gunnarsson, 1990). Low wages in female-dominated occupations imply that many women with responsibility for rearing small children alone will be dependent on social assistance. As previously described, the high proportion of young people receiving social assistance is dominated by young unemployed men and young unemployed mothers, a shift from private to public support among these women. Contrary to the USA, the Scandinavian welfare states provide support for these young mothers.

In conclusion, modernity involves new options for young people and creates new patterns in the transition to adulthood, especially for young women. However, this also implies increased differences among young women both regarding ways of living, economy and social position. Increased educational participation by females tends to reduce culturally determined gender gaps and increase the potential for political participation. Inglehart (1990) found in his study based on data from the Euro-barometer surveys that formal education tends to erase the gender gap in politicization. The sex difference is largest among the least educated, and shrinks almost to zero among the highly educated.

Even if social change over the last decade indicates increased differentiation of young people's careers and gender roles, there are also traits in this development pulling in the other direction. The exclusion of employment as an alternative to school in adolescence leads to limitation rather than increased options for young people. Changes in young women's careers do not undermine the fact that gender still is one of the most important predictors of individual trajectories in adolescent development (Banks *et al.*, 1992). Furthermore, young women suffer from more mental health problems and lower self-esteem than young men in the same age group (Wichstrøm, 1993). It is, however, important to consider the impact of changing gender roles in the research on adolescence development.

The challenge to psychological research on identity formation is to take into account the changes described here. Most of these changes have taken place in several Western European countries and in North America. So far, we know little about how changes in transition to adulthood affect young people. Comparative research, including data from several countries, is required in order to identify changes in the general development of social identity in adolescence.

BIBLIOGRAPHY

Aamodt, P.O. (1992) *Nye studenter etter 1980—myter og realiteter i utdanning og arbeidsmarked (New students after 1980—myths and realities in education and the labour market)*, C.Å. Arnesen, and M. Egge (eds.), Oslo: NAVFs Utredningsinstitutt.

Banks, M.H., and Ullah, P. (1988) *Youth Unemployment in the 1980s: Its Psychological Effects*, London: Croom Helm.

Banks, M., Bates, I., Breakwell, G., Bynner, J., Emler, N., Jamieson, L., and Roberts, K. (1992) *Careers and Identities*, Buckingham: Open University Press.

Baethge, M. (1992) Changes in work and education as constituting factors of social identity. Theoretical and Political Implications, in T. Halvorsen, O.J. Olsen (eds.), *Det kvalifiserte samfunn (The educated society)*, pp. 31–42, Oslo: Gyldendal.

Beck, U. (1992) *Risk Society*, London: Sage.

Bem, S. (1974) The measurement of psychological androgyneity, *Journal of Consulting and Clinical Psychology, 42: 634–43.*

Berger, P.A., Steinmuller, P., and Sopp, P. (1993) Differentiation of life-courses? changing patterns of labour-market sequences in West Germany, *European Sociological Review* 9, 1: 43–59.

Bois-Reymond, M., Guit, H., Peters, E., Ravesloot, J., and Van Rooijen, E. (1994) Life-course transition and future orientation of Dutch youth, *Young, Nordic Journal of Youth Research* 2, 1: 3–20.

Buchmann, M. (1989) *The Script of Life in Modern Society. Entry into Adulthood in a Changing World*, Chicago and London: University of Chicago Press.

Central Bureau of Statistics (CBS) (1991) *Survey of Standard of Living*, Oslo.

—— (1993) *Sosialt utsyn (Social Survey)*, Oslo.

—— (1994) *Arbeidsmarkedsstatistikk (Labour market statistics)*, Oslo.

Daly, M. (1992) Europe's poor women? Gender in research on poverty, *European Sociological Review*, 8, 1: 1–12.

Elder, G.H. (1991) Lives and social change, in W.R. Heinz (ed.), *Theoretical Advances in Life Course Research*, Weinheim: Deutscher Studien Verlag.

Ellingsæter, A.L., Noack, T., and Rønsen, M. (1993) Utdanning, arbeid og inntekt: hvor likestilte har kvinner og menn blitt (Education, work and income: How equal have women and men become), *Samfunnsspeilet*, 1: 2–9.

Elm Larsen, J., and Andersen, J. (1990) *Arbejdsløshed og offentlig forsørgelse i Danmark (Unemployment and public support in Denmark)*, Copenhagen: Forlaget Sociologi.

European Commission (1994a) *Employment in Europe. Employment Observatory*, SYSDEM publications, no 17, Brussels.

—— (1994b) *Growth, Competitiveness, Employment. The Challenges and Ways forward into The 21st Century*, White Paper. Brussels.

Fauske, H. (1994) *Å bli voksen. Overgang til voksenstatus i 1980-årene (Growing up. Transition to grown-up status in the 1980s)*, Rapport Lillehammer distrikthøyskole.

Furlong, A., and Cartmel, F. (1997) *Young People and Social Change: Individualization and Risk in Late Modernity*, Buckingham: Open University Press.

Furstenberg, F., Winquist Nord, C., Peterson, J.L., and Zill, N. (1983) The life course of children of divorce: marital disruption and parental contact, *American Sociological Review*, 48: 656–68.

Gunnarsson, E. (1990) Kvinnors fattigdom i velferdsstaten (Women's poverty in the welfare state) *Kvinnovetenskaplig Tidsskrift*, 2: 28–35.

Hammer, T. (1993a) Explanations of youth unemployment, *Young, Nordic Journal of Youth Research*, 1: 11–26.

—— (1993b) Unemployment and mental health among young people: a longitudinal study, *Journal of Adolescence*, 16: 407–20.

—— (1996) Consequences of unemployment in the transition from youth to adulthood in a life course perspective, *Youth and Society*, 27: 450–68.

—— (1997) History dependence in youth unemployment, *European Sociological Review*, 13, 1: 1–17.

Inglehart, R. (1990) *Culture Shift in Advanced Industrial Society*, Princeton: Princeton University Press.

Jeffs, T., and Smith, M. (1990) *Young People, Inequality and Youth Work*, London: Macmillan.

Jensen, A., Jensen, M., Moen, B., and Clausen, S. (1991) *Enebarn, delebarn eller stebarn (Only child, part child, or step child)*, report no. 14, Oslo: NIBR (Norwegian Institute for City and Region Research).

Jensen, M. (1990) *Tall om barn (Figures about children)*, report no. 113, Oslo: NIBR (Norwegian Institute for City and Region Research).

—— (1993) *Barns levekår i 1980-åra (Children's life circumstances in the 1980s)*, report no. 11, Oslo: NIBR (Norwegian Institute for City and Region Research).

Jørgensen, T. (1993) Studenttallseksplosjonen (The explosion in student numbers) *Samfunnsspeilet*, 4: 12–14.

Kerckhoff, A.C. (1990) *Getting Started, Transition to Adulthood in Great Britain*, San Francisco: Westview Press.

Kristiansen, J.E. (1989) *Ungdoms levekår (Youth's living conditions)*, Oslo: Universitetsforlaget.

Kroger, J. (1993) The role of historical context in the identity formation process of late adolescence, *Youth and Society* 24, 4: 363–76.

Meyer, J.W. (1988) Levels of analysis. The life course as a cultural construction, in M.W. Riley (ed.), *Social Structures and Human Lives*, Newbury Park and London: Sage and American Sociological Association Presidential Series.

Moen, K. (1991) *Ungdomsundersøkelsen 1990. Foreløpig rapport* (*Youth investigation 1990. Preliminary report*), report no. 2, Oslo: Arbeidsdirektoratet.

Organization for Economic Co-operation and Development (OECD) (1991) *Quarterly Labour Force Statistics*, no. 4. Paris.

Pearce, D.M. (1985) Toil and trouble: women workers and unemployment compensation, *Signs*, 10, 3: 439–59.

Rosvold, E.O., and Hammer, T. (1991) En longitudinell studie av arbeidsløshet og økonomisk mestring relatert til mental helse (A longitudinal study of unemployment and economic mastering related to mental health), *Tidsskrift for samfunnsforskning*, 32, 2: 121–42.

Skogen, K., and Wichstrøm, L. (1995) Kriminalitet og klasse (Crime and class) *Nordisk Tidskrift for Kriminalvidenskap*, 82, 1: 32–49.

Sørensen, A.B, Weinert, F.E, and Sherrod, L.R. (1986) *Human Development and the Life Course*, London: Erlbaum.

Wallace, C. (1987) *For Richer Or Poorer. Growing Up In and Out of Work*, London: Tavistock.

Warr, P., Jackson, P., and Banks, M.H. (1988) Psychological effects of unemployment, *Journal of Social Issues*, 44, 4: 47–68.

Wichstrøm, L. (1993) *Hvem sprang? Hvem sto igjen og hang? Ungdomsskoleelevers skolemotivasjon* (*Who ran? Who were left behind? School motivation among pupils in youth school*), report no. 4, Norwegian Center for Youth Research (Ungforsk) Oslo.

—— (1994) *Mental helse blant ungdom i Norge. Oslo som særtilfelle? (Mental health among youth in Norway. Oslo as a special case)*, report no. 3, Norwegian Center for Youth Research (Ungforsk), Oslo.

Willis, P. (1979) *Learning to Labour*, London: Saxon House.

Ziehe, T., and Stubenrauch, H. (1983) *Ny ungdom og usædvanlige læreprocesser (New youth and exceptional learning processes)*, Copenhagen: Politisk Revy.

Zinnecker, J. (1994) *Leaving the family home in the third decade of life. Patterns of housing among young Germans in a comparative perspective*, paper presented to the Fourth Nordic Youth Research Symposium University of Stockholm.

5   Self-concept development during adolescence

Do American truths hold for Norwegians?

Lars Wichstrøm

Self-concept has been one of the most researched topics of adolescent development. Despite this, several inconsistencies in findings exist. From the late 1970s and onwards there has been a growing consensus that self-esteem is multidimensional, and this is reflected in the three most frequently used self-report schemes for assessing self-concept during adolescence: namely, the Offer Self-Image Questionnaire (OSIQ) (Offer, 1969), Marsh's Self Description Questionnaires (SDQ) (Marsh, 1988) and Harter's Self Perception Profile for Adolescents (SPPA) (Harter, 1988a). After the introduction of multidimensional scales, findings have converged to a greater extent. However, inconsistencies and controversies still exist. Reviewers have concluded that a number of studies are hampered by methodological problems which pertain to both scale construction and the samples involved (Wylie, 1974, 1979; Marsh, 1989).

There may, however, be a more theoretically meaningful reason for seeming inconsistencies. Self-concept is by definition relational and social. Most contemporary researchers would agree, at least to some extent, with William James' (1892) contention that self-esteem is generated from the relation between the ideal and perceived self and with Cooley's (1902) notion of "the looking glass self," implying that self-evaluations are based on generalizations of others' reactions toward ourselves. This means that culturally defined standards for the ideal self, cultural variations in which aspects of the self-concept are important, as well as the relative importance and the pace of normative developmental challenges in the adolescent's life course may be hypothesized to have a profound impact on their self-concept. This pertains to its structure, its development, and to gender differences. So far studies have been conducted in English-speaking countries only, that is in Australia (Marsh, 1989; Trent *et al.*, 1994), the UK (Cairns *et al.*, 1990; Eiser *et al.*, 1995; Hoare *et al.*, 1993) and the USA (Harter,

1988b). Some exceptions do exist: two European studies have addressed self-derogation in adolescence (Alsaker, 1992; Silbereisen *et al.*, 1989), and the OSIQ has been administered to adolescents in various different cultures (Offer *et al.*, 1988). However, the data analysis in the latter study did not go beyond simple comparisons of mean values between countries. Thus, at present these analyses have not been carried far enough to address the more theoretically oriented questions regarding self-concept. In conclusion, doubts may be raised about the generalizability of this large body of research. In this chapter we will address some of the profound inconsistencies which exist in order to investigate whether data from a large representative and nationwide sample can shed some light on these issues. It will also address topics on which a more coherent picture can be drawn from present American findings in order to see if these findings can be replicated among Norwegian youth.

DIFFERENTIATION OF THE SELF

The newborn has no sense of self. According to Harter (1988b), during pre-school years the "Me" emerges, but self-descriptions for the most part consist of specific examples of observables such as behavior, possessions and abilities. Limited by the constraints of pre-operational thought these specific examples are not organized into a coherent picture of self, and the distinction between the ideal self and the real self is blurred. During middle childhood the content of self-descriptions become *traits* and they are organized logically into different domains. Moving into adolescence, self-descriptions then become abstractions and a coherent theory of oneself emerges. Thus, according to several theories of self-development, the self should become increasingly differentiated during both childhood and adolescence (Harter, 1988b; Shavelson *et al.*, 1976). Marsh *et al.* (1984) argued that if self-concept becomes increasingly differentiated, one should expect a decrease in the correlations between self-concept domains with age, and they found such a decline from grades 2 to 4. These findings were replicated in later studies (Marsh and Hocevar, 1985; Marsh, 1989), but the two studies that have addressed the question of increased differentiation during adolescence failed to document this (Cairns *et al.*, 1990; Marsh, 1989). Harter and Monsour (1992) claimed to have found evidence for an increased differentiation in different social roles from grade 7 to grade 11. However, the sample was very small ($n = 64$), and one therefore has to await replications before adhering to this finding.

GENDER DIFFERENCES

Two much cited reviews of potential gender differences in global self-esteem published two decades ago concluded that no such difference could be established (Maccoby and Jacklin, 1974; Wylie, 1974). More recently Hattie (1992) claimed that a meta analysis of 77 studies yielded a correlation between gender and self-concept of merely 0.006. In many of these studies, global self-esteem was calculated as the sum of different subscales tapping into different domains or social roles. However, as pointed out by James (1892), the individual's global self is constructed on the basis of competencies in those areas one considers *important*. Thus, if boys and girls differ in their evaluation of their competencies in different domains, sex differences in global self-esteem will depend heavily on what domains are put into the different self-esteem scales. For example, if girls devalue their appearance more than boys do, gender differences in global self-esteem will probably be different in a scale which includes appearance, compared to one which does not. Drawing on the works of James (1892) and Cooley (1902), Harter (1982) argues that global self-esteem should be evaluated directly by asking the subjects about their own evaluations of themselves as a whole, thereby letting the person's center–periphery distinctions rule, and not by mathematically summing all items, by treating each self-concept domain as equally important to all persons.

Later reviewers applying more strict methodological criteria and extending the review period into the 1980s (Marsh, 1989; Skaalvik, 1986) have concluded that when subdomains are considered, gender differences are commonly found which match prevailing sex-role stereotypes. However, what constitutes "prevailing sex-role stereotypes" may differ considerably between cultures. Due to a longer history of a policy towards gender equality, one may, optimistically, hypothesize that gender differences in self-evaluations are fewer and smaller in Scandinavian countries as opposed to the USA and other English speaking countries. For example, Intons-Peterson (1988) found that the gender concepts of Swedish adolescent boys and girls were more similar than their American counterparts. Even so, sex stereotypes among Swedish adolescents were clear and for the most part followed the same pattern as in the USA. Thus, although gender differences may be diminishing in some areas this is a slow process. In Norway this is supported by the fact that gender segregation in the labour market still prevails (see Hammer, Chapter 4), and we should therefore expect to find the traditional gender differences in self-concept, albeit possibly to a lesser extent.

Reviewers also commonly find evidence for a small difference favoring boys in global self-esteem. This gender difference in global self-esteem was also found in the normative studies of the SPPA (Harter, 1988a) and in other studies applying it from England (Eiser *et al.*, 1995), Northern Ireland (Cairns *et al.*, 1990), Scotland (Hoare *et al.*, 1993); and Australia (Trent *et al.*, 1994). Thus, having some reservations about potential smaller gender differences in Norway as compared to these other Western countries, girls are expected to score higher than boys on close friendship and boys to score higher than girls on athletic competence, physical appearance and global self-worth. Boys and girls should be expected to score equally high on school competence.

AGE TRENDS

In her review of the self-concept research, published in 1974, Wylie concluded that there was no convincing evidence of any age effect in global self-esteem from the age of 5 to age 50. As for the adolescent period, later reviewers (O'Malley and Bachman, 1983; Marsh, 1988) have concluded that there seems to be an increase in global self-esteem as well as in many subdomains of self-concept during late adolescence and early adulthood. One study published after these reviews found girls'—but not boys'—cognitive competence to show an increase from when it was measured at age 17 to the second observation point 18 months later (Cairns *et al.*, 1990). This study also documented an increase in social competence and overall self-esteem for both boys and girls, but no change in athletic competence was observed. Thus there seems to be considerable support for an increase during late adolescence. Some evidence suggests a *drop* in self-esteem during the early years of adolescence (Hoare, *et al.*, 1993; Marsh, 1988; Rosenberg, 1985), implying a U-shaped curve potentially covering up a linear trend. But, such age effects have not been found in other studies (that is, Eiser *et al.*, 1995). However, only a few researchers have addressed the possibility of such curvilinear effects; therefore more data—preferably from different cultures—need to be accumulated before conclusions can be drawn.

SEX AND AGE EFFECTS IN SOURCES FOR GLOBAL SELF-WORTH

The self may become increasingly differentiated with age. However, we know comparatively little about what areas contribute to overall self-esteem; if those areas which become crystallized as the child grows older also contribute to global self-esteem; and if important differences exist between groups in the impact of self-concept subdomains on global self-esteem. Harter has repeatedly found physical attractiveness to be highly correlated with global self-worth, followed in magnitude by peer social acceptance. This is also the principal finding of other studies in English-speaking cultures (Cairns *et al.*, 1990; Hoare *et al.*, 1993; Trent *et al.*, 1994). Harter (1990) claims that good looks are more important to girls as compared to boys. This may in part be due to American society's preoccupation with good looks. Intons-Peterson (1988), for example, did not find weight and dieting concerns to be a central part of the Swedish girl's gender concept, in marked contrast to American girls. On the other hand, this single finding should be contrasted with the fact that there is nothing to indicate that eating disorders are less prevalent in Scandinavia as opposed to the USA (Götestam *et al.*, 1995) and Wichstrøm (1995a) found 42 percent of the Norwegian female population to "often" or "always" be "Preoccupied with a desire to be thinner," which is comparable to American results.

However, high correlation between a particular subscale and global self-worth does not necessarily mean that the subscale contributes highly to the variance in global self-worth. Positive correlations between self-concept subscales are commonly found, thus the effect may be confounded by other subscales. Only one study (Cairns *et al.*, 1990) seems to have addressed the question of sources of overall self-esteem multivariately. They found that peer social acceptance was the most important predictor of self-esteem, with cognitive competence and locus of control contributing modestly, and athletic competence being unpredictive. This, again, should be expected to vary according to culture. In a study of determinant of Chinese children's self-concept it was found that physical appearance was rated lowest whereas scholastic competence and behavioral conduct (viz. not breaking social rules) were the most important areas (Meredith *et al.*, 1993).

It has been suggested that peer regard is more important to girls than to boys, and that girls therefore become more vulnerable to stress (Simmons *et al.*, 1987). Cairns *et al.* (1990) found no support for such a contention. Rather, the data might suggest that peer acceptance was more important for boys, but this possibility was not tested statistically.

In sum, despite hundreds of studies on adolescent self-esteem, relatively little has been established as facts about what areas are important for adolescents when their overall sense of worth is created.

Consequently, we do not know if the way self-esteem is constructed differs among girls and boys, or if its sources change during the adolescent period, or to what extent there are differences between cultures.

PUBERTAL DEVELOPMENT

From studies conducted during the 1970s and 1980s on North American subjects, an overall consensus has emerged stating that self-esteem is affected by pubertal development, particularly by the adolescent's own *perception* as regards the *timing* of puberty (Petersen and Crockett, 1985). Early developing girls fare worst as compared to those who are on time or late developers (Brooks-Gunn, 1987; Simmons and Blyth, 1987). The effects cover a broad range of areas related to adjustment and self-perception, but the two areas most consistently and most strongly affected are satisfaction with appearance and global self-esteem (Petersen, 1988; Petersen, and Crockett, 1985; Tobin-Richards *et al.*, 1983). The effect seems to be reversed for boys; early developers have better self-esteem, and in particular they are more satisfied with their appearance. Late developing boys, however, are found to have lower self-esteem as compared to those who are on time or early developers (Simmons and Blyth, 1987; Tobin-Richards *et al.*, 1983). These findings are commonly interpreted according to the "deviance hypothesis." According to this hypothesis, adolescents who are off-time in their physical maturation are socially deviant compared to their peers of the same sex and age. Early maturing girls are the first to enter this deviant position, and their adaptation is therefore believed to be particularly affected. Similarly, late maturing boys will form a particularly deviant category in middle adolescence, because most of their same-aged peers will have reached puberty.

Few studies have been conducted outside the USA. One study analyzing data collected in Sweden in the early 1970s (Stattin and Magnusson, 1990), found girls' self-image to suffer from early pubertal development. However, the few recent European studies so far carried out have not fully confirmed these rather well established American findings. Silbereisen *et al.* (1989) did not find any negative effects of early pubertal development among German adolescent girls, and Alsaker (1992) noted that although the American findings generally were confirmed for Norwegian girls, early development was inconsistently related to self-esteem among boys. Thus, questions may be raised about the external validity of the prevailing body of research on the effects of pubertal development on self-esteem. There is an obvious need for more studies outside North America, preferably using representative samples.

METHOD

In order to overcome some of the problems with previous research a large scale and representative survey was conducted among Norwegian adolescents.

Sample

The gross sample in the *Young in Norway* study comprised 12,287 students from 67 schools in grades 7 through 12. They completed a questionnaire covering a broad range of areas central to the adolescent period. Each grade was equally represented. Cluster sampling was applied with the school as the unit. Every school in the country was included in the register from which the schools were selected. The sample was stratified according to geographical region and school size—which in Norway is closely related to degree of urbanization. Each school's sampling probability was proportional to the number of students at the school. In Norway 98.5 percent of the age cohorts between 12 and 16 attend the ordinary public junior high schools. After graduating from these, 97 percent begin in senior high school. Due to drop out and courses which take less than three years to complete, about 80 percent of the 18-year-olds are still in high school.

The only exclusion criterion was a severe lack of reading capability. I excluded 1.5 percent due to this. There are two main reasons for this lack of reading skills. In Norway mentally retarded children are regularly integrated into the ordinary schools. Those most handicapped (for example having Down's syndrome, severe brain damage or childhood autism) were excluded. Other groups excluded due to lack of reading skills were immigrants and refugees recently arrived in the country.

The response rate was 97 percent. The missing replies, 3 percent, were due to lack of student consent ($n = 206$), lack of parental consent ($n = 55$) and 117 students who could not fill in the form due to prolonged hospitalization or who were untraceable. Seventeen subjects were excluded because they had obviously given incorrect or humorous responses. Students who were younger than 13 years of age and older than 19 years of age were excluded, owing to the fact that they were most likely unrepresentative of their age group, that is, they consisted of particularly early school-starters or students with delayed, prolonged or discontinued schooling, respectively. The resulting net sample was *n* = 10,462.

Procedure

Consent from the Ministry of Research and Education, the local school authorities and the school boards was obtained. At each school one of the teachers was appointed as "liaison officer" serving as the research team's link to the school, the students and the parents. This person was trained in a one-day seminar arranged by the research group. Every student gave his/her consent in writing based on both an oral and written description of the project formulated according to the standards prescribed by the Norwegian Data Inspectorate. According to these standards, a written informed consent was also obtained from the parents of students below the age of 15. Because this sampling was the first wave of a longitudinal study, the students were informed that records connecting an ID number with name and address would be kept in the school archives. The questionnaire took two regular school hours of 45 minutes each to complete. The students put the completed questionnaires in an envelope and sealed it themselves. Thus, the school had access to the ID numbers and the names but not the questionnaires, whereas the researchers had the ID number and the questionnaires, but not the names. A teacher trained by the liaison officer monitored the students in the class during completion. In order to avoid students influencing each other's responses, all eligible students at each school completed the questionnaire at the same time. Students who had consented to participate but who were not present in class during those two hours completed the questionnaire together on a later occasion. Students completing the questionnaire were rewarded by a lottery ticket, the winner getting a vacation of choice for NOK 30,000 (approx. USD 4,200).

Instruments

Self-concept

The adolescents' self-concept was measured by a revised version of SPPA, SPPA-R (Wichstrøm, 1995b). Two subscales, job competence and behavioral conduct, were excluded due to time considerations.

Pubertal development

Pubertal status was measured by the Pubertal Development Scale (PDS) (Petersen *et al.*, 1988). PDS is a self-report measure of pubertal development which asks for ratings of the level of development on five pubertal indices on a 4-point scale ranging from "not begun" to "development completed." Indices for boys and girls were pubic hair, growth spurt, and skin changes. In addition, boys rated their development of facial hair and voice change whereas girls rated their breast development and whether they had reached menarche. The sum of the scores on the five indicators was divided by five to preserve the original metric. In addition, pubertal status scores were categorized into levels of development ranging from "pre-pubertal" (1) to "post-pubertal" (5). Only adolescents in junior high school completed the PDS. The internal consistency was *alpha* = 0.88 for girls and *alpha* = 0.97 for boys. Current perceived pubertal timing was measured by one item which previously have been shown to accurately assess perceptions of timing (Alsaker, 1992; Dubas *et al.*, 1991), namely "Does your physical development seem to be earlier or later than most of the girls/boys your age?" using seven options ranging from "Much later" to "Much earlier."

Body mass (BMI) (kg/cm^2) was based on self-report. Perceived obesity was measured by one item: "How would you characterize yourself?" with the options "Very thin" (1), "Fairly thin" (2), "Normal" (3), "Fairly obese" (4) and "Very obese" (5).

RESULTS

Age and sex differences

The norms for SPPA-R are provided in Table 5.1. As can be seen, sex-differences were found in every self-concept domain, except for social acceptance. These differences were all highly statistically significant ($p<0.0001$).

The largest difference was found for physical appearance, where boys scored 0.63 SD above girls. All sex differences were in favor of boys, except for close friends where girls scored half a SD above boys. There were slight increases in close friends, social acceptance, physical appearance and romantic appeal as the adolescents grew older. These three self-concept domains correlated positively with age: 0.07, $p<0.001$; 0.06, $p<0.001$; 0.03, $p<0.01$; and 0.07, $p<0.001$, respectively. School competence and athletic competence declined with age, as

Table 5.1 Normative data for SPPA-R according to age and sex. Means and (SD)

SPPA-R Sub-domains	Sex	Age groups Means and (SD)							
		13 n=1,355	14 n=1,667	15 n=1,768	16 n=1,835	17 n=1,505	18 n=1,386	19 n=578	13–19 n=10,094
Close friends	Girls	3.18 (.60)	3.23 (.58)	3.27 (.60)	3.38 (.51)	3.36 (.52)	3.35 (.53)	3.37 (.52)	3.30 (.56)
	Boys	3.00 (.60)	2.97 (.59)	3.00 (.58)	3.01 (.57)	3.05 (.60)	3.04 (.62)	3.06 (.64)	3.01 (.59)
School competence	Girls	2.83 (.52)	2.78 (.55)	2.75 (.58)	2.80 (.51)	2.77 (.51)	2.73 (.49)	2.82 (.50)	2.78 (.53)
	Boys	2.96 (.54)	2.90 (.54)	2.88 (.55)	2.85 (.48)	2.85 (.50)	2.83 (.49)	2.82 (.50)	2.87 (.52)
Social acceptance	Girls	3.03 (.54)	3.03 (.56)	3.04 (.54)	3.13 (.45)	3.14 (.46)	3.08 (.46)	3.13 (.48)	3.08 (.50)
	Boys	3.06 (.50)	3.02 (.50)	3.08 (.51)	3.11 (.45)	3.11 (.49)	3.10 (.47)	3.11 (.48)	3.08 (.49)
Athletic competence	Girls	2.34 (.58)	2.37 (.59)	2.33 (.60)	2.28 (.59)	2.29 (.61)	2.19 (.59)	2.19 (.60)	2.29 (.60)
	Boys	2.62 (.60)	2.64 (.61)	2.68 (.62)	2.58 (.62)	2.59 (.64)	2.59 (.63)	2.60 (.61)	2.62 (.62)
Physical appearance	Girls	2.46 (.69)	2.33 (.70)	2.32 (.67)	2.36 (.64)	2.41 (.65)	2.44 (.63)	2.46 (.65)	2.39 (.66)
	Boys	2.77 (.66)	2.76 (.63)	2.79 (.63)	2.76 (.61)	2.83 (.59)	2.82 (.59)	2.85 (.59)	2.79 (.62)
Romantic appeal	Girls	2.48 (.62)	2.46 (.62)	2.51 (.61)	2.56 (.56)	2.57 (.56)	2.59 (.56)	2.58 (.60)	2.53 (.59)
	Boys	2.63 (.63)	2.65 (.59)	2.69 (.58)	2.70 (.51)	2.74 (.55)	2.71 (.55)	2.79 (.52)	2.69 (.56)
Global self-worth	Girls	2.81 (.58)	2.71 (.59)	2.68 (.57)	2.76 (.53)	2.77 (.53)	2.76 (.51)	2.83 (.55)	2.75 (.55)
	Boys	3.00 (.56)	2.95 (.53)	2.99 (.53)	2.97 (.49)	2.99 (.52)	2.96 (.49)	3.00 (.53)	2.98 (.52)

evidenced by negative correlations with age: -0.05, $p<0.001$ and -0.06, $p<0.001$, respectively. The global self-worth scores, however, remained unchanged over these years.

In order to investigate sex and age differences more closely, age, sex, age squared and the interaction between age and sex were regressed on each self-concept domain as well as on global self-worth. The results revealed a U-shaped age slope for the following domains: school competence—which was most likely due to the increase between age 18 and age 19; physical appearance—which probably was due to the decrease from age 13 to age 14; and global self-worth—which also declined from age 13 to age 14, and increased thereafter. Negative quadratic terms, that is, inverted U-slopes, were observed for the close friends—which showed an increase from age 14 to age 16, after which no change was observed—and for social acceptance, which increased from age 14 to age 17 and declined again. The analyses also revealed three sex-by-age interactions, namely for close friends, school competence and athletic competence. Close inspection of Table 5.1 shows that an increase in close friends was only observed for girls. Furthermore, the bell-shaped curved detected in the analyses can most likely be attributed to the rapid increase in close friends from age 13 to age 16 and the following consolidation observed only among girls. Boys' school competence declined steadily throughout the adolescent period. Girls' perceived competence, however, fluctuated somewhat, with the exception of their perceived school competence which did not change during adolescence. With respect to athletic competence, girls' scores steadily declined from age 14 and onwards. Boys' scores increased slightly from age 13 to age 16, followed by a minor recession.

Due to multicollinearity problems, the gender by age squared term could not be tested directly. Separate regressions were therefore performed for each sex. The analyses showed that the observed age effects on physical appearance were only found among girls; t-values for age and age squared were 0.82 and -0.67 for boys and -4.38 and 4.48 for girls, respectively. This was due to a sudden drop in physical appearance score between age 13 and 14 among girls followed by a slow recovery from the age of 16. These changes were paralleled in the global self-worth scores. The t-values for the linear and quadratic age components were -0.58 and 0.58 for boys and -4.11 and 4.20 for girls, respectively.

Differentiation of the self-concept during adolescence

Shavelson *et al.* (1976) proposed that if self-concept becomes more differentiated with age, the correlations between self-concept domains should decline with age. Marsh (1989) and Cairns *et al.* (1990) found no support for such a decline during adolescence. However, it may be that adolescents become increasingly more consistent in their responses to self-report instruments as they grow older. Thus, the changes in intercorrelations may be confounded with changes in reliability, thus preserving the correlations at the same level. In order to account for this the reliability (a values) on each age level were calculated. The results were clear cut: there was no evidence of a systematic decline or increase during this age period, except for a drop in the reliability of school competence after the age 15 (from $a = 0.72$ to $a = 0.65$) and a rise in the reliability of athletic competence (from $a = 0.72$ to $a = 0.80$) during early to mid-adolescence. The mean intercorrelations between each self-concept domain and the other domains for each age level were calculated after initial z transformation. The mean intercorrelations were remarkably stable over this period, and no deviations beyond chance were detected (Bonferroni correction).

Sources for global self-worth

Even though the *mean* intercorrelations between self-concept domains do not diminish during adolescence—thereby indicating a lack of differentiation of the self-concept—the relative *importance* of self-concept domains for constructing global self-esteem may change. Furthermore, the relative importance of these self-concept domains may differ for boys and girls, and separate analyses should therefore be performed for each sex. The results showed that for the whole age period 13 to 19 years there was one single most important source of variation in global self-worth, namely physical appearance (β for boys $= 0.59$ and $\beta = 0.66$ for girls). School competence ($\beta = 0.15$ for boys and $\beta = 0.14$ for girls) and social acceptance ($\beta = 0.17$ for boys and $\beta = 0.16$ for girls) followed thereafter. Close friends contributed also marginally ($\beta = 0.09$ for boys and $\beta = 0.06$ for girls) The sex by physical appearance interaction was significant: $t = 3.68$, $p<0.002$ (sex controlled), indicating that physical appearance contributed more to girls' global self-worth than to boys'.

In order to check for potential developmental differences, a series of multiple regressions, one for each sex on each age group were carried out, in which all self-concept domains were regressed on global self-worth. The overall picture was one of stability throughout the adolescent period.

The impact of pubertal development on self-concept

Table 5.2 shows the correlations between the self-concept domains and age, perceived pubertal timing and perceived pubertal development for boys and girls separately. Most self-concept domains correlate modestly with all three measures. The correlations involving pubertal timing are generally higher than the ones involving age or pubertal development. As can be seen, numerous sex-differences exist between these correlations. With respect to age and pubertal timing, correlations differing more than 0.046 between the two sexes are significant on the $p<0.01$ level ($z>2.56$), whereas for pubertal development—which was obtained only for junior high school students—differences in correlational magnitudes have to exceed 0.072 to reach significance on this level. This implies that both pubertal timing and pubertal development were more strongly positively correlated with all self-concept domains among boys compared to girls except for close friends and school competence. This was most clearly seen with respect to physical appearance and global self-worth, for which advanced pubertal development and early pubertal timing were associated with higher scores for boys but lower scores for girls.

Table 5.3 shows the mean values for each level of perceived pubertal timing. No negative effects of being an early developer can be detected. Scores on all self-concept domains increase according to how early developed the adolescent was, and this was the case for both sexes. The increases were greatest in the lowest levels of pubertal timing. Generally, the increase took place in the area ranging from "much later" to "slightly later," after which the self-concept score leveled off, except for physical appearance among girls. Here girls who considered themselves to be exactly on time had the highest score and girls who were early developed scored slightly lower, but yet higher than girls who were late developers. The romantic appeal scores for both sexes also increased beyond the point of being on time.

One effect of pubertal development is increased tissue fat, especially among girls. Thus, the alleged negative impact of (early) pubertal development on self-concept, particularly physical appearance, may therefore partly be mediated by increased chubbiness. However, for the extra pounds put on to have any effect, they must alter one's *perception* of oneself, that is, as having become slightly overweight. Some girls may not have perceived themselves as overweight if they gain some

Table 5.2 Correlations between self-concept domains and age, perceived pubertal timing and perceived pubertal development

		Age	*Perceived*	*Perceived*
Close friends	Boys	.04	.09	.04
	Girls	.11	.06	.07
School	Boys	−.07	.08	.02
competence	Girls	−.03	.04	.04
Social acceptance	Boys	.05	.15	.12
	Girls	.07	.08	.03
Athletic	Boys	−.03	.18	.12
competence	Girls	−.09	.02	−.01
Physical	Boys	.04	.16	.07
appearance	Girls	.02	.01	−.10
Romantic	Boys	.07	.17	.14
appeal	Girls	.08	.11	.05
Global self-	Boys	.00	.12	.05
worth	Girls	.02	.01	−.09

Note: Correlations >.03 are significant on the p<.01 level

pounds, others would consider this as an important change. The linear and quadratic effects of pubertal timing were therefore controlled for age, BMI and perceived obesity. First, the analyses showed that these variables explained only a very small proportion of the variance in self-concept among adolescents, viz. between 1 percent and 5 percent. The only exceptions were girls' physical appearance (11 percent) and questionably their global self-worth (7 percent). However, the moderately high levels of explained variance in these two areas were for the most part due to the negative association between perceived obesity and self-concept—particularly physical appearance (t = 21.89). This perceived overweight might not only stem from pubertal changes, but rather characterize the girl as such. To disentangle the relations between pubertal development and overweight BMI was entered first, perceived overweight next, and finally pubertal timing (both linear and quadratic terms) were included in the equation. BMI was non-significantly correlated with physical appearance (r = 0.02). However, it seemed that a case of statistical suppression existed, because the effect of BMI became significant when perceived obesity was entered: β for BMI = 0.09, t = 8.58, p<0.00001 and *beta* for perceived obesity = −0.26, t = −25.95, p<0.00001. These two variables explained 6.49 percent of the variance. When pubertal timing, both linear and quadratic terms, were added, the R^2 increased marginally to 0.0764.

Table 5.3 Mean self-concept values for each level of perceived pubertal timing

		Level of perceived pubertal timing						
		1	2	3	4	5	6	7
Boys (n)		79	244	673	2,561	651	578	156
Girls (n)		56	183	511	2,779	698	585	153
Close	Boys	2.77	2.90	2.95	3.03	3.05	3.07	3.10
friends	Girls	2.93	3.22	3.22	3.32	3.32	3.35	3.26
School	Boys	2.63	2.79	2.85	2.87	2.92	2.96	2.87
competence	Girls	2.73	2.74	2.76	2.77	2.82	2.80	2.85
Social	Boys	2.70	2.87	2.99	3.11	3.15	3.16	3.15
acceptance	Girls	2.73	2.89	2.99	3.10	3.12	3.11	3.07
Athletic	Boys	2.19	2.40	2.50	2.61	2.72	2.81	2.75
competence	Girls	2.08	2.19	2.29	2.30	2.33	2.28	2.23
Physical	Boys	2.23	2.53	2.68	2.82	2.86	2.89	2.89
appearance	Girls	2.12	2.25	2.34	2.43	2.36	2.33	2.36
Romantic	Boys	2.50	2.47	2.63	2.67	2.73	2.86	2.96
appeal	Girls	2.21	2.39	2.44	2.52	2.57	2.60	2.73
Global self-	Boys	2.55	2.80	2.90	3.00	3.03	3.03	3.03
worth	Girls	2.43	2.69	2.71	2.79	2.73	2.72	2.72

Note: Levels of perceived pubertal timing: 1 = much later, 2 = somewhat later, 3 = slightly later, 4 = exactly as the others, 5 = slightly earlier, 6 = somewhat earlier, 7 = much earlier

Although bordering on substantial significance this increase was still statistically significant: F change = 60.27, $p<0.00001$. Furthermore, the impact of BMI and perceived obesity remained unchanged: $t = 6.75$ and $t = -26.62$, respectively. Reversibly, when pubertal timing was entered first and BMI and perceived obesity next, the effect of pubertal timing remained unchanged. The t value of the linear term changed from 8.10 to 8.55 and the t value of the quadratic term changed from -6.88 to -6.87. Thus, we may conclude that the strong effect of perceived obesity on physical appearance did not originate from early pubertal development. Furthermore, the effect of pubertal timing is not mediated through increased obesity. In conclusion, the effects of pubertal timing and obesity on physical appearance are completely separate: perceived obesity was by far the most important variable and the effect of such perceptions were only weakly related to actual body mass.

The analyses identified several curvilinear relationships, that is, inverted U-slopes, between pubertal timing and most areas of self-concept. These effects were strongest for physical appearance, social acceptance, and global self-worth, and somewhat smaller for close friends (girls only) and athletic competence (girls only). The question thus arises if this drop was due to the early or late developers, or both. Table 5.3 suggested on an univariate basis that the curvilinearity was due to particularily low scores among the late developers. However, this has to be tested multivariately. Separate multivariate regressions were performed on those who were average or later developed (perceived pubertal timing levels 4 to 1) and on those who were average or earlier developed (perceived pubertal timing levels 4 to 7).

The results in Table 5.4 showed that the β-values for pubertal timing among the late to average group were higher than in the early to average group. This can be interpreted as supporting the conclusion that the curvilinear effects generally were due to the increase from late to average timing. Further, none of the *beta* were negative in the average-to-early group, thus indicating no negative effects of early timing. In sum, boys and girls alike, the important thing is *not* to be late: those who perceive themselves to be late suffer in every area of their self-concept, but those who are on time and early score almost equally high.

DISCUSSION

The present study addressed five topics relevant to self-concept development in a large, representative, nationwide sample of Norwegian

Table 5.4 Betas of perceived pubertal timing stemming from multiple regressions including BMI, perceived obesity and age as predictors of self-concept. Late and early developers separate.

| | Pubertal timing level | | | |
| | Boys | | Girls | |
	Late to average	Early to average	Late to average	Early to average
Close friends	.09	.04	.09	.00
School competence	.07	.05	.04	.05
Social acceptance	.20	.05	.15	.02
Athletic competence	.14	.12	.08	.00
Physical appearance	.21	.07	.13	.00
Romantic appeal	.10	.15	.11	.10
Global self-worth	.17	.04	.13	.00

Note: βs>.04 are significant on the p<.01 level

adolescents with a very good response rate. These topics were: differentiation of self during adolescence; gender differences; age trends; the sources of global self-worth; and the impact of pubertal development on self-concept.

Differentiation of the self

In line with previous research (Cairns *et al.*, 1990; Marsh, 1989), no evidence was found for an increased differentiation of self between the ages 13 and 19. This, however, is in marked contrast to generally acknowledged theories of self-concept formation (James, 1892; Harter, 1988b; Shavelson *et al.*, 1976).

For some writers "self-concept" is synonymous to "identity," viz. the content of the self: what one *is* (current self), what one *would like to become* (ideal self), or what one thinks one can *actually* become (possible self). Such identities might be highly idiosyncratic, at least among adults. However, standard measurement instruments, such as SPPA, SDQ and OSIR, measure self-esteem, that is one's attitude towards one's current self; they do not measure identity itself. As for self-esteem, ones identity might go through a developmental process during adolescence which is characterized both by increase in complexity and in coherence. Our "self" might be the cognitive scheme that we are most experts on. Experts' schemes are abstract, complex, highly organized and compact (Fiske and Taylor, 1991). The adolescent's strive for identity achievement might be interpreted as the efforts of an expert emerging, equipped with new cognitive resources, that are trying to work out an abstract, highly organized and compact, self-scheme. Thus, the developmental process taking place after pre-adolescence should not be described as differentiation, implying that the interrelationships between a person's competencies becomes weaker, but rather as versatility and coherence. The content of the self-concept (identity) may change because new self-concept domains emerge, which in part may be idiosyncratic, based on new competencies and new social roles. However, in this process the *structure* between the original domains are neither lost nor weakened.

Age and sex differences

Generally, the presented hypotheses concerning gender differences in self-concept subdomains were confirmed: boys scored higher than girls on athletic competence and physical appearance, whereas girls perceived themselves as having more intimate peer relations. These findings conform to prevailing sex-role stereotypes. In addition, boys scored slightly higher on school competence and romantic appeal as compared to girls. These results are in line with findings from both the UK, the USA and Australia, when it comes to the size of the gender differences. Thus, the contention that the gender egalitarian policy in Scandinavia might have boosted girls' self-esteem seems to have no bearing.

It may come as some surprise that girls perceive themselves as less competent in the academic domain, given the fact that they obtain better grades than boys in all subjects except mathematics and science. In accordance with the grades obtained, other studies have found boys to have higher math self-concept and girls to score higher on academic self-concept and verbal self-concept (Marsh *et al.*, 1988). Possibly, the importance of math/science is greater than for other subjects when adolescents create their self-concept in the cognitive and academic sphere. Another explanation for this seeming discrepancy between competence and self-evaluation might be that boys, generally, have more positive views about themselves compared to girls, and that this is seen in almost every subdomain, academic self-concept being no exception. Thus, global self-worth may not only be the *result* of evaluating one's competency in different fields, the causal direction may also be the other way around: global self-worth may affect the evaluation of one's competence. A general positive view towards the self may outweigh the fact that boys receive lower grades than girls. Further, no reference group is specified in SPPA except for "other adolescents." One may therefore suspect that other adolescents of the same sex to a greater extent than adolescents of the opposite sex constitute the reference group for one's attitude towards oneself. Consequently, boys may not be plagued by the fact that the girls in their class get better grades, as long as the other boys do not. The shrinking of the gender difference in academic self-concept during late adolescence may also be interpreted according to the reference group hypothesis. During the adolescent period mixed-sex groups or cliques increase, and accordingly the possibility of including opposite-sexed persons in one's reference group will also increase. However, to disentangle the relationship between academic self-concept, gender, academic competence and reference groups, more fine-graded measures of different academic self-concept need to be included in longitudinal studies.

Drawing on previous studies, a heightened self-concept was expected in late adolescence compared to mid-adolescence. Further, some studies suggested a drop in self-concept from early to mid-adolescence. The present study identified numerous changes in self-concept during adolescence. For the most part, however, these changes were of minor magnitude compared to several of the gender differences. Although curvilinear effects were observed, there was no evidence of a general decline in self-concept from early to mid-adolescence, except for physical appearance and global self-worth among girls, which dropped slightly more than one-fifth of an SD from age 13 to 14. Although increases in self-concept as well as positive quadratic age effects (U-slopes) were noted for several self-concept domains, there was meager evidence for these changes taking place during late adolescence, as originally hypothesized.

In conclusion, the self-concept of the young teen-ager and the late adolescent is almost identical, both with respect to level of self-esteem and to the structure of the self-concept. However, gender did matter: despite several decades of gender egalitarian official policy, the self-concepts of Norwegian adolescents are as gender-stereotypic as among other Western adolescents.

Sources of global self-worth

Self-concept is best conceived of as multidimensional, but according to both James (1892) and Harter (1988b) one's overall sense of worth depends on one's competencies in those areas considered important by the individual. Consequently, in order to examine the sources of global self-worth, measures of the centrality–periphery of each self-concept domain should be obtained, otherwise it would be difficult to conclude from competence measures alone whether a different impact of a self-concept domain on global self-worth should be attributed to differences in competence, difference in the importance of that domain, or both. However, if age or sex differences in perceived *competence* are low, non-existent or in the reverse direction of what is detected by multivariate analyses of self-concept subdomains' impact on global self-worth, these differential impacts could be attributed to differences in the centrality of the subdomain in question.

The present study identified perceived physical appearance to be the single most important variable explaining the variance in global self-worth. School competence, social acceptance and close friends also added to the variance, but to a much lesser extent. Romantic appeal and athletic competence were of no importance. The importance of physical appearance to global self-worth did not change during the adolescent years. Other studies have noted very high correlations between physical appearance and global self-worth, ranging from 0.52 in Northern Ireland (Granleese and Joseph, 1993) to 0.64 in Scotland

(Hoare *et al*, 1993). In the normative studies of Harter (1988b), these correlations ranged from 0.66 to 0.73. Very high correlations between the two have also been noted in samples of children as well in adulthood (Harter, 1988a). The extreme importance of appearance may be understandable during the height of egocentrism during adolescence (Elkin, 1967). Findings showing correlations at the same level of magnitude during pre-adolescence as well as in adulthood are more difficult to interpret. Such findings have led Harter to speculate that the physical appearance subdomain may not be conceived of as one of many subdomains. Rather, physical appearance could be understood as a manifestation of the outer self, and global self-worth as a manifestation of the inner self. It is not entirely clear whether this implies that there is a *causal* relation between physical appearance and global self-worth or if the self is *expressed* in two different ways: *if* the relation is considered causal, the direction of this causality has yet to be established. Further, it is difficult to see why only physical appearance should be a representation of the outer self, that is, how one thinks others perceive oneself. The importance of appearance should not be underestimated, but why not also true behavioral competencies such as the ability to affiliate with friends, athletic abilities, academic abilities and so forth? To sum up, the *process* of construing one's self needs to be examined in more detail. In this endeavor both longitudinal studies and experimental designs should be applied.

The results showed that physical appearance contributed more to girls' self-worth than to that of boys'. This is in accordance with Harter's (1988b) contention, and fits the notion of female value in the dating "market" depending heavily on their attractiveness, whereas male value tends to be rated more in terms of their status (Wade, 1991). Simmons and Blyth (1987) found US mid-western girls to rate the importance of good looks and popularity higher than boys did. At first glance the present finding may be interpreted in accordance with the contention that physical attractiveness is more *important* to girls. However, data from a study of a large random sample of Norwegian senior high school students (Wichstrøm, 1994) showed that the mean score for a scale measuring the importance of appearance (arithmetic mean = 2.5) was lower (score = 2.67) for girls compared to boys (score = 2.80), $F(1,14585) = 154.74$, $p<0.00001$. Thus, it is possible that the centrality judgment may not be a completely conscious process, implying that although Norwegian girls—when questioned—downplay the importance of good looks as compared to boys, its importance is still higher than they "admit." It is, however, difficult to see what processes supposedly underlie girls being less conscious or open about these matters as compared to boys. Apart from this modest difference, the sources of self-worth were remarkably similar for Norwegian boys and girls. Yet another minor difference might be found: Girls' score higher on intimate relationships than boys, and at the same time there is a non-significant trend for boys' close friends score to contribute more to their global self-worth compared to girls during early adolescence. Adhering to the competency/importance distinction of William James, one might argue that, if anything, intimate relations may be of less importance to girls as compared to boys. Possibly, the value put on intimacy in the female role (Chodorow, 1978; Maccoby and Jacklin, 1974) is diminishing among contemporary Norwegian youth: girls perceive themselves to be better at it, that is, more competent, but it is not that important to them.

The impact of pubertal development

The present study failed to confirm studies from the USA and earlier studies from Scandinavia which generally conclude that early pubertal development affects girls' self-esteem negatively and boys' self-esteem positively. The main conclusion from the present study was that both late developed girls and boys suffer, whereas early developers and on-time adolescents have equally high self-esteem. Stemming from a very large nationally representative sample with a very high response rate, these findings seriously question previous attempts to theorize on the importance of pubertal development. So far, two out of several possible theories about the social and psychological effects of pubertal development have been advocated, namely the "deviance hypothesis"—previously described—and the "developmental readiness hypothesis" (Simmons and Blyth, 1987). The latter theory is sometimes also called the "stage termination hypothesis" (Petersen, 1988), and resembles Coleman's "focal theory of change" (Coleman, 1974). This theory has some psychoanalytical bearing, stating that several chronologically ordered developmental tasks have to be successfully completed during the children's and adolescents' life in order to ensure proper ego development and adjustment. If puberty comes too soon and too suddenly, too little time will have been spent on ego development during latency. This will affect girls the most because they are the first to enter puberty. Both the "deviance hypothesis" and the "developmental readiness hypothesis" are universal theories, supposedly equally relevant across time and culture. Thus, these hypotheses *not* being supported in some contexts, that is, contemporary Europe, seriously questions their applicability in our attempts to understand the impact of pubertal change. The "cultural ideal hypothesis" (Simmons and Blyth, 1987), stating that puberty will bring the young boy closer to his physical ideal—by growth in height and muscles—and the girl's further away from the prevailing lean female ideal—by increased tissue fat—fits previous American and European findings. It is, however, difficult to claim that these ideals have changed drastically in Europe during the last decade. Further, although the chubby pubertal girl does not conform to the female body ideal, neither does the pre-pubertal lean girl. She may resemble the fashion model, but this boyish look is far from the cultural ideal portrayed in commercials and men's magazines. When asked directly by an open-ended question "Who would you like to resemble the most?," the junior high school girls in this study for the most part answered "myself" (26.7 percent), "no one in particular" (8.8 percent) or "don't know" (16.6 percent). However, when indicating a person or a character, 21.6 percent named a person who is primarily known for her good looks. The most frequently cited persons were Cindy Crawford (8.6 percent), Julia Roberts (4.6 percent) and Mona Grudt, a Norwegian Miss Universe winner (1.5 percent). None of these persons are overweight, but none can possibly be characterized as having a pre-pubertal look; adolescent idols are slim but definitely post-pubertal. Thus, the suggestion that the pubertal girl is led further away from the Western stereotyped female ideal may not be true. Both boys and girls are led closer to their respective ideals, provided that they do not put on weight. Possibly, contemporary Western adolescent girls succeed in this endeavor. They certainly try hard: 42.5 percent of the girls in the present sample state that they are "often" or "always" "preoccupied with a desire to be thinner."

The theories put forward so far are not mutually exclusive. The discrepant findings may therefore be accounted for by an interplay of several of these mechanisms. A cultural ideal effect superimposed on a social deviance effect may fit the data quite well: the early developer gains in physical attractiveness, and possibly also in social status by becoming more mature and adult-like, but at the same time belonging to a minority of off-timers is stressful and this deflates the self-concept. This combination of theories also explains why on-timers do not score higher than early developers (i.e. because of their lagging behind in adult-likeness compared to the early developers) and why the late developers fare worst (because they have the double impact of both being deviant and far from the cultural body ideal).

How can the fact that this pattern of effects was not found in previous studies be explained? The "cultural ideal hypothesis" is sensitive to changes in time and context. Possibly current Norwegian society places less emphasis on the stereotypical male stature as compared to the USA. It is also possible that the embarrassment and negative affect experienced by American girls when they start menarche and become sexually responsive individuals (Greif and Ulman, 1982; Ruble and Brooks-Gunn, 1982) are less among Norwegian girls due to the comparatively greater openness about adolescent sexuality which is prevalent in this country.

BIBLIOGRAPHY

Alsaker, F.D. (1992) Pubertal timing, overweight, and psychological adjustment, *Journal of Early Adolescence*, 12: 396–419.
Brooks-Gunn, J. (1987) Pubertal processes: their relevance for developmental research, in V.B. Van Hasselt, and M. Hersen (eds.), *Handbook of Adolescent Psychology*, pp. 111–30, New York: Pergamon.
Cairns, E., McWhirter, L., Duffy, U., and Barry, R. (1990) The stability of self-concept in late adolescence: Gender and situational effects, *Personality and Individual Differences*, 11: 937–44.
Chodorow, N. (1978) *The Reproduction of Mothering: Psychoanalysis and the Sociology of Gender*, Berkeley: University of California Press.
Coleman, J.C. (1974) *Relationships in Adolescence*, Boston: Routledge and Kegan Paul.
Cooley, C.H. (1902) *Human Nature and Social Order*, New York: Schribner's.
Dubas, J.S., Graber, J.A., and Petersen, A.C. (1991) A longitudinal investigation of adolescents' changing perceptions of pubertal timing, *Developmental Psychology*, 27: 580–6.
Eiser, C., Eiser, J.R., and Havermans, T. (1995) The measurement of self-esteem: practical and theoretical considerations, *Personality and Individual Differences*, 18: 429–32.
Elkin, D. (1967) Egocentrism in adolescence, *Child Development*, 38: 1024–38.
Fiske, S.T., and Taylor, S.E. (1991) *Social Cognition*, New York: McGraw-Hill.
Götestam, K.G., Agras, W., and Stewart, W.S. (1995) General population-based epidemiological study of eating disorders in Norway, *International Journal of Eating Disorders*, 18: 119–26.
Granleese, J., and Joseph, S. (1993) Factor analysis of the Self-Perception Profile for Children, *Personality and Individual Differences*, 15: 343–5.
Greif, E.B., and Ulman, K.J. (1982) The psychological impact of menarche on early adolescent females: a review of the literature, *Child Development*, 53: 1413–30.
Harter, S. (1982) The Perceived Competence Scale for Children, *Child Development*, 53, 87–97.
—— (1988a) *Manual for the Self-Perception Profile for Adolescents*, Denver: University of Denver.
—— (1988b) Developmental processes in the construction of the self, in T.D. Yawkey and J.E. Johnson (eds.), *Integrative Processes and Socialization: Early to Middle Childhood* pp. 45–78, Hillsdale: Erlbaum.

—— (1990) Self and identity development, in S.S. Feldman, and G.R. Elliott (eds.) *At the Threshold. The Developing Adolescent*, pp. 352–87, Cambridge: Harvard University Press.

Harter, S., and Monsour, A. (1992) Developmental analysis of conflict caused by opposing attributes in the adolescent self-portrait, *Developmental Psychology*, 28: 251–60.

Hattie, J. (1992) *Self-Concept*, Hillsdale: Erlbaum.

Hoare, P., Elton, R., Greer, A., and Kerley, S. (1993) The modification and standardization of the Harter Self-Esteem Questionnaire with Scottish school children, *European Child and Adolescent Psychiatry*, 2: 19–33.

Intons-Peterson, M.J. (1988) *Gender Concepts of Swedish and American Youth*, Hillsdale: Erlbaum.

James, W. (1892) *Psychology: The Briefer Course*, New York: Holt, Rinehart, and Winston.

Maccoby, E.E., and Jacklin, C.N. (1974) *The Psychology of Sex Differences*, Stanford: Stanford University Press.

Marsh, H.W. (1988) *The Self Description Questionnaire (SDQ): A Theoretical and Empirical Basis for the Measurement of Multiple Dimensions of Preadolescent Self-Concept: A Test Manual and a Research Monograph*, San Antonio: The Psychological Cooperation.

—— (1989) Age and sex effects in multiple dimensions of self-concept: preadolescence to adulthood, *Journal of Educational Psychology*, 81: 417–30.

Marsh, H.W., Barnes, J., Cairns, L., and Tidman, M. (1984) The Self Description Questionnaire (SDQ): age effects in the structure and level of self-concept for preadolescent children, *Journal of Educational Psychology*, 76: 940–56.

Marsh, H.W., Byrne, B.M., and Shavelson, R.J. (1988) A multifaceted academic self-concept: its hierarchical structure and its relation to academic achievement, *Journal of Educational Psychology*, 80: 366–80.

Marsh, H.W., and Hocevar, D. (1985) The application of confirmatory factor analysis to the study of self-concept: first and higher order factor structures and their invariance across age groups, *Psychological Bulletin*, 97: 562–82.

Meredith, W.H., Wang, A., and Zheng, F.M. (1993) Determining constructs of self-perception for children in Chinese culture, *School Psychology International*, 14: 371–80.

Offer, D. (1969) *The Psychological World of the Teen-Ager*, New York: Basic Books.

Offer, D., Ostrov, E., Howard, K.I., and Atkinson, R. (1988) *The Teen-age World. Adolescents' Self-Image in Ten Countries*, New York: Plenum Medical Book Company.

O'Malley, P., and Bachman, J.C. (1983) Self-esteem: change and stability between ages 13 and 23, *Developmental Psychology*, 19: 257–68.

Petersen, A.C. (1988) Adolescent development, *Annual Review of Psychology*, 39: 583–607.

Petersen, A.C., and Crockett, L. (1985) Pubertal timing and grade effects on adjustment, *Journal of Youth and Adolescence*, 14: 191–206.

Petersen, A.C., Crockett, L., Richards, M., and Boxer, A. (1988) A self-report measure of pubertal status: reliability, validity, and initial norms, *Journal of Youth and Adolescence*, 17: 117–33.

Rosenberg, M. (1985) Self-concept and psychological well-being in adolescence, in R.L. Leahy (ed.), *The Development of the Self*, pp. 55–121, Orlando: Academic Press.

Ruble, D.N., and Brooks-Gunn, J. (1982) The experience of menarche, *Child Development*, 53: 1557–66.

Shavelson, R.J., Hubner, J.J., and Stanton, G.C. (1976) Self-concept: validation of construct interpretations, *Review of Educational Research*, 46: 407–41.

Silbereisen, R.K., Petersen, A.C., Albrecht, H.T., and Kracke, B. (1989) Maturational timing and the development of problem behavior: longitudinal studies in adolescence, *Journal of Early Adolescence*, 9: 247–68.

Simmons, R.G., and Blyth, D.A. (1987) *Moving into Adolescence. The Impact of Pubertal Change and School Context*, New York: Aldine de Gruyter.

Simmons, R.G., Burgeson, R., Carlton-Ford, S., and Blyth, D.A. (1987) The impact of cumulative change in early adolescence, *Child Development*, 58: 1220–34.

Skaalvik, E.M. (1986) Sex differences in global self-esteem: a research review, *Scandinavian Journal of Educational Research*, 30: 167–79.

Stattin, H., and Magnusson, D. (1990) *Pubertal Maturation in Female Development*. Hillsdale: Erlbaum.

Tobin-Richards, M.H., Boxer, A.M., and Petersen, A.C. (1983) The psychological significance of pubertal change: sex differences in perceptions of self during early adolescence, in J. Brooks-Gunn and A.C. Petersen (eds.) *Girls at Puberty: Biological and Psychosocial Perspectives*, pp. 127–54, New York: Plenum Press.

Trent, L.M.Y., Russell, G., and Cooney, G. (1994) Assessment of self-concept in early adolescence, *Australian Journal of Psychology*, 46: 21–8.

Wade, T.J. (1991) Race and sex differences in adolescent self-perceptions of physical attractiveness and level of self-esteem during early and late adolescence, *Personality and Individual Differences*, 12: 1319–24.

Wichstrøm, L. (1994) Predictors of Norwegian adolescents' sunbathing and use of sunscreen, *Health Psychology*, 13: 412–20.

—— (1995a) Social, psychological and physical correlates of eating problems. A study of the general adolescent population in Norway, *Psychological Medicine*, 25: 567–79.

—— (1995b) Harter's Self-Perception Profile for Adolescents: reliability, validity and evaluation of the question format, *Journal of Personality Assessment*, 65: 100–16.

Wylie, R.C. (1974) *The Self-Concept*, vol. 1, *A Review of Methodological Considerations and Measurement Instruments*, Lincoln: University of Nebraska Press.

—— (1979) *The Self-Concept*, vol. 2, *Theory and Research on Selected Topics*, Lincoln: University of Nebraska Press.

6 Language and ethnic identity in indigenous adolescents

Siv Kvernmo

Language and ethnicity are usually recognized to be closely inter-related. The salience of language in ethnic relations can be illustrated in several ways; language can often be a critical attribute to group membership, an important cue for ethnic categorization, an emotional dimension of identity and a means of facilitating in-group cohesion (Giles and Coupland, 1991). The formation of the ethnic identity of indigenous minority members assumes the continuity of the indigenous culture by its values, beliefs and practices from one generation to the next. The language may act as the main tool for this continuity and for the internalization of culture by the individual. For many ethnic groups language therefore becomes an important dimension of ethnic identity by symbolizing the distinctiveness from other groups (Giles and Johnson, 1981; Heller, 1987).

Different criteria for ethnic group membership can be applied, involving ancestry, religion, physiognomy and other dimensions of ethnicity (Fishman, 1977). Most ethnic groups have a distinct language or dialect, and these can often be considered necessary attributes for full and "legitimate" membership of a group. Language has also been claimed to be a stronger cue to an individual's sense of ethnic belongings than inherited characteristics such as skin color because many aspects of language performance (for example, accent) can be acquired and modified developmentally and situationally (Giles and Coupland, 1991). For "invisible" ethnic minorities with few or no physiognomic characteristics like the Samis, the language may be the major tool for categorizing and distinguishing ethnic members from the dominant group.

Even though language is generally the most common topic in research regarding cultural practice or ethnic behavior, little is known about the impact of mother tongue on the indigenous adolescents' sense of attachment to their group. The preservation or acquisition of the ethnic language is seen as a major factor for the development and maintenance of the ethnic identity among several indigenous groups such as Samis, Maoris and Native Americans (Thomas, 1993; Pfiffer, 1993; Nikora, 1993). However, the relative importance of language varies from one ethnic group to another (Driedger, 1975). Smolicz (1979) claimed that certain cultural values, such as language, will be important for the formation of ethnic identity by members in some ethnic groups, whereas the same values will be irrelevant to the formation of ethnic identity in other groups. Smolicz also suggested that each culture possesses a number of basic characteristics which are essential for the transmission and the maintenance of that culture; these core values identify a given culture. Both ethnic identity and language development are products of the socialization process the child undergoes, modified by social and psychological factors. In a study of Mexican children living in USA their use of the Spanish language at home was found to be related to their ethnic identity. Children using Spanish at home showed more frequent use of ethnic behaviors, a greater number of correct ethnic labels, more ethnic knowledge and more frequent ethnic preferences than children who did not speak Spanish at home (Knight et al., 1993).

The ethnic identity process and socialization start at an early age, and by the age of six children usually have developed some type of ethnic identity (Aboud, 1977). The social representation of language comprises shared meanings, social scripts, and the internalization of social values, which play an essential role in the development of cultural or ethnic identity (Hamers and Blanc, 1993). Individuals will identify with the ethnic group with whom they share these common cultural characteristics and values which distinguish them from those who do not. It is necessary that the group recognizes the person as a member, and that the person is perceived as a group member by others. Social network studies have revealed that close-knit, territorial-based social networks will, by norm-enforcement mechanisms, exert a pressure on their members to adapt to the group or context specific values, norms and behaviors, including those pertaining to language (Milroy, 1980). For children, parents, grandparents and siblings will represent the first close-knit personal context; then, in adolescence, the personal network widens to include neighbors, friends, school peers and teachers. The language spoken in childhood by close-knit models of the child will play an important role in the socialization. The individual is supposed to behave according to the behavior patterns of groups he or she wants to identify with, to the extent that: (1) the person can identify the group; (2) the person has adequate access to the groups and the ability to analyze their behavior patterns; (3) the person's motivation to join the groups is sufficiently powerful and is either reinforced or reversed by feedback from the groups; and (4) the person has the ability to modify his or her behavior (Le Page, 1968; Le Page and Tabouret-Keller, 1985).

THE ROLE OF LANGUAGE IN ETHNIC IDENTITY

When more than one language is used in the same society or ethnic community, language and culture are not distributed in the same way. To the extent that language is a dimension of culture, members of an ethnic group who do not share the same language will not necessarily share all the same meanings and behaviors of the specific group even though there will exist a great deal of overlap (Hamers and Blanc, 1993). This will be the reality for ethnic groups like for example the Sami, the Maori and Native Americans, who have experienced an extensive loss of ethnic language through assimilation processes, especially in the younger generations. If the child, as for multicultural or multiethnic children, has to deal with two or more ethnic groups and identify positively with members of these groups, the child must perceive these groups in a positive way (Aboud and Mitchell, 1977). If language is one of the core values of ethnicity and there is an incongruence between language and ethnic group membership, it is claimed that the child will not be able to identify with another person, especially if this person is a member of his own group but speaks the language of another group (Aboud and Mitchell, 1977; Hamers and Blanc, 1993). Thus, the inclusion of two languages in one's ethnic identity may facilitate processes such as flexibility and bicultural competence which are important for the development of the child's ethnic identity.

It seems obvious that the relationships among bilinguality, language choice and ethnic identity in bilingual individuals are complex and multifactorial. Hamers and Blanc (1993) stated that the relationship between bilinguality and ethnic identity is reciprocal. Bilinguality influences the development of cultural identity, which in turn influences the development of bilinguality. The topic of ethnic identity and mother tongue in indigenous minority adolescents has not been studied systematically. However, a recent study of ethnic identity in Sami adolescents revealed that positive attitudes towards the Sami language and Sami language practice were closely related to ethnic identity and ethnic contexts such as ethnicity of parents and type of ethnic communities (Kvernmo and Heyerdahl, 1996).

LANGUAGE SHIFT OR LANGUAGE CONTINUITY: THE CASE OF THE SAMIS—THE INDIGENOUS PEOPLE OF SCANDINAVIA

From the nineteenth century the Norwegian authorities started an overt assimilation policy to eradicate Sami language and culture. Prejudice and discrimination towards the Samis were widespread in all parts of the society (Magga, 1994). Economic sanctions were imposed on Samis who refused to enter into the Norwegian lifestyle and culture. From the beginning of this century it was stipulated by law that only persons with Norwegian names, those who spoke and wrote Norwegian, were allowed to buy land. The use of the ethnic language was virtually forbidden in school and all teaching was done in the dominant language, an unknown language for most Sami children. Teachers were encouraged to spread the Norwegian language at any time and at any place. Cultural specific knowledge and skills in Sami language and way of living were rejected by the school and the dominant Norwegian society.

However, during the last decades an ethnic revival and cultural mobilization have taken place providing an increased sense of ethnic group membership and in-group solidarity (Stordahl, 1994). Several Sami institutions such as education, health services, research, media and art have been funded, most of them located in the highland of Finnmark which is the major Sami area in Norway. The cultural revival among the Samis has resulted in increased use of ethnic language and traditional ethnic clothes as cultural paraphernalia expressing or betraying one's ethnic group membership.

LANGUAGE CONTEXTS AND ACCULTURATION

The acculturative process has been different in the geographical areas, the coast and the highland, and this has lead to different language contexts for the Samis. The early assimilative process has had the greatest impact on the coastal communities where the Samis became a minority (Aubert, 1978). Due to assimilative pressure, Samis in this area often have tried to enter into the Norwegian culture by hiding and changing their Sami background, such as their ethnic behavior and language (Magga, 1994). A language death due to a language shift is the result of this process, not only because of forced language policy from the authorities, but also as a reflection of a pragmatic desire for social mobility and an improved standard by the Samis themselves. Today only 10 percent of the overall adult population in coastal areas, and even fewer among the children and adolescents, are Sami speakers. Due to interethnic marriages and Norwegian settlements the ethnic density in these areas is relatively low. The dispersal of Sami speakers threatened the maintenance of the Sami language as reported for other minority languages (Edwards, 1985). The structural and practical support to the Sami group is fragmented and sporadic, even though a positive revival of the Sami culture is evident also in this area.

In the highland communities the ethnic density is high; about 80–90 percent of the population are Samis. The influence of the national assimilation policy has been weaker there. Norwegian settlements and interethnic marriages were rare up to the Second World War. The Sami language survived because the ban of the forbidden Sami language was not enforced as strictly as in the coastal area. About 90 percent of the overall adult population are Sami speakers or bilingual. Both Sami and Norwegian are official languages in all public areas (for example, schools, health care, radio, church) in the highland communities. The ethnic revitalization process in this area was initiated by highly educated Samis. The founding of several bilingual and Sami institutions (theater, college, research institutions, Sami Parliament, health services and broadcasting), mainly staffed by highly educated Samis, have provided successful indigenous role models. A high density of Sami speakers created an extensive use of the Sami language in several arenas. The status of Sami language has had a remarkable progress during the recent years, especially in this area, resulting in a new language legislation with the right to learn Sami at school and to use the language in public offices.

The effect of the assimilation policy created different language contexts. In the coastal areas the assimilation policy lead first to a language shift and later to an extensive language death. The use of Sami language in this context is often limited to private arenas and mainly practiced among the elders. Because of the experience of prejudice and stigmatization Sami parents chose to teach their children the dominant language. The language shift between the generations has to a great extent resulted in a continuity break of Sami cultural values from the grandparents and parents to the children. In the highland area, however, the language continuity resulted in a Sami-dominated language context where Sami is used both in private and official contexts. The ethnic socialization and ethnic language continuity are strengthened through generational contact and through bilingual and cultural sensitive education.

In this chapter I will discuss a recent study investigating the nfluence of language contexts on ethnic identity in both Sami and non-Sami speaking Sami adolescents. The aim of the study was three-fold. First, ethnic language continuity or shift from parents to adolescents, and the impact of language context were assessed. Second, the influence of mother tongue and parental language strategy on ethnic identity was examined, and finally, the relationship between language and ethnic attitudes and behavior was investigated.

METHOD

Sample

Participants in the study comprised 247 Sami students (131 girls and 116 boys) attending 23 junior high schools in eight municipalities in Finnmark, Norway. The schools were selected to represent the region culturally and geographically. The participants were between 12 and 16 years of age ($M = 14.4$, $SD = 0.94$). Students participated on a voluntary basis, and parental consent was obtained. The study consisted of a self-report survey, administered at the schools by the teachers. All students in the same school completed the questionnaires anonymously at the same time. The questionnaire was available both in Sami and Norwegian.

The Samis are the native people of northern Scandinavia. Sapmi, the area inhabited by Samis, includes parts of Norway, Sweden, Finland and the Kola Peninsula of Russia. The Samis have their own native language, traditional costumes and folk music and originally also their own religion. There are in total about 60,000–100,000 Samis, of whom most live in Norway, mainly in the two northernmost parts.

The adolescents were included in this study if they considered themselves Sami, or if parents' ethnicity or grandparents/parents mother tongue was reported as Sami. Education in Sami language has been encouraged in Sami areas since the 1970s and has been voluntary for the participants in junior high school in this area. Many students have been educated in Sami since first grade in the ordinary school. In this study, all of the adolescents with Sami mother tongue had been taught Sami at school as first or second language, compared to 92 percent of those from bilingual homes. Among monolingual respondents with Norwegian mother tongue, 61 percent of the students had learned Sami as a second language.

Measures

The self-report questionnaire included items on sociodemographic background, ethnicity, and language use in families and among friends. Ethnic items were grouped into two categories: (1) ethnic group membership and ethnic self-identification, and (2) ethnic behavior and attitudes. Because the ethnic items were not answered by all students, the number of respondents varied in the analyses below.

Ethnic self-identification

Ethnic identity was defined by the adolescents' self-identification in response to a multiple-choice question: "I perceive myself as . . . ." The alternatives provided were "Norwegian," "Sami," "Finnish" or "Other: Please specify . . . ." The participants could choose one or more alternatives. Adolescents answering "Sami" only were categorized as having a Sami identity. Subjects selecting both "Sami" and one or more of the other alternatives were classified as having a bicultural identity. Finally, those who chose only "Norwegian" were categorized as having a Norwegian identity. Participants who chose "Finnish" or "Other" only were excluded.

Ethnic behaviors and attitudes

Items assessing ethnic behavior and attitudes, cultural awareness and cultural satisfaction, excluding mother tongue, were scored on a 3-point ordinal scale (0 = not true, 1 = somewhat or sometimes true, 2 = true or often true). Ethnic *behavior* was assessed by two items. One item concerned which languages were learned at home. Those reporting that Sami was learned at home were classified as having Sami mother tongue; all others were scored as not having Sami mother tongue. Ethnic *attitudes* were assessed by two questions: one of attitude towards the further existence of the Sami language, the other of attitude toward the usage of Sami language with friends. Ethnic *awareness in the family* was assessed by the item: "We often talk about our cultural background at home." Finally, the adolescents were asked to evaluate their *ethnic group membership* with the item: "I am satisfied with my cultural background."

RESULTS AND DISCUSSION

Language status among Sami adolescents

The results showed that there has been a more extensive language shift from Sami to Norwegian in the adolescent generation than in the parental generation. Of the 247 adolescents, 203 (82 percent) had Sami-speaking parents (51 percent both parents, 22 percent only father and 27 percent only mother as Sami lingual), and 132 (53 percent) of these respondents had learned Sami at home. As expected, nearly all monolingual families practiced monolinguality (either Sami or Norwegian), whereas 46 percent ($n = 45$) of the ninety-nine bilingual families used Sami and 39 percent ($n = 39$) used Norwegian as their main language, and 15 percent ($n = 15$) practiced equally Sami and Norwegian as main languages.

As shown in Figure 6.1, for both types of language contexts the Sami language continuity was strongest in families with both parents speaking Sami, for Sami-dominated language contexts—chi-square (4, $n = 127$) = 44, $p<0.0001$—and for Norwegian-dominated contexts—chi-square (2, $n = 76$) = 18, $p<0.001$. There was no significant difference between monolingual Sami speaking mothers and fathers as contributors in language shift even though mothers in the Sami-dominated areas showed a stronger tendency to transfer the Sami language to their children than did the fathers (see Figure 6.1).

The relatively high degree of language shift in bilingual families can be explained by the fact that most frequently both parents are competent in the dominant language but not in the ethnic one. The dominant language therefore becomes the most spoken language, especially in Norwegian-dominated communities where little support for the Sami language and culture exists. The linguistic shift in these communities may also represent a wish to enter into the dominant culture, and linguistic assimilation may have been chosen by the parents to avoid ethnic stigmatization of their children as often experienced by the parents themselves. It seems likely that this linguistic assimilation has been due to the involuntary assimilation process the Samis, like other indigenous people, went through where the ethnic language was considered as an unnecessary and a low status language. Historically, the acquirement of a more highly valued majority language was necessary for the possibility of social mobility. The effect of the ethnic revitalization process of the Sami culture was just in its beginning when the participants were born. This cultural revival was probably not strong enough to counteract the linguistic assimilation at this time.

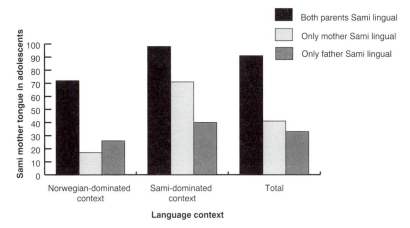

Figure 6.1 Sami language transference from parents to adolescents in different language contexts

In Sami-dominated communities, however, being competent in Sami language is highly valued and institutions outside the family support the ethnic language continuity. The increasing pattern of bilinguality may also illustrate a greater integration of the majority and the ethnic culture and thereby the need for being bicultural and bilingual. Being exposed to two or more different cultures forces the child to deal with the challenge of integrating two different cultures expressed by the two languages.

The impact of language on ethnic self-identification

In both types of language contexts, ethnic self-identification and mother tongue was strongly related: chi-square (4, $n = 247$) = 111, $p<0.0001$). Not surprisingly, of the adolescents with Sami mother tongue 89 percent ($n = 31$) labeled themselves strongly as Sami, 9 percent ($n = 3$) as bicultural, and only one respondent as Norwegian. In the bilingual group the adolescents mostly identified themselves as Sami; 41 percent ($n = 41$) as monoethnic Sami, 39 percent ($n = 39$) as bicultural. Nineteen percent ($n = 19$) identified themselves as Norwegian. Norwegian speakers identified mostly in accordance with their mother tongue as did those with Sami mother tongue; 63 percent ($n = 70$) of Norwegian speaking Samis identified themselves as Norwegian, 32 percent ($n = 35$) as bicultural, and only 5 percent ($n = 6$) as Sami. However, as shown in Table 6.1, the relationship between ethnic self-identification and mother tongue varied with type of language community.

Children's first language(s) is the prime symbol of identification with significant agents, such as parents, and of the cultural values they represent as important role models. Subsequent identifications with other role models such as teachers and friends, if associated with another language, are symbolized by the second language (Northover, 1988). Each language is a symbol of its respective culture. In this study the impact of mother tongue on ethnic self-identification was illustrated. These findings support results from other studies (Knight *et al.*, 1993). Language context created important variations for the relationship between ethnic identity and mother tongue. In Sami-dominated areas Sami identity was strengthened in all three language groups compared to Norwegian-dominated contexts. Surprisingly, the majority of adolescents in Sami areas with Norwegian mother tongue identified as Samis, and mostly biculturally. In the Norwegian-dominated context, however, Norwegian identity was very strong in this language group. This may be due to the fact that Sami adolescents in these areas are embedded in a context rich in cultural supportive factors stimulating Sami group membership and identity, where language constitutes only one of the factors. A recent study of the impact of the ethnic context on Sami adolescents' ethnic identity supports this finding (Kvernmo and Heyerdahl, 1996).

It has been claimed that in order to develop an additive balanced binguality, the two languages and cultures have to be favorably perceived and equally valued by the individual. Sociocultural factors important to the child's ethnic identity plays an important role, but depends on the child's social network and contacts with members of both groups (Hamers and Blanc, 1982; Lambert, 1974). In this study, bilinguals' ethnic identity varied significantly with the cultural and linguistic context. The Sami context provided more ethnic identification; half of the adolescents identified themselves as Sami and one third as bicultural. In the Norwegian context the bicultural and the Norwegian identity were strengthened; about half of the group identified themselves as bicultural and a little more than one-third as Norwegian. These findings may illustrate the fact that ethnic identity choice in adolescence is influenced by the surroundings represented by, for example, friends and school, whereas the impact of parents and family are weakened. Regarding bilingual adolescents in the Norwegian-dominated contexts identifying strongly bicultural, this may represent a successful integration of two cultures and two languages at the individual level.

Table 6.1 Ethnic self-identification and mother tongue in Sami adolescents and type of language context (%)

	Mother tongue					
	Sami dominated language context			Norwegian dominated language context		
Ethnic self identification	Sami (n=72)	Bilingual (n=40)	Norwegian (n=17)	Sami (n=6)	Bilingual (n=37)	Norwegian (n=73)
Sami	91	55	15	67	7	2
Bicultural	6	34	54	33	54	25
Norwegian	3	11	31	0	39	73
Total	100	100	100	100	100	100

Ethnic identity and language shift

Ethnic self-identification was strongly related to both language strategy, chi-square (2, n = 203) = 54, $p<0.001$, and language context, chi-square (2, n = 247) = 91, $p<0.001$. Adolescents living in families with continuity of Sami language labeled themselves mainly as Samis, 55 percent (n = 72) as monoethnic Samis, and 32 percent (n = 42) as bicultural. Among adolescents in families with language shift from Sami to Norwegian, 55 percent (n = 39) identified themselves as Norwegian, 37 percent (n = 26) as bicultural, and only 9 percent (n = 6) as monoethnic Sami.

However, when parental language strategy and language context were considered together, shifts appeared (see Table 6.2). In language communities dominated by Sami the Sami identification was strengthened in families where the adolescents learned Sami, just as Norwegian identification was strengthened in families with language shift living in Norwegian-dominated communities. Families with language shift in Sami language-dominated communities and those with language continuity in Norwegian-dominated communities had almost equally as many labeling into the three categories, about one third as Norwegian, half of the respondents as bicultural, and about 15 percent as only Sami (see Table 6.2).

The relation between language and ethnic identity was also illustrated by the impact of language continuity on ethnic self-identification. Adolescents exposed to language continuity in families were more frequently identifying as Samis in both types of language contexts. On the other hand, adolescents who experienced an ethnic language shift in the family were more dominant identified. Both language continuity and mother tongue showed a great flexibility and variation with language context.

Ethnic attitudes and behavior

Other components of ethnic identity such as ethnic behavior, attitudes, awareness and evaluation of ethnic group membership were also explored in relation to language continuity or shift in the family and language context. Table 6.3 shows the items representing different components and, for brevity, each cell shows a single combined percentage, representing adolescents who rated items positively.

The adolescents were asked to report which language they preferred to use when talking with friends. There was a significant correlation between mother tongue and preferred language used with friends for

Table 6.2 Ethnic self-identification in Sami adolescents in families with different parental language strategies by language context (%)

	Parental language strategy				
	Sami dominated language context		Norwegian dominated language context		
Ethnic self-identification	Continuation (n=103)	Shift (n=24)	Continuation (n=29)	Shift (n=47)	Total (n=203)
Sami	66	17	14	4	39
Bicultural	25	54	55	28	34
Norwegian	9	29	31	68	28
Total	100	100	100	100	100

both types of language contexts: chi-square (4, *n* = 127) = 63, *p*<0.0001, for Sami-dominated, and chi-square (4, *n* = 118) = 6, *p*<0.05, for Norwegian-dominated contexts. In the Sami area both groups with monolingual mother tongue (Sami or Norwegian) mainly wanted to practice their mother tongue with their friends; respectively, 77 percent (*n* = 24) of the Sami speakers preferred Sami, and 84 percent (*n* = 21) of the Norwegian speakers preferred Norwegian. Only 16 percent (*n* = 5) of the Sami linguals and 12 percent (*n* = 3) of the Norwegian linguals reported that they wanted to be bilingual in their communication with friends. In the bilingual group, however, 47 percent (*n* = 33) wanted to practice biliguality, 29 percent (*n* = 20) only Sami and 24 percent (*n* = 17) only Norwegian. In the Norwegian-dominated communities no adolescents wanted to speak only Sami with friends. All the three Sami monolinguals wanted to use Norwegian with friends, whereas 98 percent (*n* = 84) of the Norwegian speakers preferred their mother tongue with friends. Two Norwegian speakers preferred to be bilingual. Among the bilingual adolescents 86 percent (*n* = 24) would like to practice Norwegian and 14 percent (*n* = 4) biliguality with friends.

The role of language in the formation of ethnic identity can be described dually. First, it gives access to participation in different arenas or different activities in the formation of social networks and group boundaries. Second, language can act as a central means of shared experiences (Heller, 1987). Bilingual competence is assumed to give access to both Norwegian and Sami arenas and thereby enhance the possibility of social interaction. Surprisingly, relatively few monolingual adolescents in the Sami-dominated, but bilingual context, wanted to be bilingual in their communication with friends. The

Table 6.3 Ethnic behavior and ethnic attitudes and parental strategy in different language contexts (%)

| | Parental language strategy by language context | | | | | |
| | Continuation | | Shift | | | |
	Sami (n=101)	Norwegian (n=29)	Sami (n=24)	Norwegian (n=47)	Total (n=201)	Differences for total groups (language context and parental language strategy)
Ethnic behavior						
– traditional clothes	92	57***	75[a]	25***[b]	61	***c
Ethnic attitudes						
– Sami language	97	86*[a]	87	85	88	***[a]
– traditional clothes	94	79*	83	87	86	**
Ethnic awareness	60	51	44	64	52	N.s.
Evaluation of ethnic group membership	90	93	86	96	91	N.s.

Differences by language context: *$p<0.05$; **$p<0.01$; ***$p<0.001$
Differences by language strategy: [a]$p<0.05$; [b]$p<0.01$; [c]$p<0.001$

bilingual group, however, reported the strongest wish for bilinguality, but also a strong wish for only using Sami in these communities. In the Norwegian context, the influence of the dominant language showed a greater impact than the ethnic language in the Sami area and may be due to the monolingual character of this context. Norwegian was the most preferred language in contact with friends.

These findings illustrate that children establish social networks of peers with similar mother tongue. Because co-members of a group, also a linguistic group, obviously interact more with each other than they do with anyone else, their need for being bilingual is not present. Their experiences are limited to certain contexts not only dominated by the specific language but also by cultural values and symbols connected to or expressed by the language. In the Norwegian context the Sami adolescents have to interact with Norwegian peers and are faced with the majority culture to a much stronger degree than in the Sami context. Their challenges are to integrate these cultures and to resolve the conflicts between these cultures on an individual level. Being bilingual is a necessary means for access to and understanding of the different cultural contexts.

Another expression of ethnic behavior examined in the present study was the use of ethnic clothes which was strongly related to both parental language strategies—chi-square $(2, n = 201) = 41$, $p<0.0001$—and language context—chi-square $(2, n = 246) = 87$, $p<0.0001$). Wearing ethnic clothes highlights one's ethnic group membership just like using the ethnic language. This kind of ethnic exposure depends on the context; culturally supportive contexts are assumed to provide more expression of ethnic membership than contexts characterized by prejudice. In this study Sami adolescents living in Sami-dominated contexts were wearing their Sami traditional clothes significantly more frequently than did their peers living in Norwegian-dominated contexts.

Internal and invisible aspects of identity, such as ethnic attitudes, have been found in other studies to be more resistant to cultural change than external ones such as ethnic behavioral change (for example, Bond and Yang, 1982; Rosenthal and Feldman, 1990, 1992; Triandis *et al.*, 1986). In this study ethnic attitudes towards the use of the Sami language and traditional clothes were generally positive in all groups, but were also strongly associated with both language strategies—chi-square $(2, n = 200) = 19$, $p<0.001$, for attitude towards the Sami language, and chi-square $(2, n = 200) = 27$, $p<0.001$, for attitudes towards ethnic clothes)—and language context—chi-square $(2, n = 244) = 27$, $p<0.001$, for attitude towards Sami language, and chi-square (2, n = 245) = 43, $p<0.001$, for attitudes towards ethnic clothes.

Ethnic awareness in the family was not significantly associated with parental language strategies or language context, but it was lowest in families with language shift living in Sami language-dominated contexts and in families maintaining their Sami language living in Norwegian-dominated language contexts. Evaluation of ethnic group membership was generally high in all groups.

CONCLUSION

Several indigenous minorities have experienced language shifts as a part of an assimilation process to the dominant group resulting in loss of ethnic language especially in the younger generations. This change has had a significant impact on the formation of ethnic identity in minority adolescents as shown in this study. The linguistic socialization plays an important role in children's identification with their ethnic group. To preserve childrens' and adolescents' ethnic affiliation, there needs to be a linguistic revitalization of the ethnic language. This revitalization has to take place both on the family and the community level. Parents have to be encouraged to transfer their ethnic mother tongue to their children to make their children have access to all arenas of the ethnic community and be able to cooperate through binguality. On the community level, the kindergartens and the schools represent the most obvious institutions for providing ethnic language competence and support to parents' language strategies. Many parents are not able to teach their children the ethnic language because they themselves have not had the opportunity to learn it. The risk of not feeling attached to one's ethnic group or to be excluded by other group members, may be higher among adolescents being competent only in the dominant language. For Norwegian-speaking children, offers of language education in the community are very important and may be the only way to obtain the binguality and complete integration and acceptance of these adolescents in the community.

Positive ethnic attitudes, ethnic awareness and ethnic behavior all seem to be closely related to parental language continuity and contexts appreciating indigenous values, and finally to identification with the ethnic group. The strategy of elevating the status of the minority language and minority culture therefore should be provided by the dominant or majority group but also by the parents. This strategy can make indigenous children and adolescents feel more comfortable and safe with their ethnic group membership.

BIBLIOGRAPHY

Aboud, F.E. (1977) Interest in ethnic: a cross-cultural developmental study, *Canadian Journal of Behavioral Science*, 9: 134–46.

Aboud, F.E., and Mitchell, F.G. (1977) Ethnic role taking: the effects of preference and self-identification, *International Journal of Psychology*, 12: 1–17.

Aubert, W. (1978) *The Lappish Population in Northern Norway*, paper from Central Bureau of Statistics no. 107, Oslo: Aschehoug/Universitetsforlaget.

Bond, M.H., and Yang, K.S. (1982) Ethnic affirmation versus cross-cultural accommodation: the variable impact of questionnaire language on Chinese bilinguals in Hong Kong, *Journal of Cross-Cultural Psychology*, 13: 169–85.

Driedger, L. (1975) In search of cultural identity factors: a comparison of ethnic students, *Canadian Review of Sociology and Anthropology*, 12: 150–62.

Edwards, J. (1985), *Language, Society and Identity*, Oxford: Blackwell.

Fishman, J.A. (1977) Language and ethnicity, in H. Giles (ed.), *Language, Ethnicity and Intergroup Relations*, London: Academic Press.

Giles, H., and Coupland, N. (1991) *Language: Contexts and Consequences*, Pacific Grove: Brooks/Cole Publishing Company.

Giles, H., and Johnson, P. (1981) The role of language in ethnic group relations, in J.C. Turner, and H. Giles (eds.), *Intergroup Behavior*, Oxford: Blackwell.

Hamers, J.F., and Blanc, M.H.A. (1982) Towards a social-psychological model of bilingual development, *Journal of Language and Social Psychology*, 1: 29–49.

—— (1993) *Bilinguality and Bilingualism*, Cambridge: Cambridge University Press.

Heller, M.(1987) The role of language in the formation of ethnic identity, in J.S. Phinney, and M.J. Rotheram (eds.), *Children's Ethnic Socialization*, pp. 180–200, Newbury Park: Sage.

Knight, G.P., Bernal, M.E., Cota, M.K., Garza, C.A., and Ocampo, K.A. (1993) Family socialization and Mexican American identity and behavior, in M.E. Bernal, and G.P. Knight (eds.), *Ethnic Identity. Formation and Transmission among Hispanics and Other Minorities*, Albany: State University of New York Press.

Kvernmo, S., and Heyerdahl, S. (1996) Ethnic identity in indigenous Sami adolescents; the impact of family and ethnic community context, *Journal of Adolescence*, 19: 453–63.

Lambert, W.E. (1974) Culture and language as factors in learning and education, in F.E. Aboud, and R.D. Meade (eds.), *Cultural Factors in Learning*, Bellingham: Western Washington State College.

Le Page, R.B. (1968) Problems of description in multilingual communities, *Transactions of the Philological Society*, 189–212.

Le Page, R.B., and Tabouret-Keller, A. (1985) *Acts of Identity: Creole-Based Approaches to Language and Ethnicity*, Cambridge: Cambridge University Press.

Magga, O.H. (1994) The policy towards the Sami people in Norway, *Diedut*, 1: 57–62.

Milroy, L. (1980) *Language and Social Networks*, Oxford: Blackwell.

Nikora, L.W. (1993) *For Us, Our Children, or Grandchildren to Come?: Maori*

Development and Identity, paper presented at the conference "From Generation to Generation—From People to People," Kautokeino, Norway.

Northover, M. (1988) Bilinguals or "dual linguistic identities?", in J.W. Berry, and R.C. Annis (eds), *Ethnic Psychology: Research and Practice with Immigrants, Refugees, Native Peoples, Ethnic Groups and Sojourners*, Berwyn: Swets North America.

Pfiffer, A.B. (1993)*Laanaa Nisin: Dinè. Education in the Year 2003*, paper presented at the conference "From Generation to Generation—From People to People," Kautokeino, Norway.

Rosenthal, D.A., and Feldman, S.S. (1990) The acculturation of Chinese immigrants: effects on family functioning of length of residence in two cultural contexts, *Journal of Genetic Psychology*, 4: 495–514.

—— (1992) The nature of stability of ethnic identity in Chinese youth, *Journal of Cross-Cultural Psychology*, 1: 214–27.

Smolicz, J.J. (1979) Core values and cultural identity, *Ethnic and Racial Studies*, 4: 75–90.

Stordahl, V. (1994) Identity and saminess: expressing world view and nation, *Diedut*, 1: 57–62.

Thomas, D.R. (1993), *Culture, Ethnicity and Learning. Applications for Educational Policy and Practice*, Waikato: University of Waikato.

Triandis, H.C., Kashima, Y., Shimada, E., and Villareal, M. (1986) Acculturation indices as a means of confirming cultural differences, *International Journal of Psychology*, 21: 43–70.

Part III
Life Span Development

7 The ethic of care[1]

Issues in moral development

Eva Elisabeth Aspaas Skoe

> The motives of love and sympathy, if sufficiently enlightened and impartial, would achieve the purposes of moral rules better than the moral rules do, and would also achieve other good purposes beyond them.
>
> (Garnett, 1969, p. 91)

Referring to what Aristotle has called our "second nature," that is, our moral personality, Baumrind (1992) noted that moral reasoning is an everyday activity engaged in by the average person. Human beings in all cultures are responsible for their own lives; they are required to plan and take charge of their actions and to answer to themselves and to the community for the consequences. Research in the area of moral judgment has been dominated by Lawrence Kohlberg's conception of the development of justice, perhaps at times to the exclusion of other aspects of practical, everyday morality. As stated by Garnett (1969) in the opening quotation, sympathetic care for others is also central to everyday moral life. And so is proper care for self.

JUSTICE, CARE AND GENDER

Carrying forward into adolescence Piaget's (1932) pioneering investigation of moral thinking in children, Kohlberg (for example, 1981; 1984) derived six stages of justice-based moral development based on extensive case analyses of boys ranging in age from about 10 to 16 years. Gender bias and gender differences, however, have for the last decade or so been controversial and difficult issues in moral development. Carol Gilligan, a colleague of Kohlberg, connected the recurrent problems in interpreting women's development to the repeated omission of women from the critical theory-building studies of psychological research (see for example 1982). She put forth a critique of Kohlberg, pointing out that in the research from which Kohlberg derived his theory, females simply do not exist.

Consequently, Gilligan argues, Kohlberg's model is insensitive to women's voice and views on morality. Gilligan's observation echoes the voice of the Norwegian playwright, Henrik Ibsen. More than one hundred years ago, Ibsen wrote in his first notes for "A Doll's House," dated October 19, 1878:

> There are two kinds of spiritual laws, two kinds of conscience, one in men and a quite different one in women. They do not understand each other; but the woman is judged in practical life according to the man's law, as if she were not a woman but a man.
>
> (1917, p. 4)

Based on her own work with women, Gilligan proposed an alternate theory of moral development. In her view, there are two gender related, if not gender specific, moral orientations: (1) justice and individual rights, which is more representative of men's ethical judgment; and (2) the ethic of care, which is more representative of women's judgment. The care ethic develops from the individual's early childhood experiences of attachment to others and reflects an ideal of love, connection and mutual responsiveness; the justice ethic develops from early experiences of inequality and reflects an ideal of reciprocity, fairness and equality (Brown, Tappan, and Gilligan, 1995). Whereas women traditionally are urged toward a morality of responsibility and care in relationships, men are socialized toward a morality of rights, a concern for autonomy in judgment and action as well as for freedom and non-interference with the abstract rights of individuals. These two patterns, of rights and justice versus responsibility and care as foci, are distinct approaches to moral judgment, according to Gilligan, and maturity involves a greater understanding of both points of view. "In the representation of maturity, both perspectives converge in the realization that just as inequality adversely affects both parties in an unequal relationship, so too violence is destructive for everyone involved" (1982, p. 174).

Several theorists (for example, Chodorow, 1978; Gilligan, 1982; Josselson, 1987; Miller, 1984; Noddings, 1984) have argued that due to interactions between biologically-determined roles and cultural norms, women value the continuance of relationships with others more than do men. Social norms for men, on the other hand, have defined their responsibilities as securing provisions and protecting family members from outside dangers (Zahn-Waxler *et al.*, 1991). Chodorow (1978) and Gilligan (1982) attribute the differences that characterize masculine and feminine personality to the fact that women, traditionally, are largely responsible for early child care. Being parented by a person of the same gender, girls identify with their mothers and stay longer in close proximity to them than do boys. In this way, creating and maintaining connection with others becomes more central to girls' gender identity and self-esteem. Boys, in contrast, focus more on the experience of inequality, and separation or independence becomes more crucial for their identity and self-esteem. Furthermore, Gilligan (1982) has proposed that since masculinity is defined through separation whereas femininity is defined through attachment, male gender identity is threatened by intimacy whereas female gender identity is threatened by separation. Thus, men tend to have difficulty with relationships whereas females tend to have problems with individuation.

There is, however, little empirical evidence supporting Gilligan's claim that Kohlberg's moral reasoning measure is biased against women in terms of stage level. In his extensive reviews and meta-analyses Walker (1984, 1991, 1995) observed that most studies (85.5 percent) have not found significant gender differences in justice-based moral thought. In early adolescence, a small percentage of studies found a stage difference favoring girls. With adults, in the few studies where women scored lower than men, they also tended to have less formal education. Walker (1995) noted that in every case where researchers controlled in some manner for education and/or occupation, gender differences in stage levels disappeared; thus, he concluded that the overall review pattern is one of non-significant gender differences.

Regarding justice versus care (thinking/orientation), research has provided mixed support for Gilligan's original claim of gender differences in moral orientation. Lyons (1983) developed a coding scheme for analyzing moral considerations presented by participants when discussing moral conflicts in their lives. Considerations were categorized as either response (care) or rights (justice), and the predominant, most frequent, mode of reasoning was used as score. Lyons (1983) reported that the majority of women (75 percent) used considerations of care whereas the majority of men (79 percent) used considerations of justice. With more refined analyses, Gilligan and Attanucci (1988) observed that most people use both care and justice perspectives, but care-focused dilemmas are more likely to be presented by women and justice-focused dilemmas by men. Other researchers, however, failed to find gender differences in reasoning about real-life moral problems (for example, Rothbart *et al.*, 1986; Derry, 1989; Pratt *et al.*, 1988). Using another research paradigm, in which stimuli are more standardized (Walker, 1995), Ford and Lowery (1986) found no gender differences in students' rating of the degree to which they used care or justice orientation in thinking about a moral conflict in their lives. Similarly, Friedman, et al. (1987) failed to find gender differences in students' rating of the importance of care and justice considerations in resolving dilemmas. The above approaches have attempted to assess Gilligan's proposed gender differences in moral orientation (justice versus care), frequently by analyzing people's reasoning about their own dilemmas and/or about Kohlberg's dilemmas. However, as observed by Eisenberg et al. (1989), in Kohlberg's dilemmas issues related to caring are not central; the focus is more on justice, rights and prohibition-related concerns. Furthermore, in the real-life moral dilemmas used in some studies (for example, Gilligan and Attanucci, 1988; Lyons, 1983; Walker et al., 1987), issues related to justice, rights, care, or other moral or social conventional concerns all might be central. Because care-related issues are less relevant to some real-life moral dilemmas than others it is difficult to examine relative use of care-related reasoning (Eisenberg et al., 1989). Similarly, Walker (1991, 1995) has noted the importance of the content or nature of the moral dilemma. Both men and women tend to use the care orientation more than the justice orientation when discussing personal/relational real-life dilemmas. Conversely, both genders tend to use justice more than care when discussing impersonal/non-relational dilemmas. Although this shows that type of conflict can predict moral orientation better than gender, overall women generate more relational conflicts than men, which means that women actually show more care responses than men (Turiel, 1998).

The large body of research (see Turiel, 1998; Walker, 1995, for recent reviews), examining gender differences on justice versus care orientations has tended to obscure a second very important implication of Gilligan's work: the concept that care-based reasoning, like justice-based reasoning, also follows specific developmental pathways and varies from individual to individual. This chapter focuses on an increasingly used care-based morality measure, the Ethics of Care Interview (EC1), designed to empirically test the developmental aspects of Gilligan's theory, which largely have been overlooked. The ECI parallels Kohlberg's stage model of justice-based moral development in that it measures hierarchical levels of development in the care ethic. The levels of care move from an initial perspective of *self-concern*, through a questioning of this as a sole criterion, to primarily *other-concern*, through a similar questioning of this as a sole criterion, to a final perspective of *balanced self-and-other concern*. Because the ECI assesses levels of care, using a real-life dilemma in addition to standardized dilemmas which specifically focus on care issues—the conflict between the needs of self and the needs of others—it is a useful tool for investigating development as well as potential gender differences in care-based moral thought. In this chapter I will give a review of existing studies with the ECI. Findings point to the importance of care-based morality for general human development, especially personality development. Directions for further research are also discussed.

THE ETHIC OF CARE INTERVIEW

The ECI consists of four dilemmas administered in a structured interview format. In addition to a real-life conflict generated by the participant, there are three standardized interpersonal dilemmas, involving conflicts surrounding (1) unplanned pregnancy, (2) marital fidelity, and (3) care for a parent. The interviews are tape-recorded and take about 30 minutes to administer. They are scored according to the ECI Manual (Skoe, 1993), which contains descriptions consistent with those outlined by Gilligan (1982) and sample responses for five ethic of care levels. The five levels involve a progressively more complex understanding of human relationships and an increasing differentiation of self and other. Thus, the ethic of care reflects a cumulative understanding of relationships based on the perception that self and other are interdependent and that activities of care benefit both others and self (see Skoe and Marcia, 1991; Skoe and Diessner, 1994, for further details).

The following are brief descriptions of each ECI level and examples of responses to a dilemma involving care for a lonely parent. Men are presented with a male protagonist, and women are presented with a female protagonist:

> Kristine/Chris, a 26 year old woman/man, has decided to live on her/his own after having shared an apartment with a friend for the last three years. She/he finds that she/he is much happier living alone as she/he now has more privacy and independence and gets more work and studying done. One day her/his mother/father, whom she/he has not seen for a long while as they do not get along too well, arrives at the doorstop with two large suitcases, saying that she/he is lonely and wants to live with Kristine/Chris. What do you think Kristine/Chris should do? Why?

Level 1 is survival (caring for self). This perspective is characterized by caring for the self in order to ensure survival and personal happiness. The person's concern is pragmatic, and what the person "should" do is undifferentiated from what the person "wants" to do. The question of "rightness" emerges mainly if the person's own needs are in conflict. The aims are basically to protect the self, to ensure one's own happiness and to avoid being hurt or suffering. There is little, if any, evidence of caring for other people.

Open the door, let his father in, put the suitcases down. Don't unpack, Dad. Let's talk about this. You don't just walk in, I'm 26. That's the basic argument. Chris would do himself in, basically, because he'd lose his privacy and his father isn't exactly doing a good thing for himself by becoming dependent on Chris . . . Dad should find his own place; unless his father's senile, crazy or something. Then maybe he should consider a nursing home.

Level 1.5 is the transition from survival to responsibility. Movement is toward responsibility that entails an attachment to others. Concepts of "selfishness" and "responsibility" first appear. Although there now is some concern for other people, survival of the self is still the main aim.

I suppose she has to let her stay for a little while, anyway. You can't very well turn your own mother away. But after awhile you have to have a heart-to-heart discussion about why it is not fair for the mother to dump on her daughter. Hopefully, they could figure out something, she could rent an apartment near her daughter and they could visit. Because after awhile they are going to realize how little they get along anyway, so the mom is probably wanting to leave anyway, hopefully. If not, the daughter has no choice but to ask her to leave. They don't get along anyway. She is infringing upon her life and not making her any happier, so she has to go. (WHY WOULD YOU TAKE HER IN IN THE FIRST PLACE?) Because if somebody landed on your doorstop you at least want to hear the story. You don't talk to somebody through the keyhole, so you have to let them in and let them stay for breakfast and then they can go.

Level 2 is conventions of goodness (caring for others). This perspective is characterized by a strong emphasis on responsibility, obligation and commitment. The person adopts societal values, and conventionally-defined goodness becomes the primary concern because survival is now seen to depend on the acceptance of others. "Good" is equated with self-sacrificing caring for others, and "right" is externally defined, for example, by the church, parents, or society. Conflict arises specifically over the issue of hurting, and others are helped or protected, often at the expense of self-assertion.

Bring him in. I've been living without a father for a long time. I wouldn't think twice . . . . Not only because too many people in this world don't have the second chance that Chris is having, family should be upper most in his mind. In a family if you can't take in your own father, you can't take in anyone else. Then you are shutting off life, and what a way to live . . . . If the father had put up with this guy for as long as he had, I think it is just common courtesy for Chris to do the same thing. You owe it to your father to take care of him.

Level 2.5 is the transition from a conventional to a reflective care perspective (from "goodness" to truth about relationships). This transition phase is marked by a shift in concern from goodness to truth and honesty. There is a reconsideration of the relationship between self and other as the person questions the "goodness" of protecting others at one's own expense.

If her mother is very old and needs attention, I feel she should be taken in. Because the mother has supported the child when she was growing up. This is depending on the idea that the mother does need help. But if mother is completely self-sufficient and just suddenly feels a whim to go live with the daughter, the daughter should say "you can stay for a week or two, but I don't feel we should be living together because I want my independence". But if the mother needs help, I feel she should give it to her. (WHY?). It's got to do with parental devotion. My parents have always been good to me. I would look after them if they had problems. I could not just put them into a home and just visit them. But if mother is only lonely, she could live somewhere on her own, and Kristine could visit her or she should try to get involved with people her own age. She will probably cause a rift between herself and her daughter because of different values and views. It would be very hard on the two of them.

Level 3 is the ethic of care (caring for both self and others). This perspective emphasizes the dynamics of relationships and achieves a balance between selfishness and responsibility through a new understanding of the complexity of connections between others and self. No longer restricted by social convention, individuals are able to make their own choices and accept responsibility for decisions as criteria for goodness move inward. There is now a balance of moral considerations between self and other, and both are included in the compass of care. Attempts are made to minimize hurt to all parties.

If I were Chris I would make it plain that certainly my father would be welcome on a temporary basis . . . and I would say to my father if you're lonely maybe we can find you something nearby or maybe in the same building but I still need my space. At this point Chris has a life of his own and seems to be expressing a real need for some solitude and just to have his own domain for a time. His father's dilemma is that he is lonely and he wants to live with Chris. I think that could be resolved quite well if his father lived nearby. That would afford them to be able to get together occasionally or often. Chris could be there for him and in emergency he could be right there . . . . So I think that's a good compromise.

The ECI yields a total score across the four dilemmas, with a potential range from 4.00 to 12.00 for any single participant. It also yields a classification into one of five discrete levels. Based on the interview, the participant is given a level score for each dilemma. If necessary, quarter scores (for example, 1.25, 2.75) can be assigned when the response seems to fall between two levels. Total scores are the summed ratings on the four dilemmas; overall level scores for the ECI are determined by dividing the total scores by four[2] and then rounding to the nearest 0.5 level (for example, 1.56 = level 1.5, 1.94 = level 2.0, 2.45 = level 2.5)[3].

The ECI has established levels of interrater reliability correlations ranging from 0.76 to 0.95 for the four individual dilemmas, and from 0.87 to 0.96 for the total scores (Cohen's Kappa 0.63–1.00)[4]. Internal consistency assessed via intercorrelations of scores on the four dilemmas have generally ranged from 0.73 to 0.92, and the dilemma-total score correlations from 0.82 to 0.97. Cronbach's *α*s of 0.94–0.97 have also been calculated (for example, Skoe and Diessner, 1994; Skoe and Marcia, 1991; Sochting, Skoe, and Marcia, 1994).

FINDINGS

In an initial study (Skoe and Marcia, 1991) of 86 college women, 17–26 years old, the ECI was found to be positively related to age and ego identity development (for example, Marcia, 1980) as well as to a Kohlbergian justice reasoning measure (Gibbs and Widaman, 1982). Also, as predicted, the ECI for these women was more closely related to ego identity than was the Kohlbergian measure. These findings are in line with Gilligan's (1982) assertion that women's conceptions of self and morality are intricately linked and that the care ethic has relevance for women's personality development. They are also congruent with Josselson (1987), who noted that skill and success in relatedness become keystones of ego development for women. Because the sample in the above study was restricted to women, however, it could not address possible gender differences or whether care-based moral reasoning is more applicable to women than to men, as argued by Gilligan. Furthermore, the ECI and identity were both assessed in interviews whereas the Kohlbergian measure was a paper and pencil test; hence, the finding that the ECI was more closely related to identity than was the Kohlbergian test may have been confounded by method differences.

A subsequent study (Skoe and Diessner, 1994) of 58 men and 76 women (age 16–30 years) was therefore conducted, examining the relations among ego identity, care-based, and justice-based moral thought, with use of Kohlberg's (Colby and Kohlberg, 1987) interview. In addition, possible gender differences in the nature (personal or impersonal) of real-life dilemmas were examined. This extended study showed that care-based moral reasoning, as measured by the ECI, was positively related to age, ego identity, and justice-based morality for both men and women. Also, there were no significant gender differences on the ego identity, justice stages, and ECI measures themselves. Although these findings suggested that gender differences may not be as pronounced as Gilligan has asserted, further analyses indicated that the ethic of care may nevertheless operate differentially in men and women in important ways. For example, significantly more women (88 percent) than men (72 percent) showed the predicted pattern of high identity/high ECI or low identity/low ECI. Moreover, the partial correlation (controlling for age) between care levels and identity was significantly higher than the correlation between justice levels and identity for women, but not for men (see Skoe and Diessner, 1994, for further details). Thus, it appears that the care ethic may be a more central component of ego identity for women than for men.

The finding that for women care was more highly related to ego identity than was justice replicates the results of Skoe and Marcia (1991) and precludes the interpretation that the ECI and identity were more strongly related because of common method variance. This time all three variables were assessed by interview. Hence, the care ethic may influence women's everyday life experiences and thinking more than men's, perhaps because of socialization, culture, and activity preferences.

The findings of no significant average gender differences on the ECI in late adolescence and young adulthood have been replicated by several independent studies at different locations, both in North America (for example, Skoe and Nickerson, 1997; Sochting, 1996; Sochting *et al.*,

1994) and in Norway (for example, Skoe, Kristensen, *et al.*, 1997; Skoe and von der Lippe, 1997; Skoe *et al.*, 1997). The lack of gender differences observed in these studies may reflect the current emphasis on gender equality and the fact that the samples consisted mainly of university students. During the past twenty years, gender stereotypes in Western cultures have been diminishing, expanding the roles and opportunities for men as well as women. The impact of such ideological changes may have been greatest on young, well-educated adults.

Gilligan and others have claimed that women have traditionally been socialized to be concerned with care and responsibility for others. Hence, it seems especially appropriate to test Gilligan's theory in older samples from the North American population. Stronger gender differences might be expected in older cohorts because of more marked differences in the socialization of men and women in such older samples. Older people grew up in a more restrictive, gender-stereotyped society, and they were raised by parents adhering to more conservative values and norms. Thus, in order to test further the hypothesis that mature women are more sophisticated with regard to care and responsibility in relationships than are men because of traditional gender roles (for example, Gilligan, 1982; Miller, 1984; Noddings, 1984), two separate studies examined care-based moral reasoning and real-life moral dilemma content in older men and women (Skoe *et al.*, 1996). Ages ranged from approximately 40 to 84 years.

Consistent with the theory that women's conventional encouragement toward caring for others will be reflected in moral reasoning patterns, the results suggested clear gender differences with regard to care-based moral thought in older participants. In both studies women scored at higher levels of care reasoning than did men, and women also generated significantly more personal, relational real-life dilemmas (and fewer impersonal, non-relational ones) than did men. In young adulthood, however, gender differences seem to be more subtle and complex than the simple main effects on the ECI found with these older adults. It is likely that cohort differences in social experiences may account for these differential age patterns. The differences in gender with age could also be due to participants' different position within the life cycle, rather than to different historical cohorts.

Considering the use of care-based moral thought in the broader context of life span development, the findings by Skoe *et al.* (1996) indicated that more sophisticated capacities in reasoning about care of self and others may serve as an important resource in adapting to the central tasks of later life, such as achieving a sense of generativity and ego integrity (for example, Erikson, 1982). Higher levels of care reasoning were found to be associated with more intimate social interactions and cognitive reflectiveness as well as with better personal adjustment (see Skoe *et al.*, 1996, for further details). Furthermore, replicating previous results in younger samples (Skoe and Marcia, 1991; Skoe and Diessner, 1994), a moderately positive relationship between care and justice reasoning levels as assessed by the standard Kohlberg Moral Judgment Interview measure was found in mature men and women. Other noteworthy findings were that the ECI showed no age differences in maturity across both studies, and relative stability over a period of approximately five years in mid-to-late adulthood in the second. Thus, longitudinal as well as cross-sectional data indicated that care reasoning levels were relatively stable in mature adulthood. This is congruent with earlier findings on justice-based moral thinking (for example, Pratt *et al.*, 1996, 1991; White, 1988).

Another age group that may be especially appropriate to examine in order to test Gilligan's theory is early adolescence, because she has noted that, in adolescence, girls are likely to focus on the strength of connection "especially when norms of feminine behavior impede strivings toward equality" (Gilligan and Wiggins, 1987, p. 282). North American research has provided some support for this proposal. For example, in a longitudinal study, Eisenberg *et al.* (1991) observed that the initial increase in other-oriented moral reasoning in late elementary school was primarily for girls. Similarly, Cohn's (1991) extensive meta-analysis of personality development showed that gender differences arose around 11 years of age, with girls being less egocentric and more concerned with social approval and acceptance than boys. These gender differences disappeared a few years later (Cohn, 1991; Eisenberg *et al.*, 1991).

A study investigating care-based moral reasoning and real-life moral dilemma content in early adolescence was conducted by Skoe and Gooden (1993). The sample comprised 23 girls and 23 boys, 11–12 years of age, and was drawn from grade 6 in a small Canadian east coast town. The ECI standardized dilemmas were revised for use with children, involving conflicts surrounding family and friends. For example:

Nicole/Jason has been invited by her/his friend, Janice/Erik, to come with her/him for dinner after school on Friday. The next day, another friend, Pam/Danny, invites Nicole/Jason on the same Friday to see their favorite rock band perform as she/he has tickets for two good seats. What do you think Nicole/Jason should do? Why?"

As expected, the results showed that early adolescent girls scored higher than boys on the ECI. Furthermore, significantly more girls than boys scored at ECI level 2 (conventions of goodness, caring for others), and more boys than girls scored at the lower, egocentric levels (levels 1 and 1.5). The girls also generated more personal, relational real-life dilemmas than did the boys, whereas the boys generated more impersonal real-life issues than did the girls. These findings of gender differences in development, favoring early adolescent girls, but not young adult women, are congruent with research in related areas such as justice-based moral development (for example, Silberman and Snarey, 1993), pro-social moral reasoning (for example, Eisenberg *et al.*, 1991), ego development (for example, Cohn, 1991), and religious judgment (for example, Oser, 1991). The results from these studies, using a variety of different measures in independent samples and locations, all suggested essentially that in early adolescence girls are more concerned about responsibility and care for others than are boys, although this difference decreases in young adulthood.

Most theories and studies in the area of moral development, however, have been North American. The developmental context for children may vary across cultures. As stated by Dasen and Jahoda (1986), human development always occurs in a specific cultural context. And although it is probable that many aspects of human development are universal, such universality must be demonstrated empirically across a variety of human populations. Also, any theory claiming generality must be able to account for cultural diversity (Dasen and Jahoda, 1986). Cross-cultural comparisons may, for example, illuminate how the environment shapes personality, attitudes, values, beliefs and behavior. Such comparisons "afford special opportunities for assessing the relative influence and interaction of biological and environmental variables in development" (Intons-Peterson, 1988, p. 30).

In order to examine possible cultural differences, care-based moral reasoning and real-life moral dilemma content in northern Norwegian early adolescents were examined, and the results were compared with those obtained in the above Canadian study (Skoe, Bakke, *et al.*, 1997). Fewer gender differences were expected in Norway because gender equality has been successfully reinforced in this country for many years. For example, a woman has been prime minister in Norway for more than 15 years, and 40 percent of the members in the Norwegian government are women. In contrast, Canada has only once had a female prime minister for a very short time (about three months), and women constitute only 18 percent of members of the Canadian parliament (Young, 1997). Furthermore, there are more Norwegian than Canadian women in the workforce (71 percent versus 57 percent), and in 1994–95, the average annual income of Norwegian women was roughly 93 percent of the average income of men (Likestillings Rådet, 1996), in contrast to the comparable figure of 58 percent in Canada (Statistics Canada, 1995). Hence, the norms of feminine behavior, the role models and the developmental context may be different in Norway, where expectations for young girls include being independent, self-assertive, and willing to take risks.

In line with this suggestion, recent research showed no gender difference in the tendency among Norwegian adolescents to be self-oriented, independent and self-reliant (Vikan and Claussen, 1994). Also, in contrast to North America where boys tend to score higher on masculinity than do girls (for example, Intons-Peterson, 1988), no such differences have been found in Norwegian adolescents (Wichstrøm, 1994). Vikan and Claussen (1994) explained Norwegians' apparent concern with individualism by noting that historically people in Norway have lived in isolated, small communities and in a challenging natural setting. Particularly in northern Norway, the challenging living conditions have necessitated women's initiative and self-reliance. While the men were away for long periods, mostly at sea fishing, the women were left behind to take care of not only the home and the children, but also to administer to the whole community (Holtedahl, 1986). This in turn must have influenced their children. Furthermore, people in northern Norway live in a rough natural landscape (large mountains and the North Sea) and in a harsh climate (long and dark winters). In contrast, the Canadian population is clustered in the southernmost part of the country, most of it today in urban centers. The history of Canadian settlement is primarily agricultural, with men present on the farms and predominant in community affairs.

In accordance with this hypothesized cultural difference, there were no significant gender differences on the ECI, nor in real-life dilemma content, in the Norwegian sample. Also, as predicted, significantly more Canadian than Norwegian girls scored at ECI Level 2 (conventions of goodness, caring for others). As noted above, both culture and nature are factors which may, at least partly, explain the findings of girls being more survival-oriented, or perhaps slower to become more other-oriented, in northern Norway. Certainly, longitudinal research is necessary, and the findings of such cross-cultural differences need replication with large, representative samples. Nevertheless, they point to the possibility that North American research findings may not necessarily be representative of all Western cultures, and call attention to the need for developmental psychologists to attend more closely to the influence of cultural factors.

Table 7.1 is a summary of research conducted so far on the ECI in North American and Norwegian samples. It presents frequencies of participants from studies with late adolescents and adults in North America (Canada and the USA) and in Norway across the various ECI levels. (The participants included people from late adolescence to late adulthood, but consisted primarily of young adult students.) As can be seen from the table, the distributions are fairly similar. In both North America and Norway about 50 percent of the participants were scored at the higher levels (2.5 and 3), around 20 percent were scored at Level 2, and about 20–30 percent were scored at the two lowest levels. Relatively few people (about 15 percent in both Norway and North America) were scored at the highest ECI level (Level 3), which is also the case with Kohlberg's justice model. In fact, it is not unusual to find no people at Kohlberg's post-conventional level (stage 5), even in samples consisting primarily of well-educated adults (for example, Colby and Kohlberg, 1987; Skoe and Diessner, 1994). These initial distributions seem to illustrate some degree of "universality" of the ECI model, although many more samples from other cultures are needed to assess this issue. Also, these samples comprised mainly university students, and there may be fewer cultural as well as gender differences in well-educated young adults. Further research with people from several different walks of life and from different countries is therefore necessary.

In conclusion, the issue of gender differences in moral development is controversial for good reasons. Especially in late adolescence and young adulthood (which are the age groups most frequently studied), gender differences seem to be complex and subtle. Rather than showing up as simple main effects on standardized measures, gender differences have been found mainly in the relations between standardized tests, and in the nature of participants' spontaneously reported self-chosen real-life conflicts. Regardless of employment or marital status, in North American studies women have consistently been found to generate more relational real-life dilemmas than men, whereas men generate more non-relational ones than women (for example, Pratt *et al.*, 1991; Skoe and Diessner, 1994; Skoe and Gooden, 1993; Walker *et al.*, 1987). In line with Gilligan's theory, this indicates, at least indirectly, that women may have a preference for the care orientation because such relational real-life dilemmas tend to evoke more care-based moral judgment than other types of dilemma (Walker, 1991, 1995). More direct support for Gilligan has been provided by a recent

Table 7.1 Frequencies of participants in the various Ethic of Care Interview (ECI) levels – North America and Norway

ECI level	Females		Males		Combined	
	N	(%)	N	(%)	N	(%)
			North America			
1	7	(5.2)	8	(6.9)	15	(6.0)
1.5	26	(19.1)	32	(27.6)	58	(23.0)
2	26	(19.1)	24	(20.7)	50	(19.8)
2.5	48	(35.3)	43	(37.1)	91	(36.1)
3	29	(21.3)	9	(7.7)	38	(15.1)
			Norway			
1	2	(1.1)	8	(4.6)	10	(2.8)
1.5	39	(21.3)	32	(18.5)	71	(19.9)
2	46	(25.1)	41	(23.7)	87	(24.4)
2.5	68	(37.2)	65	(37.6)	133	(37.4)
3	28	(15.3)	27	(15.6)	55	(15.5)

study examining gender and dilemma differences in real-life moral judgment. Wark and Krebs (1996) found that women both made more care-based moral judgments on personal, relational real-life dilemmas and reported more care-pulling pro-social dilemmas than did men. Men, in contrast, reported more justice-pulling antisocial dilemmas than did women.

These findings may reflect the possibly important distinction between what people *can* do (competence) when it is required of them and what they *will* do (preference) on their own initiative. Both Kohlberg's measure, the Moral Judgment Interview, and the ECI are essentially cognitive tests, measuring moral competence or moral understanding. Whereas there may be no significant gender differences in moral cognition or competence, at least in young adulthood, women's apparent stronger tendency to focus on personal, relational issues than men seems most readily to become evident in situations which allow people to respond more freely and spontaneously. Again, it must be noted, however, that the samples were mainly restricted to university student populations, and gender differences (and perhaps cultural differences also) may be minimized in these samples. In any case, research findings show that many additional variables must be considered in understanding moral development besides gender, such as cultural background, cohort variations, sex role orientation, situational context, sample and location characteristics, and stage or period in life. Similarly, Snarey (1997) has noted that there is a multitude of major life experiences "behind" gender, such as variations in biological maturation, family relationships, and social opportunities. All these factors must be considered when investigating growth and change in development.

DIRECTIONS FOR FUTURE RESEARCH

Longitudinal research across the life span and across cultures that includes both the justice ethic and the care ethic is necessary to further assess developmental issues in morality. Longitudinal data may, for example, shed some further light on the developmental progression of care-based moral reasoning levels, and show whether gender differences in moral thought, or the lack thereof, remain stable over the life cycle or fluctuate as, for example, gender roles and "connected" self-concepts have been found to do (for example, Abrahams *et al.*, 1978; Pratt *et al.*, 1990). There are indications that care-based morality follows a developmental path. In samples consisting primarily of late adolescents and young adults, the ECI has been found to be positively related to age as well as to other developmental measures such as Marcia's ego identity status, Loevinger's ego developmental test, and Kohlberg's justice measure. Longitudinal data, however, are required to determine whether or not the ECI levels represent invariant, qualitative stages.

Future research should also attempt to determine what kind of mechanisms or factors may facilitate change and growth in care-based moral thought. Advances in moral thought are based on questioning of previous positions and the formulation of a new, more inclusive position (for example, Gibbs, 1995; Skoe and Marcia, 1991). These processes are clearly similar to the processes of disequilibration and accommodation, assumed to underlie general cognitive development in the Piagetian theory (for example, Kohlberg, 1969). A related suggestion has been discussed by Garnett (1969) who elevated the cognitive element in conscience, the judgment of right and wrong, in distinguishing between the critical and the traditional conscience. Whereas the latter adheres to traditional moral ideas and rules without critical re-evaluation of them, the critical conscience questions and tries to improve the tradition. More recently, Baumrind (1992) has reminded us that the contradictions and complexities implicit in human social adaptation require both conformity and non-conformity to social rules and, therefore, the capacities to both observe and critique conventions and culture. As noted by Garnett (1969), reasons for moral rules have to be found in their relevance to the needs, peace and security of the community and the well-being of the persons themselves. But it is always a distinguishing mark of a moral rule that it is one for which it is believed that reasons can be given, according to Garnett. He has suggested that original critical thinking about moral rules is therefore stimulated whenever the reasons given seem inadequate, beginning with the child's "Why?" (especially when told that she ought to do something she does not want to do), and whenever there is a conflict of rules.

Hence, one might expect the ethic of care to be positively related to cognitive development, and to certain social experiences. It has been asserted that the essence of a developmental approach is that crisis reveals, as well as creates, character (for example, Gilligan, 1982). If this is true, one might predict that crisis, at least certain types of crisis (for example, divorce, illness or death of significant others), will stimulate personal growth. In line with this, Josselson (1987) and Skoe and Marcia (1991) reported that women who had experienced painful conflicts and events, for example, the turbulent ending of important relationships and terminal illness, also were highly developed in terms of identity and care-based moral reasoning at a relatively young age. Future research should examine more specifically what kind of experiences, at what stage in life, may affect moral development and, conversely, how moral reasoning affects the way one deals with crisis.

Because many would argue that morality ultimately is directed toward action (Blasi, 1980), future research should examine more closely the connection between the ethic of care and actual behavior. Sochting *et al.* (1994) investigated the relation between the ECI and willingness to help another person complete a task. Contrary to the hypothesis, no significant relation between care-based moral reasoning and willingness to assist was found. However, as stressed by Blasi (1980), moral phenomena ought not to be limited to objectively observable behavior. Moral action is complex and involves a variety of feelings, questions, doubts, judgments and decisions. Because every moral situation is a unique situation having its own irreplaceable good (and bad), the best or right course of action is not self-evident but has to be searched for (Dewey, 1957). Moral judgments of a person must take account of every feature of the person's personality concerned in the performance of his or her acts, that is, motives, intentions, beliefs, abilities and so forth (Garnett, 1969). Hence, merely looking at a person's behavior in isolation, for example, in a constructed laboratory setting, or even in a more naturalistic setting, may not tell us much about the nature or extent of the person's moral qualities.

A more valid test of moral behavior may therefore be how a person conducts his or her life in the long run, because only a whole life perspective can more fully provide a true picture of a person's quality of moral integration (Blasi, 1995). Thus, a more appropriate unit of moral behavior should comprise at least a stretch or longer period of a person's life. In line with this, in a recent study by Skoe *et al.* (1997) participants reported how many hours in their life time they had spent helping others by volunteering in charity organizations, hospitals, and nursing homes. Also, the reasons or motivation for engaging in such pro-social activities were probed and scored as follows: (1) no activities and consequently no reasons were given; (2) pressure by others, such as family, friends, and teachers; (3) partly because it was required of them, and partly because they wanted to be involved themselves because they thought it was interesting; and (4) own initiative because they thought it was both interesting and meaningful. A preliminary analysis of the responses of 60 women and 49 men, age 19–34 years, indicated a positive relationship between the ECI and hours spent on caring activities, as well as between the ECI and motivation for engaging in such behavior. People high in care reasoning levels, 2.5 and 3 (caring for both self and others), scored significantly higher on pro-social activities and on motivation than did both level 2 (conventional, self-sacrificing), and levels 1 and 1.5 (caring primarily for self). Thus, men and women who demonstrated more integrated care reasoning also tended to be more active as well as internally motivated to help people in need such as the elderly and sick, and to see these activities as personally meaningful.

Little is known about the role of emotions in moral development in general (Rich, 1986), and further research on the relations among justice-based moral reasoning, and care-based moral reasoning, and emotions should be undertaken. Garnett (1969) has connected moral feelings and thinking in stating that the emotive drives of moral approval and disapproval are moved by the thought of the effect of our actions upon other people. The feeling-tone of moral approval and disapproval is distinct and different from, for example, mere liking and disliking, in that there is in them a distinct element of concern for human welfare which is gratified by what promotes it and distressed at what seems injurious or hurtful. Moral philosophers have therefore often identified moral emotions with compassion or sympathy (for example, Dewey, 1957; Garnett, 1969), but they are not mere passive feeling states. Moral emotions have in them an element of active concern for human values with an impulse to give help when it seems needed, according to Garnett (1969).

Another important moral emotion is guilt, which could be considered an example of moral self disapproval. Williams and Bybee (1994) have found that more males than females report guilt over externally aggressive behaviors (for example, property damage, fighting and victimization of animals), and more females than males report guilt over incidents that violate norms of compassion and interpersonal trust (for example, inconsiderateness and lying). The findings that females generate more interpersonal real-life moral conflicts and also report feeling more guilty about interpersonal transgressions than males suggest that perhaps females consider care-oriented, relational moral issues more important, or more intrinsically moral, than do males (Wark and Krebs, 1996). These issues require further investigation. Again, it should be noted that these gender differences appeared not on standardized tests, but in more open-ended, free-responding situations.

So far, the link between the ethic of care and emotions is unclear. For example, in maturity both men and especially women who scored higher on care reasoning showed more positive feelings about their own aging, but not necessarily about their lives in general (Skoe *et al.*, 1996). It seems that people high in the care ethic may not necessarily feel more happy or satisfied than people at the lower levels, but they may possess a greater acceptance of the many ambiguities and hard realities in life, and a greater tolerance for their own as well as others' imperfections and misfortunes. In support of this suggestion, the ECI has been found to be positively related to social support satisfaction and empathic perspective-taking, but negatively related to right-wing authoritarianism and personal distress, that is, anxiety and unease in the presence of people with problems (Skoe *et al.*, 1996; Skoe and Nickerson, 1997). Sochting (1996) also found that persons at the highest level of ethic of care, while they scored highly on a Thematic Apperception Test measure of cognitive sophistication, scored lower than level 2 persons in general positive emotional tone of stories. In fact, it is my impression from interviewing people that "being happy" is much more of a concern and goal for people at the lower care levels. With maturity, at least as measured by the ECI, honesty, truth and personal meaning seem to become more essential.

An important area requiring investigation is the effects of family interactions and parenting styles of child-rearing on the development of the care ethic. For example, Sochting (1996) has recently examined the links between care reasoning and standardized measures of attachment, object relations and social cognition. She found that people scoring at the lower levels of the ECI (primarily self-oriented) scored higher on the fearful attachment style and were less mature in both affective and cognitive dimensions of object relations and social cognition than people who scored at the higher ECI levels. It might be hypothesized that a parenting ideology (Newberger, 1980), which employs mutuality between parents' and children's needs, would provide a better model for the subsequent development of care-based moral thought than would parental styles which emphasizes only the parents' concerns or only the child's needs. In particular, one would expect authoritative parenting, which involves a give-and-take between parents and children in terms of control (see Grotevant and Cooper, Chapter 1, for further discussion) to be more facilitative for growth in the care ethic than would either permissive or authoritarian parenting, where control in relationships moves primarily in one direction (either from parents to children, or from children to parents) (for example, Baumrind, 1991, 1992).

In addition, the nature of morality and gender in different cultures should be studied further. It has been argued that Kohlberg's justice model of morality does not sufficiently take into account social class and cross-cultural differences in moral reasoning. In his review of cross-cultural studies that had used Kohlberg's standardized measure, Snarey observed genuine forms of communitarian-like conventional and post-conventional reasoning, stressed in folk cultural groups and working-class communities, that seemed to be missing from the current Kohlbergian scheme. The missing values included, for example, " . . . understanding, reciprocity, role relationships, and the unity of life" (1995, p. 120). Investigations on culture and the self (for example, Kashima et al., 1995; Triandis, 1989) have indicated that Western cultures generally focus on the importance of being an autonomous, independent person, which inevitably involves competition with others. In contrast, non-Western cultures emphasize the importance of maintaining harmonious interdependence among people, which of necessity involves cooperation with others. Thus, one would expect less self-oriented and more other-oriented people (perhaps especially women) in non-Western societies than in the West.

Future use of the ECI with different ethnic groups and cultures must consider the questions of generalizability and the appropriateness of dilemmas in different settings. People from cultures where the extended family and the old are revered may see no dilemma or conflict in a lonely parent's request to live with them. Instead, the request may be an honor or duty which they would not dream of rejecting. In contrast, for several Norwegian participants, such a parental request was also not seen as a difficult dilemma because they would not dream of taking in the parent. A comprehensive collection of what kind of issues and situations generally constitute moral conflicts for people in various parts of the world, and a close examination of how these conflicts are resolved, might be enlightening in terms of cultural variations in values and views on the self–other relationship.

Finally, it may be useful to relate the ethic of care to mental as well as physical health. In a study of elderly people, ratings of better physical health were linked with higher care levels, particularly for men (Skoe *et al.*, 1996). In a sample of younger women, ECI scores were found to be positively related to general well-being regarding health, self-esteem and marital satisfaction (Redd, 1992). A more recent study in Norway also showed that the ECI was positively correlated with emotional adjustment and emotional stability for both men and women (Skoe, Kristensen *et al.*, 1997). Future research could attempt to establish whether, and how, people at higher ECI levels do take better care of themselves: for example, do they spend more time on things they enjoy, exercise more, eat better, smoke and worry less.

CONCLUSIONS AND IMPLICATIONS

Generally, research to date with the ECI has demonstrated the relevance of a care-based approach to moral thought. Findings indicate that variations in care levels of reasoning may have implications for personal adaptation across the life cycle for both men and women. Levels of care have, for example, been found to be positively related to androgyny, empathic perspective-taking, and ego development as well as identity achievement in young adults (for example, Nicholls-Goudsmid, 1997; Skoe, 1990, 1995; Skoe and Diessner, 1994; Skoe and von der Lippe, 1997; Skoe and Nickerson, 1997; Sochting *et al.*, 1994), and to cognitive complexity, perceived social support, and physical health in maturity (Skoe *et al.*, 1996). Care levels have also been found to be negatively related to personal distress and right-wing authoritarianism, suggesting that people higher in the care ethic also have a greater tolerance for ambiguity and for people with problems (Skoe and Nickerson, 1997; Skoe *et al.*, 1996). Furthermore, older individuals who scored higher on care showed more positive feelings about aging. Hence, balanced care for self and others may be an important aspect of personal and psychosocial maturity for men as well as women.

More specifically, within the framework of Erik Erikson's life span developmental theory, a balance between care of self and others may have important implications for achieving the stages of identity, intimacy, generativity and ego integrity (for example, 1982). Each one seems to integrate these two components (self and other), although somewhat differently, across adulthood. Following this, ego identity achievement in young adults has been found to be strongly linked to levels of care development, as noted earlier (for example, Skoe and Diessner, 1994). With regard to generativity versus stagnation and self-absorption (for example, Bradley, 1997; McAdams *et al.*, 1993; Snarey, 1993), Erikson has proposed that adulthood or middle age is the period in life when caring for the life cycles of others is a predominant concern. Yet, care for other people must be balanced by care for oneself; otherwise generativity may degenerate into mere martyrdom (Marcia, Chapter 9). The greatest and most difficult identity or life cycle challenge exits perhaps in old age, when one must rely increasingly on psychological rather than physical strength and resources, as observed by Marcia (Chapter 9). Balanced care for self and others may constitute an important psychological resource and a vital part of integrity or wisdom (for example, Birren and Fisher, 1990; Hearn, 1993).

Blasi (1995) has proposed that the integration of moral understanding and motives with "the agentic system" (that is, strength of the will or character) should produce "a sense of mastery and ownership of one's moral demands, and, therefore, the acceptance of moral accountability toward oneself and others" (p. 22). Adolescence may be a particularly crucial period in the life cycle for the development of moral reasoning and a sense of moral accountability. The transitions from childhood to adolescence and from adolescence to adulthood involve many major changes, choices and challenges, both physically and psychologically. Teen-agers face new experiences and important decisions, and the way they respond may profoundly affect themselves and the people around them, such as family and friends. Petersen *et al.* (1992) have stated that "adolescence will be the first phase of life requiring, and presumably stimulating, mature patterns of functioning that may persist throughout life. Conversely, failure to cope effectively with the challenges of adolescence may represent deficiencies in the individual that bode ill for subsequent development" (1992, p. 22).

The adolescent years involve increased independence from parents, and increased involvement with peers and a wider social world. The changes and challenges of adolescence may stimulate the need and the ability to transcend both egocentrism and conformity to external rules. In turn, this could lead to increased self–other differentiation and internalization of self-chosen principles and values. The family as well as the cultural environment may, however, enhance or hinder such development within the individual. As stated by Snarey (1997), development represents a life time of significant influences and experiences, such as family history, leisure and work place experiences, and socially defined seasons of life. Further cross-national research across the life span is required to understand the impact of various contextual factors on morality and personality development.

Because individuals are social from inception, and thus an individual's rights are inseparable from his or her responsibilities to the community, Baumrind (1992) has argued that socialization of the child should include training in construing what she calls "true" or "enlightened" self-interest. Such self-interest includes compassionate regard for others and an inclination to behave justly, as well as existential obligations to oneself. It is by honoring one's obligations to self that one comes to understand one's obligations to others; in asserting one's own rights, one at the same time affirms the rights of others. Similarly, one cannot take proper care of others until one has learned to take proper care of oneself. The process of becoming moral is the process of decentration which is not to deny self, "but rather to increase progressively the scope of self" (Baumrind, 1992, p. 268). As suggested by Baumrind, moral judgments should be directed at avoiding as well as resolving situations that create moral conflicts. Considering the increase in violence and in adolescent suicide (for example, Fombonne, 1996), it seems that moral education, including both the care ethic and the justice ethic, deserves a more prominent place in our societies. Teaching and training young people to include both self and others in the compass of care, and to practice justice as well as mercy, might serve the future well.

I close this chapter with the words of Peter Høeg, the Danish author, well known for his best selling book, turned into the film *Smilla's Sense of Snow*. Recently, he has so eloquently expressed, in thought and in action, the essence of the highest level of the care ethic. In 1996 he established the Lolwe Foundation which supports women and children in Africa and Tibet. All the revenues from his latest book, *Woman and the Ape*, go to this foundation. Talking in an interview about the Lolwe Fund, Høeg said:

> There's an egoistic perspective . . . . At a certain point in life, the difference between helping others and helping oneself disappears. You see it as a parent, that there's no difference in giving love to a child and receiving it. That perspective can be broadened to reach outside the family, to receive love from the universe somehow.
>
> (Porcelli, 1997, p. 65)

NOTES

1 The preparation for this chapter was assisted by a Fulbright Fellowship and a Norwegian Research Council, Medicine and Health grant. I thank Carol Gilligan and James Marcia for their inspiration and valuable support and the participants of these studies for their thoughtful interest.
2 If the participant does not generate a real-life dilemma, the mean score for the other three dilemmas may be used in place of a real-life score (Skoe 1993).
3 If a person's overall level score falls exactly between two levels (for example, 2.25), a second rater independently scores the person at one of the two adjacent levels.
4 Kappas are calculated based on a difference between the two raters no greater than quarter of a level score (for example, 2.50 and 2.75 are considered agreement, 2.50 and 3.00 are considered disagreement).

BIBLIOGRAPHY

Abrahams, B., Feldman, S., and Nash, S. (1978) Sex-role self-concept and sex-role attitudes, *Developmental Psychology*, 14: 393–400.
Baumrind, D. (1991) Effective parenting during the early adolescent transition, in P.E. Cowan and E.M. Hetherington (eds.), *Family Transitions: Advances in Family Research*, vol. 2, pp. 111–63, Hillsdale: Erlbaum.
—— (1992) Leading an examined life: the moral dimension of daily conduct, in W.M. Kurtines, M. Azmitia, and J.L. Gewirtz (eds.), *The Role of Values in Psychology and Human Development*, pp. 256–80, New York: Wiley.
Birren, J., and Fisher, L. (1990) The elements of wisdom: overview and integration, in R. Sternberg (ed.), *Wisdom: Its Nature, Origins, and Development*, pp. 317–32, Cambridge: Cambridge University Press.
Blasi, A. (1980) Bridging moral cognition and moral action: a critical review of the literature, *Psychological Bulletin*, 88: 1–45.
—— (1995) Moral understanding and the moral personality: the process of moral integration, in W.M. Kurtines and J.L. Gewirtz (eds.), *Moral Development: An Introduction*, pp. 229–53, Boston: Allyn and Bacon.
Bradley, C.L. (1997) Generativity-stagnation: development of a status model, *Developmental Review*, 17: 262–90.
Brown, L., Tappan, M., and Gilligan, C. (1995) Listening to different voices, in W.M. Kurtines and J.L. Gewirtz (eds.), *Moral Development: An Introduction*, pp. 311–35, Boston: Allyn and Bacon.
Chodorow, N. (1978) *The Reproduction of Mothering: Psychoanalysis and the Sociology of Gender*, Berkeley: University of California Press.
Cohn, L.D. (1991) Sex differences in the course of personality development: a meta-analysis, *Psychological Bulletin*, 109, 2: 252–66.
Colby, A., and Kohlberg, L. (eds.) (1987) *The Measurement of Moral Judgment*, New York: Cambridge University Press.
Dasen, P.R., and Jahoda, G. (1986) Preface to the special issue on cross-cultural human development, *International Journal of Behavioral Development*, 9: 413–16.

Derry, R. (1989) An empirical study of moral reasoning among managers, *Journal of Business Ethics*, 8: 855–62.

Dewey, J. (1957) *Reconstruction in Philosophy*, Boston: Beacon Press.

Eisenberg, N., Fabes, R., and Shea, C. (1989) Gender differences in empathy and pro-social moral reasoning: empirical investigations, in M.M. Brabeck (ed.), *Who Cares? Theory, Research, and Educational Implications of the Ethic of Care*, pp. 127–43, New York: Praeger.

Eisenberg, N., Miller, P.A., Shell, R., McNalley, S., and Shea, C. (1991) Prosocial development in adolescence: a longitudinal study, *Developmental Psychology*, 27: 849–57.

Erikson, E.H. (1982) *The Life Cycle Completed: A Review*, New York: Norton.

Fombonne, E. (1996, August), *Suicidal Behaviors in Young People: Time Trends and their Correlates*, poster presented at the XIVth Biennial International Society for the Study of Behavioural Development Conference, Quebec City.

Ford, M.R., and Lowery, C.R. (1986) Gender differences in moral reasoning: a comparison of the use of justice and care orientations, *Journal of Personality and Social Psychology*, 50: 777–83.

Friedman, W.J., Robinson, A.B., and Friedman, B.L. (1987) Sex differences in moral judgments? A test of Gilligan's theory, *Psychology of Women Quarterly*, 11: 37–46.

Garnett, A.C. (1969) Conscience and conscientiousness, in J. Feinberg (ed.), *Moral Concepts*, pp. 80–92, London: Oxford University Press.

Gibbs, J.E. (1995) The cognitive developmental perspective, in W.M. Kurtines and J.L. Gewirtz (eds.), *Moral Development: An Introduction*, pp. 27–48, Boston: Allyn and Bacon.

Gibbs, J.E., and Widaman, K.F. (1982) *Social Intelligence: Measuring the Development of Sociomoral Reflection*, Englewood Cliffs: Prentice-Hall.

Gilligan, C. (1982) *In a Different Voice: Psychological Theory and Women's Development*, Cambridge: Harvard University Press.

Gilligan, C., and Attanucci, J. (1988) Two moral orientations: gender differences and similarities, *Merrill-Palmer Quarterly*, 34: 223–37.

Gilligan, C., and Wiggins, G. (1987) The origins of morality in early childhood relationships, in J. Kagan and S. Lamb (eds.), *The Emergence of Morality in Young Children*, Chicago: University of Chicago Press.

Hearn, S. (1993) *Integrity, despair, and in-between: development of integrity statuses*, unpublished doctoral dissertation, Simon Fraser University, Burnaby.

Holtedahl, L. (1986), *Hva Mutter Gjør er Alltid Viktig (What mother does is always important)* Oslo: Universitetsforlaget AS.

Ibsen, H. (1917) A doll's house, introductions by William Archer, in *The Works of Henrik Ibsen. The Viking Edition*, vol. VII, New York: Schribner's.

Intons-Peterson, M.J. (1988) *Gender Concepts of Swedish and American Youths*, Hillsdale: Earlbaum.

Josselson, R.L. (1987) *Finding Herself: Pathways to Identity Development in Women*, San Francisco: Jossey-Bass.

Kashima, Y., Yamaguschi, S., Kim, U., Choi, S., Gelfand, M.J., and Yuki, M. (1995) Culture, gender, and self: a perspective from individualism–collectivism research, *Journal of Personality and Social Psychology*, 69, 5: 925–37.

168   *E. Skoe*

Kohlberg, L. (1969) Stage and sequence: the cognitive-developmental approach to socialization, in D.A. Goslin (ed.), *Handbook of Socialization Theory and Research*, pp. 347–80, San Diego: Academic Press.

—— (1981) *The Meaning and Measurement of Moral Development*, Worcester: Clark University Press.

—— (1984) *The Psychology of Moral Development*, San Francisco: Harper and Row.

Likestillings Rådet. (1996) *Mini-fakta om likestilling* (Mini-facts about equality), Oslo.

Loevinger, J. (1987) *Paradigms of Personality*, New York: W.H. Freeman.

Loevinger, J., and Wessler, R. (1970) *Measuring Ego Development*, vols. 1 and 2, San Francisco: Jossey-Bass.

Lyons, N.P. (1983) Two perspectives: on self, relationships, and morality, *Harvard Educational Review*, 53: 125–44.

Marcia, J.E. (1980) Identity in adolescence, in J. Adelson (ed.), *Handbook of Adolescent Psychology*, New York: Wiley.

McAdams, D.P., Aubin, E. de St., and Logan, R.L. (1993) Generativity among young, midlife, and older adults, *Psychology and Aging*, 8: 221–30.

Miller, J. (1984) *The Development of Women's Sense*, Wellesley: Stone Center Working Papers Series.

Newberger, C.M. (1980) The cognitive structure of parenthood: designing a descriptive measure, in R.L. Selman, and R. Yando (eds.), *Clinical-Developmental Psychology: New Directions for Child Development*, pp. 45–67, San Francisco: Jossey-Bass.

Nicholls-Goudsmid, J. (1997) *To Have and Have Not: Procreative Choice and the Ethic of Care*, unpublished doctoral dissertation, Simon Fraser University, Burnaby.

Noddings, N. (1984) *Caring: A Feminine Approach to Ethics and Moral Education*, Berkeley: University of California Press.

Oser, F.K. (1991) The development of religious judgment, in F.K. Oser and W.G. Scarlett (eds.), *Religious Development in Childhood and Adolescence*, pp. 5–25, San Francisco: Jossey-Bass.

Petersen, A.C., Silbereisen, R.K., and Sørensen, S. (1992) Adolescent development: a global perspective, in W. Meeus, M. de Goede, W. Kox, and K. Hurrelmann (eds.), *Adolescence, Careers, and Cultures*, pp. 3–34, Berlin: Walter de Gruyter.

Piaget, J. (1932) *The Moral Judgment of the Child*, New York: The Free Press, 1965.

Porcelli, K. (1997, March) Monkey business, *Scanorama. The Inflight Magazine of SAS*, pp. 62–5.

Pratt, M.W., Diessner, R., Hunsberger, B., Pancer, S.M., and Savoy, K. (1991) Four pathways in the analysis of adult development and aging: comparing analyses of reasoning about personal-life dilemmas, *Psychology and Aging*, 6: 666–75.

Pratt, M.W., Diessner, R., Pratt, A., Hunsberger, B., and Pancer, S.M. (1996) Moral and social reasoning and perspective-taking in later life: a longitudinal study, *Psychology and Aging*, 11: 66–73.

Pratt, M.W., Golding, G., Hunter, W., and Norris, J. (1988) From inquiry to judgment: age and sex differences in patterns of adult moral thinking and information-seeking, *International Journal of Aging and Human Development*, 27: 109–24.

Pratt, M.W., Pancer, S.M., Hunsberger, B., and Manchester, J. (1990) Reasoning about the self and relationships in maturity: an integrative complexity analysis of individual differences, *Journal of Personality and Social Psychology*, 59: 575–81.

Redd, M.C. (1992) *An Examination of the Relationship between a Woman's Level of Moral Development and her Health, Self Esteem and Marital Satisfaction*, unpublished masters thesis, Utah State University, Logan.

Rest, J.F. (1983) Morality, in J.H. Flavell and E.M. Markam (eds.), *Handbook of Child Psychology*, vol. 3, *Cognitive development*, 4th edn., pp. 556–629, New York: Wiley.

Rich, J.M. (1986) Morality, reason and emotions, in S. Modgil, and C. Modgil (eds.), *Lawrence Kohlberg: Consensus and Controversy*, pp. 209–22, London: Falmer Press.

Rothbart, M.K., Hanley, D., and Albert, M. (1986) Gender differences in moral reasoning, *Sex Roles*, 15: 645–53.

Silberman, M.A., and Snarey, J. (1993) Gender differences in moral development during early adolescence: the contribution of sex-related variations in maturation, *Current Psychology: Developmental, Learning, Personality and Social*, 12, 2: 163–71.

Skoe, E.E. (1990) Ego identity and moral development in college men and women, in P.J.D. Drenth, J.A. Sergeant, and R.J. Takens (eds.), *European Perspectives in Psychology*, vol. 1, *Theoretical, Psychometrics, Personality, Developmental, Educational, Cognitive, Gerontological*, Chichester: Wiley.

—— (1993) *The Ethic of Care Interview Manual*, unpublished manuscript, University of Tromsø, Tromsø, available from the author upon request.

—— (1995) Sex role orientation and its relationship to the development of identity and moral thought, *Scandinavian Journal of Psychology*, 36: 235–45.

Skoe, E.E., Bakke, I., Hoffmann, T.A., Larsen, B., Aasheim, M., and Mørch, W. (1997) *Ethic of Care and Real-Life Moral Dilemma Content in Norwegian and Canadian Early Adolescents: A Cross-Cultural Comparison*, manuscript submitted for publication, University of Tromsø, Tromsø.

Skoe, E.E., and Diessner, R. (1994) Ethic of care, justice, identity and gender: an extension and replication, *Merrill-Palmer Quarterly*, 40: 102–19.

Skoe, E.E., and Gooden, A. (1993) Ethic of care and real-life moral dilemma content in male and female early adolescents, *Journal of Early Adolescence*, 13: 154–67.

Skoe, E.E., Kristensen, W., Martinussen, M., Moe, S., and Sunde, T. (1997) *The Relation between Ethic of Care and Personality Traits: An Exploratory Study*, manuscript in preparation, University of Tromsø, Tromsø.

Skoe, E.E., and Marcia, J.E. (1991) A care-based measure of morality and its relation to ego identity, *Merrill-Palmer Quarterly*, 37: 289–304.

Skoe, E.E., and Nickerson, W. (1997) *Self and Others: Relationships among Ethic of Care, Empathy and Intimacy*, unpublished manuscript, University of Tromsø, Tromsø.

Skoe, E.E., Pedersen, A.G., and Hansen, K.L., (1997) *Thought and Action: The Relation between Care-Based Moral Reasoning and Prosocial Activities in Men and Women*, manuscript in preparation, University of Tromsø, Tromsø.

Skoe, E.E., Pratt, M.W., Matthews, M., and Curror, S. (1996) The ethic of care: stability over time, gender differences and correlates in mid to late adulthood, *Psychology and Aging*, 11: 280–92.

Skoe, E.E., and von der Lippe, A.L. (1997) *Do Moral and Ego Developments Follow Different Paths? The Relations among Care, Justice and Ego Development*, manuscript in preparation. University of Tromsø, Tromsø.

Snarey, J. (1993) *How Fathers Care for the Next Generation*, Cambridge: Harvard University Press.

—— (1995) In a communitarian voice: the sociological expansion of Kohlbergian theory, research, and practice, in W.M. Kurtines and J.L. Gewirtz (eds.), *Moral development: An Introduction*, pp. 109–33, Boston: Allyn and Bacon.

—— (1997) Ego development and the ethical voices of justice and care: an Eriksonian interpretation, in P.M. Westenberg, A. Blasi, and L. Cohn (eds.), *Personality Development: Theoretical, Empirical, and Clinical Investigations*, Hillsdale: Erlbaum.

Sochting, I. (1996) *Ethic of Care and its Relationship to Attachment, Object Relations and Social Cognition*, unpublished doctoral dissertation, Simon Fraser University, Burnaby.

Sochting, I., Skoe, E.E., and Marcia, J.E. (1994) Care-oriented moral reasoning and pro-social behavior: a question of gender or sex role orientation, *Sex Roles: A Journal of Research*, 31, 3/4: 131–47.

Statistics Canada (1995) *Women in Canada: A Statistical Report*, 3rd edn., Ottawa: Minister of Industry.

Triandis, H.C. (1989) The self and social behavior in differing cultural contexts, *Psychological Review*, 96: 506–20.

Turiel, E. (1998) The development of morality, in W. Damon (ed.), *Handbook of Child Psychology*, 5th edn., vol. 3, New York: Wiley.

Vikan, A., and Claussen, C.J. (1994) *Barns oppfatninger* (Children's perception), Oslo: Universitetsforlaget.

Walker, L.J. (1984) Sex differences in the development of moral reasoning: a critical review, *Child Development*, 55: 677–91.

—— (1991) Sex differences in moral reasoning, in W.M. Kurtines and J.L. Gewirtz (eds.), *Handbook of Moral Behavior and Development*, vol. 2, *Research*, pp. 333–64, Hillsdale: Erlbaum.

—— (1995) Sexism in Kohlberg's moral psychology?, in W.M. Kurtines and J.L. Gewirtz (eds.), *Moral Development: An Introduction*, pp. 83–107, Boston: Allyn and Bacon.

Walker, L.J., de Vries B., and Trevethan, S.D. (1987) Moral stages and moral orientations in real-life and hypothetical dilemmas, *Child Development*, 58: 842–58.

Wark, G.R., and Krebs, D.L. (1996) Gender and dilemma differences in real-life moral judgment, *Developmental Psychology*, 32: 220–30.

White, C. (1988) Age, education, and sex effects on adult moral reasoning, *International Journal of Aging and Human Development*, 27: 271–81.

Wichstrøm, L. (1994) *Mental helse blant ungdom i Norge. Oslo som særtilfelle? (Mental health among youth in Norway. Oslo as a special case?)*, report no. 3, Norwegian Center for Youth Research (Ungforsk), Oslo.

Williams, C., and Bybee, J. (1994) What do children feel guilty about? Developmental and gender differences, *Developmental Psychology*, 30: 617–23.

Young, L. (1997) Fulfilling the mandate of difference, in J. Arscott and L. Trimble (eds.), *In the Presence of Women: Representation in Canadian Government*, Toronto: Harcourt Brace.

Zahn-Waxler, C., Cole, P.M., and Barrett, K.C. (1991) Guilt and empathy: sex differences and implications for the development of depression, in J. Garber and K.A. Dodge (eds.), *The Development of Emotion Regulation and Dysregulation*, New York: Cambridge University Press.

8 Adolescence as a second separation–individuation process[1]
Critical review of an object relations approach

Jane Kroger

[Several years ago] I felt that my father and I couldn't talk properly together because he always seemed to be pressing me to go to university. But underneath, I realized I was really asking him to tell me what to do with my life . . . and he was just suggesting things to explore. It wasn't until about a year after I'd left home that I realized, he just didn't know, he just couldn't tell me what was right for me to do.

(20-year-old student, adapted from Kroger and Haslett, 1988, p. 77)

Object relations theory, generally, has concerned itself with how intrapsychic processes mediate interpersonal interactions and with how differentiation of the sense of self develops and changes over the course of the life span. Simply stated, Greenberg and Mitchell have defined object relations as one's "interactions with external and internal (real and imagined) other people, and to the relationship between . . . internal and external object worlds" (1983, pp. 13–14). Greenberg and Mitchell suggested that people react to and interact with not only an actual other, but also with an internalized representation of another person. This internalized other (or psychic representation) influences not only a person's internal emotional states but also his or her overt behavioral reactions. One specific focus of interest for object relations theorists has been on the process by which the sense of self develops (Mahler *et al.*, 1975). Margaret Mahler and her colleagues have detailed a sequence of separation–individuation subphases in which infants differentiate from their primary caretakers and establish a sense of self. The internalization of a responsive caregiver enables the child to feel secure when the caregiver is not physically present. Peter Blos (1967) was quick to appreciate some parallels between Mahler's description of the infant process and a second separation–individuation sequence during adolescence. While the infant must internalize a representation of her or his primary caretaker in order to function in the absence of the external person, Blos pointed out that the adolescent must relinquish this internalized other in order to develop a more mature sense of self. The past fifteen years have seen a burgeoning of both theoretical and empirical efforts to elucidate intrapsychic and interpersonal dimensions of the adolescent separation–individuation process, and a review and appraisal of current theory and empirical work seems warranted. This chapter will provide a critical review of contemporary theory and research on the second separation–individuation process of adolescence, followed by suggestions for conceptual refinements in theory and future research directions.

THE FIRST AND SECOND SEPARATION–INDIVIDUATION PROCESSES

In the 1960s, Margaret Mahler first conducted extensive observations of healthy mother-infant and mother-toddler dyads in a naturalistic setting to delineate the process by which the child intrapsychically differentiates from the primary caretaker to become a more autonomous person and gain a sense of self-identity. Mahler defined two tracks—separation and individuation—which must be navigated if the undifferentiated young infant is to mature into a toddler with a sense of intrapsychic separateness from, yet relatedness to, the external environment. Mahler's separation track refers to the child's "emergence from a symbiotic fusion with the mother," including such intrapsychic accomplishments as differentiation, distancing, and boundary formation, while the individuation track denotes "those achievements marking the child's assumption of his own individual characteristics," the development of intrapsychic autonomy (Mahler *et al.*, 1975, p. 4). Mahler continued to elucidate the development of these tracks through a sequence of separation–individuation subphases during the first three years of life. The child's resolution to these early developmental subphases sets the foundation for later adolescent and adult identity structure. While inferences about the pre-verbal period and separation–individuation phases are difficult, Mahler believed that repeated and consensually validated observational work by her colleagues offered some safeguards against total error (Mahler *et al.*, 1975). Thus, Mahler's work is primarily concerned with the intrapsychic process of how important others become internalized and assist in the early structuralization of what she terms "self-identity."

The separation–individuation process is preceded by what Mahler and her associates have described as normal autistic and symbiotic phases. In Mahler's view, the newborn is unable to differentiate itself from its surroundings. While there may be states of alert activity and responsiveness, these are transitory and often generated by reflex actions (Mahler and McDevitt, 1982). At this normal autistic stage, there are no internal representations of the external world, for there is little awareness of external objects. It is the gradual awareness of a caretaker, described as "the awakening," that propels the child into the next stage of symbiosis which occurs at about three to four weeks of age. At this time, there is dim recognition of mother, but she is perceived only as an extension of the infant's self. In Mahler *et al.*'s observations, "the infant behaves and functions as though he and his mother were an omnipotent system—a dual unity within one common boundary" (1975, p. 44). There is a delusion of a common boundary between two physically separate individuals (Edward, *et al.*, 1992). It is from this base that the phases of separation–individuation proceed and give rise to new forms of intrapsychic organization.

Recent research on infant development, however, has found Mahler's descriptions of autistic and symbiotic stages to be incompatible with the growing knowledge regarding neonatal competencies. For example, perceptual and cognitive capacities of neonates have been found to be too sophisticated to imply the newborn's inability to differentiate itself from other people (Lyons-Ruth, 1991; Stern, 1985). This research has cast doubt on the whole existence of a symbiotic phase and the *raison d'être* for the stages of separation–individuation that lie ahead. Stern (1985) has described the time between approximately 9–18 months as the search for "intersubjective union" rather than achieving greater intrapsychic autonomy. Pine (1990, 1992) has recently responded to criticisms by Stern and other infant researchers with some refinements to Mahler's conceptualization of the separation–individuation process. In addition to the capacity for a degree of perceptual and cognitive discriminations, Pine proposes that infants experience moments of boundarylessness or merger, affectively central to the infant's day, which attain great developmental significance beyond the actual time involved in the activity itself. The concept of a symbiotic phase, quite different from the symbiotic state Mahler first advanced, is used to describe such moments as the relaxed state during feeding and prior to sleep or the synchronous movements of the caretaker walking with infant in arms, in which a child may come to feel merged with a primary caretaker. Such merger states do not characterize all experiences of the 2–5-month-old child, but hold psychological significance beyond their temporal duration. Symbiotic phase experiences, along with caretaker responses, affect the subsequent course of separation–individuation phases that lie ahead, according to Pine. Furthermore, phenomena such as stranger anxiety in the 6–8-month-old child do indicate some type of intrapsychic differentiation process.

Mahler suggests that awareness of mother's existence as a separate person precipitates the first differentiation subphase of the separation–individuation process, where the infant's attention shifts to the other-than-mother world. During this "hatching" process, the 5–10 month-old infant achieves "a certain new look of alertness, persistence, and goal-directedness" and begins investing more energy in the outside world (1983, p. 5). The infant begins actively scanning the environment, sliding from lap to floor, comfortable in exploring not-too-far-from-mother's-feet. With increased locomotion, practicing ensues, making its developmental entrance by about 15 months. Now, there is increased locomotion and exploration, escalating into an exhilarating "love affair with the world" on the part of the toddler. The primary caretaker, however, still needs to be available to provide a "home base" for emotional "refueling." Between about 15 and 22 months, representational thought has begun to develop and the toddler's elation of the previous stage has begun to subside. In this rapprochement subphase, the primary caretaker is experienced as a separate person, a self in her own right, and the finality of intrapsychic separateness begins to dawn. This understanding brings a sense of great loss to the toddler and gives rise to new strategies, seemingly regressive, in response. Attempts to re-engage the primary caretaker in externally shared activities to stave off the realization of separateness are undertaken; at the heart of the rapprochement crisis, however, the realization ultimately dawns that there is no return to the self–object fusion of earlier times.

The toddler's conflict between the need for maternal incorporation as well as separation and individuation is prodded toward resolution by father (or additional significant other), who supports the child against the backward symbiotic pull. In the final, open-ended subphase of libidinal object constancy during life's third year, the struggle becomes less painful. If developmental conditions have been favorable, several achievements can be noted by this time: "(1) the achievement of a definite, in certain aspects lifelong, individuality, and (2) the attainment of a certain degree of object constancy" (Mahler *et al.*, 1975, p. 109). Object constancy implies that the child can intrapsychically incorporate both the good and bad parts of maternal as well as self representations, enabling the child to experience both mother and self as separate whole individuals. This feat also enables the child to experience physical distance from mother, setting the foundation for an intrapsychic structure that will be the basis of identity at least until adolescence. Beyond infancy, Mahler does not comment specifically on the implications of optimal separation–individuation resolutions.

Blos appreciated the applications of Mahler's work in understanding the intrapsychic restructuring occurring during adolescence: "Adolescent individuation is the reflection of those structural changes that accompany the emotional disengagement from internalized infantile objects" (1967, p. 164). He likened the infant's "hatching from the symbiotic membrane" described by Mahler to the adolescent process of "shedding family dependencies," the loosening of ties to an internalized parent which sustained the child through earlier stages of development. Adolescent disengagement from this internalized parent allows the establishment of new extra-familial romantic attachments. Maturation of the child's own ego accompanies disengagement from the internal representations of caretakers: "[D]isengagement from the infantile object is always paralleled by ego maturation" (Blos, 1967, p. 165). Through ego maturation, a firm sense of self, different from that of parents and more capable of self-support, emerges to mark the end of the second separation–individuation process. Blos does not detail any sequence of phases, however, in elucidating this second separation–individuation process of adolescence.

While he also does not discuss Mahler's more general separation and individuation tracks and their course of development during adolescence, he does describe some possibilities for their combined derailment. Efforts at distancing from parents in ways other than through intrapsychic separation is one possible route toward avoiding separation and individuation challenges. Blos has found that some adolescents attempt to create geographical, physical, and/or ideological distance from their families and locales of childhood, which does not deal with the underlying intrapsychic task: "The incapacity to separate from internal objects except by detachment, rejection, and debasement is subjectively experienced as a sense of alienation" (1967, pp. 167–8). It is only through the intrapsychic task of restructuring internalized ties with parents that separation and individuation processes may proceed toward greater levels of maturity.

EMPIRICAL ELABORATIONS OF THE SECOND SEPARATION–INDIVIDUATION PROCESS

Several writers in the 1970s and 1980s have made proposals as to how Mahler's phases of infant differentiation might be applied to adolescent separation–individuation processes (see for example, Brandt, 1977; Esman, 1980; Josselson, 1980, 1988). Issues addressed by these writers have focused primarily on different timings in which various separation–individuation subphases might be normatively encountered (for example, proposals for the beginning of differentiation ranged from latency through late adolescence). These proposals were based primarily on theoretical conjecture, not empirical research. More recent longitudinal and narrative studies, reviewed below, have suggested the process to be normatively addressed during mid- and late adolescence.

While studies of the interpersonal reverberations of adolescent separation–individuation have been numerous, investigations of the actual intrapsychic process itself have been more limited. In a recent publication, I proposed dimensions of the intrapsychic adolescent separation–individuation phenomenon in need of exploration (Kroger, 1996). These dimensions included a description of any adolescent separation–individuation subphases that might parallel the infant stages suggested by Mahler, as well as research directed toward understanding the roles of regression, mourning, and transitional object use during restructuring. The past five years have seen an exciting array of empirical explorations of some of these areas in both normative and clinical populations; these researches suggest further theoretical elaborations and refinements to Blos's initial proposals.

Comment will first be made on instruments which have been designed to assess issues of separation and individuation during adolescence. During the 1980s, a range of instruments were developed to measure dimensions of the adolescent separation–individuation process (for example, Separation–individuation Process Inventory: Christenson and Wilson, 1985; Adolescent Separation Anxiety Test: Hansburg, 1980a, 1980b; Psychological Separation Inventory: Hoffman, 1984; Separation–Individuation Test of Adolescence: Levine *et al.*, 1986). The 1990s has seen continued refinement of some of these measures (McClanahan and Holmbeck (1992), Levine and Saintonge (1993), Kroger and Green (1994), Levine (1994), and Holmbeck and McClanahan (1994) all address refinements to Levine *et al.*'s Separation–Individuation Test of Adolescence, and Dolan *et al.*, 1992, suggest refinements to Christenson and Wilson's Separation–Individuation Inventory).

Levine *et al.*'s Separation–Individuation Test of Adolescence (SITA) has undergone the most rigorous psychometric refinement of the above instruments. The SITA was developed to evaluate dimensions of the adolescent separation–individuation process, based on the premise that separation–individuation issues of early childhood are likely to be reworked in adolescence. The most recent version of the SITA consists of nine scales: separation anxiety, engulfment anxiety, practicing mirroring, dependency denial, nurturance seeking, peer enmeshment, teacher enmeshment, healthy separation, and rejection expectancy. Internal consistency reliabilities (Chronbach's *a* s) for all scales except separation anxiety and healthy separation have generally been above 0.70 (Kroger and Green, 1994; Levine *et al.*, 1986; Levine and Saintonge, 1993). Discriminant, construct, and external criterion validity of the SITA has been demonstrated when meaningful and significant differences were found on the SITA subscales for each of five Millon Adolescent Personality Inventory scales (Levine *et al.*, 1986; Levine and Saintonge, 1993).

Additional instruments assess further dimensions of adolescent separation–individuation. The Hansburg (1980a, 1980b) Adolescent Separation Anxiety Test enables individuals to be evaluated on each of six psychological systems: attachment need, individuation capacity, painful tension, hostility, reality avoidance, and self-evaluation. Hoffman's (1984). Psychological Separation Inventory consists of four scales that pertain to an adolescent's relationship with each parent: functional independence, emotional independence, conflictual independence, and attitudinal independence. Christenson and Wilson's (1985) Separation–Individuation Process Inventory is comprised of items covering various aspects of differentiation, splitting, and various relationship issues associated with separation–individuation disturbances, such as tolerance for aloneness and object constancy. Scales of each of these instruments have shown adequate internal consistency reliabilities (Chronbach's alphas generally above 0.70) and construct validity established on significant theoretically predicted associations with various adjustment disturbances of adolescence.

Several longitudinal, cross-sectional, and narrative investigations have provided details on specific movements involved in the adolescent intrapsychic restructuring process that show parallels to those subphases of infancy described by Mahler. Kroger (1985) and Kroger and Haslett (1988) conducted a two-year longitudinal investigation focused on intrapsychic representations of self and primary caretaker in relation to ego identity status (styles of making identity-defining commitments described by Marcia, 1966). These studies, using Hansburg's (1980a, 1980b) Adolescent Separation Anxiety Test, indicated highly differentiated intrapsychic self–other representations for those late adolescents who had explored identity-defining commitments on their own terms in their external environments (the identity achieved), while those adolescents who had formed identity-defining commitments based primarily on parental values (foreclosures) showed very little intrapsychic differentiation between self and parental introjects. Moratorium adolescents (exploring potential identity-defining roles and values) were in the process of relinquishing internalized parents. A second longitudinal study over two years of late adolescence using Levine *et al.*'s (1986) SITA, found that foreclosures at the outset of the study who showed greater intrapsychic differentiation from parental introjects were more likely to form identity defining commitments on their own terms by the conclusion of the study than those foreclosures who initially showed little intrapsychic differentiation (Kroger, 1995). A further study of the changing factor structure of SITA for a university student sample over two years of late adolescence suggested that with age comes greater intrapsychic self–other differentiation and a decrease in the need to struggle against both external and internalized parents (Kroger and Green, 1994); however, this change was coupled with feelings of aloneness and a subjective sense of rejection by important others. There was also an indication from this study that as intrapsychic differentiation proceeded, peers replaced parents as sources for support, nurturance, and meeting of self-esteem needs.

Additional studies examining changing internalized representations of self and parents during adolescence include cross-sectional work by Mazor *et al.* (1993) and Mirsky and Kaushinsky (1989). Mazor *et al.* studied four age groups of kibbutz adolescents (late childhood, 9–10 years; early adolescence, 13–14 years; mid-adolescence, 16–17 years; and late adolescents, 20–22 years), assessing the child's perception of relationships with parents and the level of psychological separation from them (following Selman's 1980 procedure). Mazor found that older adolescence generally construed internalized self–other relationships in a more differentiated manner than younger age groups. Engulfment anxiety tended to be higher in early adolescence and older age groups than in late childhood. Furthermore, in mid- and late adolescent age groups there was some ambivalence between merging and separateness in object relations. A further qualitative account of intrapsychic restructuring and its interpersonal ramifications has come from Mirsky and Kaushinsky (1989), who described and analyzed the experiences of immigrant adolescent students in Israel in terms of separation–individuation processes. They noted that immigration to Israel for some Jewish students helps contain many adolescent conflicts. Moving to an independent state struggling for existence speaks to adolescents' own desires for independence, while at the same time offering an opportunity for preserving cultural heritage. Initial responses of many immigrant students was elation in the freedom and independence achieved. Such reaction could be viewed as similar to the "practicing" toddler, experimenting with newfound skills. This elation also stemmed, the authors suggested, from the feeling of having escaped the symbiotic pull of an internalized parent. After the initial elation subsided, emotional "refueling," essential to the practicing toddler, was obtained by practicing immigrant adolescents through maintaining contact with their families or substitute figures; home base needed to feel secure, and crises at home often made it difficult for such adolescents to remain in Israel. The authors observed that with time, however, these practicing adolescents began to be concerned about the loss of their home countries. They often "woke up" to the fact that they were in a foreign environment and their capacity for independence was not as assured as once believed. Similar to the rapprochement crisis of toddlerhood, immigrant adolescents then became preoccupied with attempts to restore the lost quality of symbiotic unity with their past home and families. However, like the rapprochement toddler, these immigrant students could not restore their relationships with home, and Israel was not able to adjust itself completely to their needs. The authors observed that many students did revisit their homes at this stage and experienced the futility of reinstituting past forms of both internalized and external relationships. Upon return to Israel, anger was often intense and commonly directed toward both Israel and the home country. The peer group at this point played a vital role in supporting the immigrant students through the rapprochement process. A group of peers from the home country but also living in Israel often became a family surrogate, providing support and a safe environment for the trialing of new skills. Over time, this group remained important. Eventually, though, interests outside this surrogate family began to develop; with such interests, there came repeated approaching and distancing from the group, as the immigrant students eventually began seeking commitments to new lifestyles and relationships. In parallel with Mahler's final subphase of the consolidation of emotional object constancy, these young adults were now able to maintain differentiated internal representations of self, family, Israel and the homeland, as well as the peer group of countrymen, with all their good and bad aspects. The authors also suggested helpful means in structuring student environments at various stages of the adolescent separation–individuation process. Thus, there has been support for adolescent stages of separation–individuation which parallel those of the infant process described by Mahler; however, it must be remembered that while the outcome of infant separation–individuation is the internalization of parental representations which guide behavior in the absence of the external caregivers, the outcome of adolescent separation–individuation is the internal differentiation of self from parental representations (Blos's disengagement from internalized parental introjects), in turn allowing more autonomous functioning.

In considering the adolescent separation–individuation process in greater detail, several issues warrant further consideration. The course of both separation and individuation tracks need further examination during the second decade of life. Mahler and her colleagues have suggested that separation and individuation tracks in infancy proceed generally in tandem; as the child experiences greater intrapsychic separation from the primary caretaker, she also individuates to develop her own unique characteristics. A recent narrative analysis of the second separation–individuation process by a mid-life adult, however, has called into question the concurrent development of these two tracks, at least during later adolescent and adulthood years (Kroger, 1993). From a retrospective case analysis, themes of escape and fear of dissolution characterized internal feelings and external actions for many months as a young woman began the process of intrapsychic separation from the internalized parent. There was little concern with the development of unique individual characteristics (individuation) until such intense feelings abated and pangs of guilt receded. Further examination of the course of both separation and individuation tracks is needed with larger samples of adolescents and young adults to learn whether or not developments are concurrent.

Closer scrutiny of what is actually meant by "disengaging from parental introjects" is also warranted. Frequent comment has been made by object relations writers on how adolescents differentiate self from the internalized parents or disengage from parental introjects through the second separation–individuation process. Exactly who is internalized and what role that internal representation actually plays in the adolescent's intrapsychic life needs examination. Even the most foreclosed of adolescents whom I have interviewed do not seem to experience a sense of intrapsychic merger with both parents, let alone significant others who have been internalized. It is also important to consider that not only are representations of self and significant others internalized, but so too are representations of surroundings. Levy-Warren has noted that "the surroundings themselves have representations, which evoke such comfort as was originally associated with the need-satisfying object. It is these that are the early form of what during adolescence and adulthood become mental representations of culture" (1987, p. 303). Investigations of the separation–individuation process of adolescence must examine the process of differentiation from very specific internalized representations, including social and cultural surroundings.

A further line of empirical investigation of the adolescent separation–individuation process has focused on behaviors or disorders associated with particular subphase difficulties some adolescents encounter in the process of intrapsychic restructuring; furthermore, many of these derailments may stem from childhood difficulties with the first separation–individuation process. The "borderline" adolescent, studied extensively by Masterson (1981) and Rinsley (1982), refers to those young people whose affect, behavior, object relationships, and self-images are extremely unstable. Masterson and Rinsley traced the origins of this difficulty to the rapprochement phase of toddlerhood separation–individuation, where the child's desire for independence had precipitated the withdrawal of affection from the primary caretaker, leading to the child's abandonment depression. As the push for autonomy in adolescence grows, late adolescence becomes a common time for borderline symptomatology to occur. Suicide attempts have been one focus of research into difficulties in adolescent separation–individuation and possible links with borderline phenomena. Wade (1987) conducted her research with 13–17-year-old adolescent girls who had tried to commit suicide in the preceding year and had been hospitalized or received psychotherapy as a result. All adolescents were from middle-class backgrounds with little or no previous psychotherapy. Wade's findings revealed that many of the suicidal girls were locked into borderline symptomatology with their similarly disturbed mothers. On Hansburg's Adolescent Separation Anxiety Test, the borderline adolescents suffered from separation anxiety, were less individuated, and formed more hostile attachments than adolescents who were non-suicidal. The suicidal group had not negotiated the adolescent rapprochement crisis and vacillated between acting out behavior, suggestive of independence, and regressive, smothering relationships with maternal substitutes, which attempted to recreate symbiotic safety. A further study of the relationship between adolescent suicide and difficulties in the second separation–individuation process was undertaken by de Jong (1992). University students of de Jong's sample with a history of suicidality differed from two groups of controls by showing less security of attachment, the least degree of individuation, as well as the highest incidence of parental, mother, and significant other emotional unavailability in their upbringing. Security of attachment was assessed by the Inventory of Parent and Peer Attachment (Armsden and Greenberg, 1987), while individuation from parents and peers was measured by two subscales from the Personal Authority in the Family System Questionnaire (PAFS-QVC; Bray and Harvey, 1987). It appears that appropriate support by caregivers for both infant and adolescent separation–individuation plays a critical role in successful differentiation, practicing, and resolution of the rapprochement crisis.

Eating disorders has been a further area of difficulty linked to problems of the second separation–individuation process. While eating disorders may be determined by multiple factors (including individual vulnerabilities, family attachment dynamics, a social milieu placing a high value on slimness, and more pervasive cultural attitudes), some studies have begun to examine intrapsychic issues of separation–individuation development in conjunction with attachment dynamics within the family. Armstrong and Roth (1989), Friedlander and Siegel (1990), Rhodes and Kroger (1992), Smolak and Levine (1993), and Zakin (1989) have all found difficulties in adolescent separation–individuation and/or external attachments for those adolescents with an eating disorder. From these works, the anorexic or bulimic depends excessively on the resources of others and has shown little intrapsychic differentiation between self and significant others. The general pattern of adolescent separation–individuation failure resulting in the inability to achieve a separate sense of identity has been characteristic of bulimic and anorexic adolescents reported in these studies. Hansburg's Adolescent Separation Anxiety Test, Hoffman's Psychological Separation Inventory, and Levine *et al*.'s SITA were used to assess dimensions of adolescent separation–individuation in these studies. Further investigation of optimal caregiver response through the various subphases of adolescent separation–individuation is warranted.

The role of regression in the adolescent separation–individuation process has just begun to be examined. Mahler herself noted, "To go forward and to reach a higher degree of integration, a temporary phase of regression, of disorganization, of outright minor crisis—a chaotic state–has to occur" (1983, p. 6). Certainly, the height of the rapprochement crisis for the toddler involves regressive attempts to recreate the symbiotic unity of earlier times, alternating with the desire for greater autonomy. "Shadowing" and "darting away" from the primary caretaker are the toddler's behavioral expressions of this intrapsychic predicament. A parallel phenomenon has been noted by several researchers in the "push–pull" or "rapprochement-like" relationships that some adolescents (engaged in a moratorium process) have with authority figures (for example, Donovan, cited in Marcia, 1976; Podd *et al.*, 1970). Bilsker and Marcia (1991) have also found moratorium adolescents to show a greater disposition to adaptive regression than adolescents who have made commitments to identity-defining roles and values. Moratorium adolescents behaviorally are exploring various identity-defining commitments while intrapsychically undergoing the second separation–individuation process (Kroger, 1996); regression appears to precede the ability to make identity-defining commitments on one's own terms. Measurement of regression is problematic, but instruments focusing on overt behaviors as well as reported subjective states could usefully aid efforts to understand more fully the process of adolescent separation–individuation and the disequilibrium it brings. It may be that ongoing diary accounts of subjective states could initially bring the greatest enlightenment regarding possible cycles experienced in the intrapsychic differentiation process.

A growing body of theoretical literature has been emerging on infant use of transitional objects to facilitate the first separation–individuation process; transitional object use by adolescents undergoing the second separation–individuation process has been less directly examined. Winnicott was the first writer to describe transitional objects and their function during infancy. In his terms, transitional object refers to the first "not me" possession; such objects, like a blanket or cuddly toy, are different from the infant's own body but "not fully recognized as belonging to external reality" (1953, p. 90). These objects function as a representation of the primary attachment figure, and while the child knows that the blanket or cuddly toy is not really mother, the youngster still is comforted by the transitional object in a way similar to being soothed by mother (or caretaker) herself. Tolpin (1971) indicated that such objects function as an "auxiliary soother" by symbolically recreating union with the mother or primary caretaker and thereby aiding the process of infant differentiation. As separation–individuation proceeds, the transitional object is neither forgotten nor mourned; it simply loses its meaning.

Research on the use of transitional objects in infancy suggests their importance not only to the differentiation process at the time, but also to personality characteristics in later life (Cohen and Clark, 1984; Lundy and Potts, 1987; Triebenbacher and Tegano, 1993). Significant personality differences have been found for "normal" adolescents whose self and parental reports indicated use of such a transitional object during infancy. It appears that the need for intimacy in adolescence was related to recall of the special toy or object in infancy. Those adolescents who reported no special toy in infancy, scored as significantly more reserved and aloof than transitional object users (Cohen and Clark 1984). The use of transitional objects in adolescence has been discussed by Blos (1967), who postulated that extensive diaries, all-consuming hobbies, or idolized others, functioned like transitional objects and helped facilitate adolescents' differentiation from internalized parental representations. Empirical studies of transitional object use in normative adolescent development, however, have addressed the issue only indirectly. Byrd *et al.* (1993) have explored the role that siblings play as possible transitional objects during the adolescent separation–individuation process. They found that adolescents without siblings scored lower in independence than oldest children, and they rated their families as being more enmeshed than would be expected by chance. The authors proposed that the "dethronement" process, in which first borns must relinquish only child status, may facilitate both first and second individuation processes.

One of the most extensive research programs addressing transitional object use during adolescent separation–individuation has been developed by Lapsley and his colleagues (Lapsley, 1993; Lapsley and Rice, 1988). These researchers have been examining the adolescent separation–individuation process and functions that the imaginary audience and personal fable may serve during this transition time. The imaginary audience, first described by Elkind (1967), is the tendency by adolescents to see themselves primarily as the focus of others' attention in real and imagined situations. Personal fables are adolescent constructions of stories about themselves stressing themes of personal uniqueness, omnipotence, and invulnerability (similar to beliefs of the practicing toddler). Adolescents' use of imaginary audiences and personal fables are best understood, Lapsley believes, as defensive and restitutive mechanisms that facilitate resilience and coping during the second individuation process. The restructuring of internalized self–other representations brings loss in power of the parental introjects, and Lapsley suggests the imaginary audience is constructed to fill this void. The personal fable, on the other hand, serves to deny dependency and separation anxiety by focusing on the invulnerability of the self; in other words, the imaginary audience seems to express anxiety resulting from loss of the old object ties, while the personal fable offers a defense against such loss. The imaginary audience and personal fable appear to be performing some of the very functions that transitional objects serve during adolescent intrapsychic restructuring. While Lapsley's initial research on these mechanisms has not been replicated (Goossens 1994), efforts to delineate mechanisms for coping with the

second separation–individuation process should continue. In particular, attention should be directed to defense mechanisms as well as
features of objects, people, and situations that may serve as "auxiliary
soothers" or transitional objects to ease the pain of loss and help
bridge the void that intrapsychic differentiation inevitably brings.

The role of mourning in relation to the first and second separation–individuation processes has received little empirical attention. In
earlier theoretical writing, Kestenberg (1971) believed there to be
several mechanisms by which pain becomes a critical factor in regu-
lating the separation–individuation process. As each separation–
individuation subphase requires a gradual shift in the reformulation of
self and object representations, former symbiotic bonds become
replaced by lesser symbiotic bonds or "bridges" provided by transitional objects. In this way, the degree of pain that can be tolerated
regulates the pace of intrapsychic restructuring. Additionally,
Kestenberg suggested, pain can provide an impetus for turning the loss
of an old structure into a triumph for the restructured self. Further
investigation of the ways in which tolerance for pain may regulate
adolescent separation–individuation as well as the actual mourning
process would be a fruitful direction for future research.

The present chapter has focused primarily on the intrapsychic
restructuring that occurs during the second separation–individuation
process of adolescence, including phases of movement in restructuring
internal self–other representations of self, and the roles of regression,
mourning, and transitional object use. Interpersonal ramifications of
this intrapsychic process, including styles of relating to parents, other
family members, peers, and intimate partnerships have also been the
focus of a vast array of investigations too numerous to review in detail
here. The reader is referred to Marcia (1994) for an excellent overview
of such areas. However, in conclusion, brief mention will be made of
several studies directly linking adolescent separation–individuation
processes to parenting practices and styles of intimate relationships.

Quintana and Kerr (1993) echo the pleas of many researchers to
consider adolescent separation–individuation not as a linear process in
which one moves from dependence to independence, but rather as a
process of developing new forms of autonomy and connection. Many
theoretical discussions as well as research investigations of previous
decades have conceptualized the results of adolescent separation–
individuation to be the attainment of autonomy from parents; in fact,
at least one instrument purporting to extend Mahler's scheme to assess
adolescent separation–individuation, measures only aspects of independence (Hoffman, 1984). However, such work as that of Grotevant

and Cooper (1985, 1986) and later Papini *et al.* (1989) Quintana and Kerr (1993), and Weinmann and Newcombe (1990), have consistently shown adolescents' needs for both autonomy and connectedness in the changing dynamics of relationships with parents. From Grotevant and Cooper's observational research of adolescent–parent interactions on a decision-making task, parents who could support their adolescent's needs for both individuality and connectedness had teen-agers showing more mature forms of identity resolution. Quintana and Kerr found that college students with parents who supported their autonomy, mirroring, and nurturance needs on Levine *et al.*'s SITA showed freedom from depression, while engulfment anxiety, separation anxiety, and denial of dependency were associated with depressive complaints among college students with parents who did not support such needs. Mature forms of intimacy have been directly linked with optimal resolution of the second separation–individuation process; furthermore, adolescents forming primarily enmeshed or superficial relationships have shown indications of failure to differentiate fully from internalized object ties on Hansburg's test (Levitz-Jones and Orlofsky, 1985; Millis, 1984). It remains the task of researchers in the next decade to delineate more fully the forms of adolescent connectedness and separateness that are most adaptive from those that are not. Work such as that by Fullinwider (1991), which examined varying qualities of family connectedness in relation to adolescent identity development, is a start in this direction.

CONCLUSIONS

The early 1990s have witnessed increasing empirical investigations of the adolescent separation–individuation process in both normative and clinical populations. These researches have suggested a number of refinements to Blos's initial descriptions. While precursors of the second separation–individuation process exist in latency and early adolescence, it appears to be the mid- to late adolescent years in which much intrapsychic restructuring normatively occurs. Subphases of adolescent separation–individuation that parallel the infant process have been empirically documented. Separation and individuation tracks may not generally proceed concurrently during the second separation–individuation process; escaping the regressive pull of formerly merged self–other representations and dealing with the fear of dissolution may precede the ability to develop and enjoy more individually distinct characteristics.

Many dimensions of the adolescent separation–individuation

process warrant further study. Closer scrutiny of what is actually meant by "disengaging from the parental introject" or "differentiating from merged self–other representations" is needed. Exactly who has been internalized and what role that person or persons play in the differentiation process needs to be more fully examined. Attention must also be given to internalized representations of surroundings and the functions such representations have in adolescent separation–individuation. The issues of regression, transitional object use, and mourning also need to be more fully documented and their functions examined. Some form of behavioral regression appears to precede optimal resolution to the intrapsychic restructuring process; what it is that actually regresses needs more careful scrutiny. An understanding of the intrapsychic dimensions of regression might be obtained through adolescents' diary records or description of subjective states.

Research attention might usefully be directed toward transitional objects such as the imaginary audience and personal fable and the functions they serve in intrapsychic restructuralization. The extent to which tolerance for pain regulates the pace of intrapsychic restructuring might also be investigated. While the present chapter has focused primarily on intrapsychic issues involved in adolescent separation–individuation, the relationship between internalized self–other representations and forms of relatedness with external others has begun. The second separation–individuation process not only brings greater differentiation from both internalized and external others but also new forms of connection. Researchers of the next decade must attempt to delineate more fully the actual forms of adolescent connection and separateness that are most adaptive in the course of development in the years beyond adolescence.

NOTE

1 I would like to express my grateful appreciation to Cathy Diggens for her assistance with literature searches and to the Internal Grants Committee, Victoria University of Wellington, for funding which supported the acquisition of materials reviewed in this chapter.

BIBLIOGRAPHY

Armsden, G.C., and Greenberg, M.T. (1987) The inventory of parent and peer attachment: individual differences and their relationship to psychological well-being in adolescence, *Journal of Youth and Adolescence*, 17: 527–45.
Armstrong, J.G., and Roth, D.M. (1989) Attachment and separation difficulties in eating disorders: a preliminary investigation, *International Journal of Eating Disorders*, 8: 141–55.

The separation–individuation process   189

Bilsker, D., and Marcia, J.E. (1991) Adaptive regression and ego identity, *Journal of Adolescence*, 14: 75–84.

Blos, P. (1967) The second individuation process of adolescence, *Psychoanalytic Study of the Child*, 22: 162–86.

Brandt, D.E. (1977) Separation and identity in adolescence: Erikson and Mahler—some similarities, *Contemporary Psychoanalysis*, 13: 507–18.

Bray, J.H., and Harvey, D.M. (1987), *Intimacy and Individuation in Young Adults. Development of the College Student Version of the Personal Authority in the Family System Questionnaire*, Department of Psychology, Texas Woman's University, Houston Center.

Byrd, B., DeRosa, A.P., and Craig, S.S. (1993) The adult who is an only child: achieving separation or individuation? *Psychological Reports*, 73: 171–7.

Christenson, R.M., and Wilson, W.P. (1985) Assessing pathology in the separation–individuation process by an inventory: a preliminary report, *The Journal of Nervous and Mental Disease*, 173: 561–5.

Cohen, K.N., and Clark, J.A. (1984) Transitional object attachments in early childhood and personality characteristics in later life, *Journal of Personality and Social Psychology*, 46: 106–11.

Dolan, B.M., Evans, C., and Norton, K. (1992) The separation–individuation inventory: association with borderline phenomena, *The Journal of Nervous and Mental Disease*, 180: 529–533.

Edward, J., Ruskin, N., and Turrini, P. (1992) *Separation/Individuation: Theory and Application*, 2nd edn., New York: Brunner/Mazel.

Elkind, D. (1967) Egocentrism in adolescence, *Child Development*, 38: 1025–34.

Esman, A.H. (1980) Adolescent psychopathology and the rapprochement phenomenon, *Adolescent Psychiatry*, 8: 320–31.

Friedlander, M.L. and Siegel, S.M. (1990) Separation–individuation difficulties and cognitive–behavioral indicators of eating disorders among college women, *Journal of Counseling Psychology*, 37: 74–8.

Fullinwider, N. (1991, April) *Adolescent Identity Development Within the Context of a Triangulated Family System*, paper presented at the Biennial Meeting of the Society for Research in Child Development, Seattle.

Goossens, L. (1994, February) *Separation–individuation and the "new look" at adolescent egocentrism*: paper presented at the Biennial Meetings of the Society for Research on Adolescence, San Diego.

Greenberg, J.R., and Mitchell, S.A. (1983) *Object Relations in Psychoanalytic Theory*, Cambridge: Harvard University Press.

Grotevant, H.D., and Cooper, C. (1985) Patterns of interaction in family relationships and the development of identity exploration in adolescence, *Child Development*, 56: 415–28.

—— (1986) Individuation in family relationships, *Human Development*, 29: 82–100.

Hansburg, H.G. (1980a) *Adolescent separation anxiety: a method for the study of adolescent separation problems*, vol. 1, New York: Robert E. Krieger.

—— (1980b) *Adolescent Separation Anxiety: Separation Disorders*, vol. 2, New York: Robert E. Krieger.

Hoffman, J.A. (1984) Psychological separation of late adolescents from their parents, *Journal of Counseling Psychology*, 31: 170–8.

Holmbeck, G.N., and McClanahan, G. (1994) Construct and content validity

190   *J. Kroger*

of the separation–individuation test of adolescence: a reply to Levine, *Journal of Personality Assessment*, 62: 169–72.

Jong, M.L. de (1992) Attachment, individuation, and risk of suicide in late adolescence, *Journal of Youth and Adolescence*, 21: 357–73.

Josselson, R. (1980) Ego development in adolescence, in J. Adelson (ed.) *Handbook of Adolescent Psychology*, New York: Wiley.

—— (1988) The embedded self: I and thou revisited, in D.K. Lapsley and F.C. Power (eds.), *Self, Ego, and Identity: Integrative Approaches*, New York: Springer-Verlag.

Kestenberg, J.S. (1971) From organ–object imagery to self and object representations, in J. McDevitt and C. Settlage (eds.), *Separation–Individuation: Essays in honor of Margaret S. Mahler*, New York: International Universities Press.

Kroger, J. (1985) Separation–individuation and ego identity status in New Zealand university students, *Journal of Youth and Adolescence*, 14: 133–47.

—— (1992) Intrapsychic dimensions of identity during late adolescence, in G.R. Adams, T.P. Gullotta, and R. Montemayor (eds.) "Advances in Adolescent Development", vol. 4., *Adolescent Identity Formation*, Newbury Park: Sage.

—— (1993) On the nature of structural transition in the identity formation process, in J. Kroger (ed.), *Discussions on Ego Identity*, Hillsdale: Erlbaum.

—— (1995) The differentiation of "firm" and "developmental" foreclosure identity statuses: a longitudinal study, *Journal of Adolescent Research*, 10: 317–37.

—— (1996), *Identity in Adolescence: The Balance between Self and Other*, 2nd edn., London: Routledge.

Kroger, J., and Green, K. (1994) Factor analytic structure and stability of the Separation–Individuation Test of Adolescence, *Journal of Clinical Psychology*, 50: 772–9.

Kroger, J., and Haslett, S.J. (1988) Separation–individuation and ego identity status in late adolescents: a two-year longitudinal study, *Journal of Youth and Adolescence*, 17: 59–81.

Lapsley, D.K. (1993) Toward an integrated theory of adolescent ego development: the "new look" at adolescent egocentrism, *American Journal of Orthopsychiatry*, 63: 562–71.

Lapsley, D.K., and Rice, K. (1988) The "new look" at the imaginary audience and personal fable: towards an integrative model of adolescent ego development, in D.K. Lapsley and F.C. Power (eds.), *Self, Ego, Identity: Integrative Approaches*, New York: Springer-Verlag.

Levine, J.B. (1994) On McClanahan and Holmbeck's construct validity study of the separation–individuation test of adolescence, *Journal of Personality Assessment*, 62: 166–8.

Levine, J.B., Green, C.J., and Millon, T. (1986) Separation–individuation test of adolescence, *Journal of Personality Assessment*, 50: 123–37.

Levine, J.B., and Saintonge, S. (1993) Psychometric properties of the separation–individuation test of adolescence within a clinical population, *Journal of Clinical Psychology*, 49: 492–507.

Levitz-Jones, E.M., and Orlofsky, J.L. (1985) Separation–individuation and intimacy capacity in college women, *Journal of Personality and Social Psychology*, 49: 156–69.

Levy-Warren, M.H. (1987) Moving to a new culture: cultural identity, loss, and mourning, in J. Bloom Feshbach and S. Bloom-Feshbach (eds.), *The Psychology of Separation and Loss*, San Francisco: Jossey-Bass.

Lundy, A., and Potts, T. (1987) Recollection of a transitional object and needs for intimacy and affiliation in adolescents, *Psychological Reports*, 60: 767–73.

Lyons-Ruth, K. (1991) Rapprochement or approchement: Mahler's theory reconsidered from the vantage point of recent research on early attachment relationships, *Psychoanalytic Psychology*, 8: 1–24.

Mahler, M.S. (1983) The meaning of developmental research of earliest infancy as related to the study of separation–individuation, in J.D. Call, E. Galenson, and R.L. Tyson (eds.), *Frontiers of Infant Psychiatry*, New York: Basic Books.

Mahler, M.S. and McDevitt, (1982) Thoughts on the emergence of the sense of self, with particular emphasis on the body self, *Journal of the American Psychoanalytic Association*, 30: 827–48.

Mahler, M.S., Pine, F., and Bergman, A. (1975) *The Psychological Birth of the Human Infant*, New York: Basic Books.

Marcia, J.E. (1966) Development and validation of ego identity status, *Journal of Personality and Social Psychology*, 3: 551–8.

—— (1976) *Studies in Ego Identity*, unpublished research monograph, Simon Fraser University, Burnaby.

—— (1994) Ego identity and object relations, in J. Masling and R.F. Bornstein (eds.), *Empirical Perspectives on Object Relations Theory*, Washington, D.C.: American Psychological Association.

Masterson, J. (1981), *The Narcissistic and Borderline Disorders: An integrated Developmental Approach*, New York: Brunner/Mazel.

Mazor, A., Alfa, A., and Gampel, Y. (1993) On the thin line between connection and separation: the individuation process, from cognitive and object-relations perspectives, in kibbutz adolescents, *Journal of Youth and Adolescence*, 22: 641–69.

McClanahan, G., and Holmbeck, G.N. (1992) Separation–individuation, family functioning, and psychological adjustment in college students: a construct validity study of the separation–individuation test of adolescence, *Journal of Personality Assessment*, 59: 468–85.

Millis, S.R. (1984), *Separation–Individuation and Intimacy in Young Adulthood*, unpublished doctoral dissertation, University of Cincinnati.

Mirsky, J., and Kaushinsky, F. (1989) Migration and growth: separation–individuation processes in immigrant students in Israel, *Adolescence*, 24: 725–40.

Papini, D.R., Micka, J.C., and Barnett, J.K. (1989) Perceptions of intrapsychic and extrapsychic functioning as bases of adolescent ego identity status, *Journal of Adolescent Research*, 4: 462–82.

Pine, F. (1990) *Drive, Ego, Object, and Self*, New York: Basic Books.

—— (1992) Some refinements of the separation–individuation concept in light of research on infants, *Psychoanalytic Study of the Child*, 45: 179–94.

Podd, M.H., Marcia, J.E., and Rubin, B.M. (1970) The effects of ego identity and partner perception on a prisoner's dilemma game, *The Journal of Social Psychology*, 82: 117–26.

Quintana, S.M. and Kerr, J. (1993) Relational needs in late adolescent separation–individuation, *Journal of Counseling and Development*, 71: 349–54.

Rhodes, B., and Kroger, J. (1992) Parental bonding and separation–individuation difficulties among late adolescent eating disordered women, *Child Psychiatry and Human Development*, 22: 249–63.

Rinsley, D. (1982) *Borderline and Other Self Disorders*, New York: Jason Aronson.

Selman, R. (1980) *The Growth of Interpersonal Understanding*, New York: Academic Press.

Smolak, L., and Levine, M.P. (1993) Separation–individuation difficulties and the distinction between bulimia nervosa and anorexia nervosa in college women, *International Journal of Eating Disorders*, 14: 33–41.

Stern, D.N. (1985) *The Interpersonal World of the Infant*, New York: Basic Books.

Tolpin, M. (1971) On the beginning of the cohesive self, *Psychoanalytic Study of the Child*, 26: 316–54.

Triebenbacher, S.L., and Tegano, D.W. (1993) Children's use of transitional objects during daily separations from significant others, *Perceptual and Motor Skills*, 76: 89–90.

Wade, N.L. (1987) Suicide as a resolution of separation–individuation among adolescent girls, *Adolescence*, 22: 169–77.

Weinmann, L.L., and Newcombe, N. (1990) Relational aspects of identity: late adolescents' perceptions of their relationships with parents, *Journal of Experimental Child Psychology*, 50: 357–69.

Winnicott, D.W. (1953) Transitional objects and transitional phenomena: a study of the first not-me possession, *International Journal of Psychoanalysis*, 34: 89–97.

Zakin, D.F. (1989) Eating disturbance, emotional separation, and body image, *International Journal of Eating Disorders*, 8: 411–16.

9 Peer Gynt's life cycle

James E. Marcia

Erik Erikson, artist and psychoanalyst, employed his creative, and clinical-theoretical talents in the service of constructing a portrait of psychological development across the life span (Erikson, 1959, 1982) (Figure 9.1). My students, colleagues and I have worked for a number of years to develop measures of these stages of psychosocial develop-ment (Bradley, 1992, 1997; Bradley *et al.*, 1990; Hearn, 1993; Hearn *et al.*, 1997; Kowaz and Marcia, 1991; Marcia *et al.*, 1993; Orlofsky *et al.*, 1973) (see Figure 9.2). In this chapter, I would like to join Erikson's theory and our empirical research within the context of Henrik Ibsen's witty, fantastic, and, yet, psychologically trenchant verse play, *Peer Gynt*, which he based upon a folk tale of his native Norway.

We first encounter the 20-year-old Peer trying to explain to his mother where he has been for the past few months when there was so much hard work to be done around the house. He tells her one of the many fantastic tales for which he has become noted in his village. He says that he was chasing a reindeer up to a sharp mountain ledge, trying to plunge his knife into the animal; he became pinned on its back; and they tumbled together down a chasm into a river, where Peer and the buck together swam to safety. His mother, Åse, is briefly taken in by the story until she recognizes it as a well-known legend— describing someone else. "Shame!," she says to Peer. And, indeed, *shame* is an important theme in this part of the story as we shall continue to see later.

Shame has a very definite place in Erikson's theory (see Figure 9.1). It is the negative outcome of the second psychosocial developmental period in which the young child's task is the formation of a sense of autonomy. Autonomy involves the will, and most of us are familiar with the healthy willfulness of the 2-year-old. In the necessary process of modifying this willfulness, parents may resort to shaming or ridiculing the child—for "going" where she ought not go, whether in the eliminative or locomotive sense. Shaming is a disciplinary easy way out for a parent who notices that the child has done something wrong and then ridicules her for it. Shaming is much easier than attending carefully to what the child needs and helping her to meet the social demands. But the price paid developmentally for continual shaming is either the child's lingering sense of doubt ("I must always cover my back-side"), or shameless defiance ("I'll do as I please, and damn your eyes!").

Peer seems to have internalized strongly this sense of shame in both its doubt-ridden and defiant aspects. After playfully parking his mother on a house roof, we find him next at a wedding celebration in the village. Ingrid, a girl his mother had encouraged him to marry in order that they might live off her dowry and inheritance, is about to wed another. Peer, typically, was too late in making a commitment to her, although it seems she fancied him. As he approaches the party, he anticipates his friends' ridicule, in typical adolescent personal fable, imaginary audience fashion, saying to himself: "They always whisper behind your back and their sniggering seems to burn right through you." And later: "Oh well, let them gossip—it doesn't hurt me!" Still again: "Who's that? Was there somebody laughing behind me? I was certain I heard . . . . No, there's nobody there."

In fact, when Peer does join the party, his false "friends" do spurn him, teasing him by refusing to speak with him. We should remember that Peer is a very *young* 20-year-old. And who does not recall how devastating such an incident of total rejection by one's peers can be to an adolescent! Actual shame heaped upon anticipated shame is the double indignity that Peer suffers. So he gets drunk. He is about to leave the celebration when he espies the angelic Solveig: "How lovely!" he exclaims, "I've never seen anyone like her—with her eyes on the ground and her little white apron, the way she kept hold of her mother's skirts, and carried her prayer book wrapped in a kerchief . . . I must see her again." Recovering from this moment of stunned adoration, he asks her to dance with him. She refuses. He persists. She still refuses. Then, Peer runs up the hill to where Ingrid, the bride-to-be, has locked herself in the outhouse (waiting for Peer, perhaps?). He "shamelessly" throws her over his shoulder "like a pig" and carries her off, to the dismay and consternation of the whole wedding party.

Now, in the entire wedding party scene, there is no planned action on Peer's part. This, as we shall see, often characterizes Peer's activities. He simply goes from impulse to impulse. He lays no plans to impress his friends and reverse their opinions; he has no stratagems to

CHRONOLOGICAL AGE

Identity issue at Integrity Stage →

Precursor to Autonomy at Trust Stage ←

Chronological Age	1	2	3	4	5	6	7	8
OLD AGE — VIII	T-M Intg.	A-S,D Intg.	I-G Intg.	Ind-I Intg.	Id-ID Intg.	Int-Is Intg.	G-S Intg.	Integrity and Despair · G
ADULTHOOD — VII	T-M Int. G	A-S,D G.	I-G Int.	Ind-I Int.	Id-ID Int.	Int-Is Int. G	G-S Int.	Inty-D Int.
YOUNG ADULTHOOD — VI (○ Genital, ● Mature intrusion-inclusion)	T-M Id.	A-S,D Id.	I-G Id.	Ind-I Id.	Id-ID Id.	Intimacy and Isolation · Id.	G-S Id.	Inty-D Id.
ADOLESCENCE — V	T-M Ind.	A-S,D Ind.	I-G Ind.	Ind-I Ind.	Identity and Identity Diffusion · Ind.	Int-Is Ind.	G-S Ind.	Inty-D Ind.
SCHOOL AGE — IV (○ Latent)	T-M Ind.	A-S,D Ind.	I-G Ind.	Industry and Inferiority · I	Id-ID Ind.	Int-Is Ind.	G-S Ind.	Inty-D Ind.
PLAY AGE — III (○ Phallic (oedipal), Intrusion-inclusion, ● Individuation)	T-M I	A-S,D Ind.	Initiative and Guilt · A	Ind-I I	Id-ID I	Int-Is I	G-S I	Inty-D I
EARLY CHILDHOOD — II (○ Anal, Eliminative-retentive, ● Practising)	T-M A	Autonomy and Shame, Doubt · T	I-G A	Ind-I A	Id-ID A	Int-Is A	G-S A	Inty-D A
INFANCY — I (○ Oral, Passive-active Incorporative, ● Attachment)	Basic Trust and Basic Mistrust	A-S,D T	I-G T	Ind-I T	Id-ID T	Int-Is T	G-S T	Inty-D T

○ Psychosexual zone
(grey) Related behavioral modality
● Object relational phase

Figure 9.1 Psychosocial stages

persuade Solveig. Carrying off Ingrid was more a result of her plotting (by first locking herself in the outhouse when she knew that Peer had arrived) than of his planning. And impulsiveness is not Initiative. In Erikson's terms, Peer displays little apparent initiative, the ego quality which Erikson proposes to follow from, and to rest upon, a sense of autonomy (see Figure 9.1). Initiative adds to the sheer willing of the Autonomy stage a sense of purposiveness, of conceiving and executing a project of one's own design.

Ego psychoanalytic theory has it that Initiative is learned within the oedipal context as one tries out different stratagems to gain the undivided attention of a desired parent. For optimal developmental results, one ought to succeed only moderately at this task. Failure at the oedipal project is associated with Guilt. One can experience guilt over either the means one employs to gain parental affection or over that goal, itself. On the other hand, too much success in the oedipal project produces a reluctance, even an inability, to ever progress beyond preoccupation with those parental figures.

What was Peer's family like—his "oedipal context"? Briefly, his mother, Åse, doted on the young Peer. Some of her fondest memories were of the two of them curled up in front of the fire making up fantastic tales. Small wonder that Peer should be, throughout his life, a spinner of outlandish yarns. While the young Peer and his mother were enjoying their intimacy, Peer's father, Jon Gynt, was busy drinking and wasting the family inheritance. Åse explains her closeness to Peer by saying:

> We clung together in want and sorrow for I must tell you, my husband drank, roaming the district with foolish chatter, wasting and trampling our wealth under foot while I sat at home with Little Peer . . . . What could we do but try to forget? I was too weak to face the truth—it's a terrible thing to look fate in the face, so you try to shrug your troubles away and do your best to keep from thinking: some try lies, and some try brandy, but, ah, we took to fairy tales of princes, trolls, enchanted beasts, and stolen brides . . .

The legacy of an absent and wastrel father and, especially, of an affectionate and imaginative mother to their only child, Peer, was a sense of entitlement, almost of invulnerability, an assurance that women would always love him (and, for a time, they all did). But Peer was left with almost no basis for those internalized standards that, in time, become a reference point for feelings of self-esteem. Whatever conscience Peer had, might most kindly be described as extremely flexible—and not at all serviceable as a guide to moral decision making. One of the most attractive aspects of the innocent Solveig for him was her purity—as if by having her, he might establish a connection on the outside with what he lacked inside.

I shall use the term "part-identity" to refer to those partial identifications and self-labels one adopts or constructs in childhood, and which, later on in adolescence become woven into the first integrated identity. What part-identities might Peer have carried from his childhood into his late adolescence? As we know from the nature of Erikson's theory, as reflected in the 64 square diagram, every psychosocial issue occurs at every life cycle stage (see Figure 9.1). So that there is an identity component to early childhood when the predominant issue is Autonomy, as there is at play age when the main focus is on Initiative. Peer's identity with respect to Autonomy and Shame, Doubt might be described as "one who must always show a good front"—even if that front is a fantasy. If he doesn't, his audience may see behind his facade to his shameful self.

While social self-protection is, to some extent, a normal reaction, it is exaggerated in Peer because he has never learned that "just as he is" is good enough; he has been encouraged to live only in the hyperbolic— hence, Ibsen's irony in having Peer declaim the virtue of being "one's self." Peer is most "himself" when he is telling one of his fantastic tales about his made-up self, or playing one of his imaginary roles. In fact, Peer is never *himself*. Hence, he must always be on the lookout for what is being bought socially and must package himself accordingly: not a good prognosis for healthy identity development. Peer's identity with respect to Initiative and Guilt, is "one who will do whatever it takes in the moment" with little regard for the consequences to others. Therefore, Peer is more concerned with appearance than with substance, more motivated by fear than by guilt. (This suggests that there might be another less developmentally advanced, outcome to Erikson's postulated resolutions of initiative and Guilt, viz., fear.)

A good example of Peer's disregard for the impact of his behavior on others is his brutal rejection of Ingrid, the next morning, after his "abducting" her from the wedding celebration (with her complicity, I think). Fully aware that he has spoiled her chances for a good marriage, he compares her now-soiled self with the unblemished Solveig.

PEER   Have you a prayerbook wrapped in your kerchief? Have you a
        gold plait that-hangs down your back? Do you look modestly down
        at your apron? Do you hold on to your mother's skirt? *Do* you?
INGRID   No, but—
PEER   Was it last spring that you were confirmed?

INGRID   But listen, Peer—
PEER   Do you blush and lower your eyelids? Can you deny me when
   I beg?
INGRID   Lord! I think he's out of his mind!
PEER   Do a man's thoughts grow all holy when he sees you? Do they?
INGRID   No, but—
PEER   Then what else is there that counts?

At this juncture one might expect Peer to go to another village since he cannot return to his own (which he has outraged), find a job there, and pursue the lovely Solveig. But Peer is ill-prepared to work or to plan realistically. As his mother says: "his greatest strength was in his tongue—he never did anything in his life!" His only competence seems to have been playing at button-making. When he was a child, he would ask his father for scrap metal to melt down and cast into buttons. His father, the grandiose drunkard, gave him, instead, silver coins to use. One can speculate on what concept of "worthiness" or "worthwhileness" this may have conveyed to the young Peer. At one moment, he is worth being given silver coins to use and destroy as playthings. At another, he is wholly ignored, treated as insignificant. What realistic worth has he? Is he a prince or a destitute bastard? How would a child ever develop a sense of Industry, the idea that working hard is worthwhile and will be rewarded commensurably if, willy-nilly, he is tossed precious coins to melt down? Could one look to such a father for any useful evaluation of one's worth? Did Peer in fact, actually have a father, save in biology and in fantasy?

There is almost no reference to Peer's ever having developed a sense of Industry (see Figure 9.1), a sense that working hard is worthwhile and that if one persists, one is likely to feel a competent and valued worker in his society. Peer never, in his later life, ever completes a task—including building a proper house for Solveig. He does only what is required in the present moment to fulfill immediate demands— no long-range projects requiring perseverance for him.

In developing a measure of Industry-Inferiority (see Figure 9.2) to be used with school-age children, Andrea Kowaz took special care to assess the child's developmentally necessary transition from a preoccupation with play to an interest in work (Kowaz and Marcia, 1991). Consistent with Erikson, she saw latency as a developmental period during which the child learned the technology of his culture, and, equally importantly, a sense of himself as a competent worker within that culture. Life requires a time for planning as well as for imagination, for work as well as for play, a time for reality and a time for fantasy. In order to be truly creative, one must have not only vision, but the perseverance and technical skills to realize that vision. Skill requires practice. Peer just couldn't be bothered with the tedium. He never progressed beyond imagination, play, and fantasy. He created nothing, save his tall tales, and even many of these were tales taken from others into which he wove himself. His Industry-based identity might be "one who plays at working."

Peer is 20 when we first meet him and Identity (see Figure 9.l) is the psychosocial task we would expect him to be confronting. As we have seen, he comes to this stage psychologically ill-prepared, having little sense of healthy Autonomy, Initiative, or Industry. The extent of his "flexibility" (one might say diffusion) in identity commitment is shown in the scene in the Troll-King's palace. After abandoning the hapless Ingrid, and enjoying himself with three enthusiastic herdgirls, he encounters the daughter of the Troll-King whom he says he wants to marry—and thereby succeed to the Troll-King's domain. The Troll-King is willing to consent to this provided that Peer become a troll. Peer has no immediate objection (remember, he is the one who will be "whatever it takes in the moment"), and he even consents to wearing a tail. However, even this commitment is one he cannot make when he learns that if he becomes a troll, he can not leave the Troll-Kingdom. Nobody is going to fence in Peer Gynt!

In our research, we have identified two criteria as important in identity development at late adolescence: exploration and commitment (Marcia *et al.*, 1993). The life areas in which exploration and commitment are important include occupation, ideological beliefs, and interpersonal values. Decisions about what one is to do, what kind of world outlook one is to espouse, and what values about relationships one is to hold are tasks faced by the adolescent who is in transition from childhood to adulthood. This is not the only time in one's life cycle that these decisions must be made. However, the period following puberty is the first time they *can* be made, and their content constitutes the first identity. Subsequent "adolescences," that is, subsequent identity decision-making periods, occur throughout the life cycle, at least during every major psychosocial stage (see Figure 9.l). Hence, the first identity, although it may influence the subsequent ones, is usually not the final identity. A case in which that first identity is more likely to be the final one is when the person is an *identity diffusion*: someone who fails to form an initial identity at late adolescence. Being diffuse at the close of late adolescent period, when conditions are usually optimal for exploration and commitment predisposes, but does not destine, one to lifetime diffusion—so our research tells us.

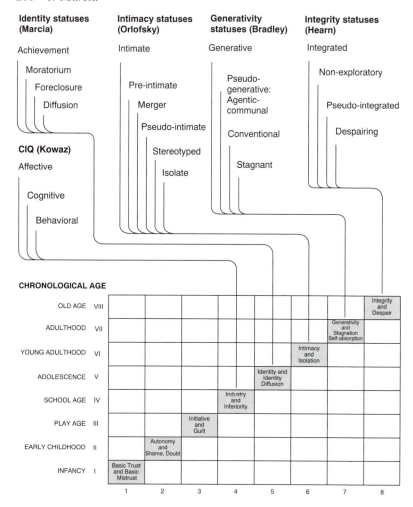

Figure 9.2 Measures of psychosocial development

Consider Peer's position. He comes to the crucial period for identity formation with three previous tentative childhood identities: "one who must always show a good front," "one who will do whatever it takes in the moment," and "one who plays at working." This is not a very sound basis for a firm, self-constructed, reliable, psychological core to take into adulthood. It sounds more like a prescription for a superficial, unscrupulous, adventurer. And that is at least a major part of what Peer becomes, although one cannot say that it is an identity he has deliberately chosen. Rather, it is one he fell into as a consequence of his largely negative resolution of previous stages. Peer never experienced what we call a "moratorium," a period during which he weighed seriously his abilities and interests with respect to his society's demands and provisions and tried to come to some resolution. Peer did not undertake an identity *exploration*; he merely wandered. As Peer comments much later in the play when he is reviewing his life: " To hell with this brooding! Once you start thinking, you trip yourself up." With respect to *commitment* he says later in the play: "The secret of success in life's affairs is very simple—it's this: to keep one's ears shut tightly against one serpent's deadly inroads . . . (that) little one that leads men to do what is irrevocable . . . keep yourself thus free to choose . . . be sure you've left behind you a bridge securing your retreat." Contrast Peer's "escape clause" with Erikson's example of Martin Luther's identity declamation at the Diet at Worms as he faces the representatives of the powerful Roman Catholic hierarchy: "Here I stand. I can do no other." Even Peer's worship of Solveig was insufficient to compel his commitment. The word "choose" in the previous quotation deserves some comment. Again, as with Peer's declaration of the necessity of being "oneself," he never made choices, any more than he was ever truly himself. It is Ibsen's irony, used to demonstrate Peer's hypocrisy, that puts these words in Peer's mouth.

So we leave Peer at late adolescence, diffuse in Identity, outcast from his village, but beloved by women, and with more than an ordinary fund of energy and imagination. The balance of Peer Gynt's life cycle awaits us.

Peer comes down from his revelry on the mountain with Ingrid, the herd-girls, and the Troll-Princess to find himself an outcast from his village. So he begins to build himself a hut in the woods. As he is working on the construction, fantasizing, of course, what a magnificent edifice it will be, he sees Solveig coming towards him and his new home. She has left her family to live with him in the woods. He is overjoyed. One can see the glimmering possibility of psychosocial redemption. He goes happily out to collect wood. In the forest, he meets the Troll-Girl, who has become an extremely unattractive woman with an equally ugly child—his own. She tells him that he can settle there in his hut in the woods if he likes with his love, but that she and the child will be nearby and will likewise demand his care. Care, except very occasionally for his mother, is something for which Peer seems to lack any capacity. Faced with having to make a costly commitment in order to stay with his beloved Solveig—that is, having to care for the Troll-Girl and their child—Peer does the Peer-like thing:

he "goes round about," as he had been advised previously by the Boyg[1], and leaves Solveig in the partially-finished house.

The psychosocial expectation in Eriksonian theory is that the development of a sense of Intimacy will succeed identity (see Figure 9.1). Intimacy refers to the capacity for sharing oneself with another in a deep, mutually satisfactory, and committed manner. Jay Orlofsky (in Marcia, *et al.*, 1993) has outlined several resolutions of the Intimacy–Isolation crisis (see Figure 9.2). The one of these that seems to fit Peer best is the *stereotyped* status. Stereotyped individuals have decidedly shallow relationships. They never really get to know the other person. Seldom do they stay around long enough, and, consequently, they are seldom known themselves. "Not here for a long time, but for a good time" is their motto. This is an apt characterization of Peer in his relationships with Ingrid, the three herd-girls, the Troll-Girl, and even Solveig. With respect to intimate relationships, Peer may be described as having been "in lust" (with Ingrid, the Troll-Girl, and later with Anitra), "in adoration" (with Solveig), but never "in love." It is difficult if you have no clear sense of who you are (no identity), to share deeply, explore mutually, or commit wholly, for fear that that tenuous self will be lost in the other person.

After leaving Solveig in the hut in the woods. Peer returns home to find his mother dying. In what I find to be one of the two most touching scenes in Ibsen's drama (the other also involves death and a mother), Peer holds and comforts Åse, and the two recall, and retell to each other, some of the old tales they shared in their warmth before the fire. It is clear that Peer loves his mother, and that Åse loves her son. At the end, Peer kisses her cheek and says: "Thank you for all that you gave me—for beatings and lullabies." The tender mutuality between them that makes us believe that at least at the very first stage of life, Peer gained from his mother a sense of Basic Trust. Although we could never trust Peer, Peer, at least, could trust life and his right to be in the world. It is likely that Peer drew upon this accrued capital of basic trust for the energy with which he lived his life, and that it helped to lend his character its lovability. Peer's earliest identity might have been: "one who can count on being cared for by Woman." Peer's deficiency in care, however, re-emerges even in this scene as he gets so caught up in the fantastic tale he is telling his mother that he seems almost unaware of her dying, and, predictably, does not stick around for her funeral!

Ibsen's drama now picks up Peer's life as a robust, middle-aged man who seems to have done quite well for himself—at least monetarily. He has left his native Norway and we find him on his yacht in conversation with three other businessmen. They applaud Peer's financial success and ply him for tips. What he has been doing, he explains, is engaging in the lucrative slave trade. As well, he has been selling idols and liquor to the Chinese—and then transporting missionaries and Bibles to them. As the conversation proceeds, even these exponents of unbridled capitalism are shocked when Peer explains that he intends to finance the Turks against whom the Greeks are fighting for their independence, simply because the Turks are the stronger and more likely to win. The businessmen commandeer his yacht, stranding Peer in a desert kingdom in Arabia. We shall follow Peer's adventures here, but first let us see what Erikson has to say about psychosocial development at middle age.

Adulthood or middle age, according to Erikson, is the time in life when caring for the life cycles of others is a predominant concern. He calls this Generativity. Generativity refers both to productiveness and care. The products may be one's offspring or one's works; the care may be for one's children, others' children, or whatever one has created. Care for others must be balanced by care for oneself or else generativity degenerates into mere martyrdom. Failure to be generative is referred to by Erikson as Stagnation and Self-absorption. One may either languish in stagnant non-productiveness and/or lavish care on oneself as one's only beloved child.

Cheryl Bradley (Bradley, 1992, 1997; Bradley *et al.*, 1990) has expanded Erikson's description of the outcomes of the generativity stage to encompass five statuses (see Figure 9.2). The criteria for these statuses are active involvement in, and tolerance for, self and other. Active involvement refers to the extent of investment of time and energy in generative pursuits and tolerance refers to the inclusivity of who qualifies for one's care. For example, *generative* persons are highly involved with caring for others and themselves. The *pseudogenerative agentic* individual is highly invested in his own work and only those persons who can aid him with his projects. He cares little for others' individual development. The *pseudogenerative communal* person, by contrast, has no projects of her own but is very highly involved with others—only others, not herself, qualify for care. (Of course, such people also expect endless indications of gratitude.) The *conventional* person is highly involved with others, but only so long as they adhere to a rather narrow set of values and follow only certain "approved" pursuits. The *stagnant* person is generally unproductive and uncaring about others.

With the possibilities of generativity resolution in mind, let us return to Peer in his desert and see further what his previous Identity and Intimacy resolutions have prepared him for. The desert is inhabited by Mohammaden tribesmen who revere men they see as prophets. Typically, Peer anoints himself Prophet. The Christian Peer has no more compunction about being a Muslim prophet than he did about becoming a troll or about being a slave trader. Peer is "the one who does what it takes in the moment." Besides, as he says, ". . . in a pinch, I can always retract—I'm in no way committed . . . ." Here he meets Anitra, a dancing-girl, whom he thinks loves him, but who turns out to be more than his match in venality. She wheedles most of his money from him and leaves him in the desert.

In the final scene of Peer's middle age, Ibsen places him in an insane asylum in Cairo where Peer is finally able to realize one of his narcissistic fantasies, that of being an Emperor. Peer gains the madmen's recognition for outdoing them in the thing at which they are expert self-absorption. They say, ". . . he's full of himself, and of nobody else." By now, we are not surprised that Peer has adapted himself to this context as well, becoming a madman among madmen. As he says: "I'm whatever you wish: a Turk or a sinner—a hill-troll . . . ." At this point, an asylum resident places a wreath on Peer's head and exclaims: "Long live . . . the Emperor of Self!"

What might we say about Peer and Generativity? He has no children, no apprentices, no students for whom he cares; he has no particular occupation or profession save for making money; and the ways in which he chooses to make money are ones which are highly exploitative. Perhaps some of his guiltless mendacity harks back to his father whose main contact with Peer seemed to be an arbitrary toss of a coin. Even his fellow capitalists can no longer stand him, nor can Anitra who was initially impressed by him. No one seems to want to be around the middle-aged Peer for long. The charm of his youth having diminished, he seems to have little to recommend him for any enduring relationships save his penchant for spreading his money around when he thinks it's to his advantage. Peer's middle age is a portrait of Stagnation and Self-absorption. But one must grant him his sheer activity, even if it produces nothing but cash. Perhaps Peer's mid-life identity might be "one who is busy on his own behalf."

Before accompanying Peer into his old age, I would like to discuss briefly the issue of adolescing throughout the life span. We have already seen Peer's part-identities in life span periods other than adolescence. But adolescing throughout the life span means more than this. By using the verb form, "adolescing," I mean to suggest that adolescence is a process that can characterize those periods following puberty when one reviews and reorganizes one's life. This might be expected to occur at least as an accompaniment to the resolution of other life cycle stages, and for many of us, more frequently than that. At a minimum, one might expect an identity crisis to accompany intimacy–Isolation, Generativity–Stagnation, and Integrity–Despair. Just as puberty and other changes at early adolescence disequilibrate the partial identities of childhood, so do the demands of intimacy require a reformulation of the initial Identity achieved at late adolescence. Likewise, the generative, care-giving requirements of middle age differ from those of being with an intimate partner. Perhaps the greatest identity challenge exists in old age when one must rely increasingly upon psychological resources rather than physical ones. It is probably when one can no longer get by on sheer strength and energy that one faces the most difficult life cycle challenge.

To put it directly, the Eriksonian virtues of fidelity, love, care, and wisdom, qualities deriving from positive psychosocial stage resolution, do not emerge without struggle. A developmentally successful adolescence requires the psychological relinquishing of childhood, just as the formation of an intimate relationship necessitates enlarging and reorganizing one's newly-formed identity to include another. Generativity requires a shift of caring attention from one special person to concern for one's children, one's works, and the life cycles of the new generations. Integrity involves some relinquishing of that generativity in order to expand psychologically and spiritually at the same time as physical capacity is decreasing. Only by *not* growing psychologically can the transitional crises be avoided. Peer, for example, seems never able to convert any of his predicaments into occasions for decisions or for psychosocial growth. He just goes along with the strongest immediate situational pull and "adjusts."

I think that periods of adolescing are normal, expectable components of life cycle growth. Furthermore, I would advocate social support for such questioning and change as one finds one's previous identity inadequate to encompass one's current and forthcoming life cycle challenges. It is not easy to undergo identity crises at any time, but especially not at middle and old age.

Returning to Peer, one of the most significant features about his life is that he really never changes. He is the same Peer at middle age as he was at late adolescence. When we are not just being entertained by his antics, we hope to see some growth, some greater solidity. If Erikson is right, then at any life cycle stage, he has the chance to make up for previously inadequately resolved stages, especially since he does have that fundamental sense of Basic Trust. But not Peer. He just goes on his same Gyntish way, never really taking hold of, or constructing, a life of his own. If we were to speak in identity status terms we might say that he had foreclosed on diffusion. Many diffusions find another person who cares for them and with whom they can develop that inner structure that seems to have been missing. Solveig might be that person for Peer, but he runs from her. Yet, still, there is a psychosocial stage left, a possibility . . . .

At the drama's end, Peer is traveling home to Norway, by ship and spots familiar landmarks along the coastline. Upon being asked by the ship's captain whether Peer will tip the crew as he had promised, he replies: "Do you think I'd fork out my money at random for other men's brats? I've sweated too hard to earn what I've made . . . . There's no one waiting for old Peer Gynt." He then gives them only enough money for liquor so that they'll all go home drunk, beat their wives, and frighten their children. We see what kind of an old man Peer is becoming.

Simon Hearn (Hearn, 1993; Hearn *et al.*, 1997) in his largely successful efforts to develop a measure of Erikson's final stage of integrity-despair has described four integrity statuses (see Figure 9.2). *Integrated* persons are those who have reviewed their lives and find them meaningful. They are currently actively involved with others, and espouse those values that have stood them in good stead their whole lives. They are no strangers to regret or even to some despair, but these feelings do not predominate. They are not necessarily sweet or likeable. But they know who they are, how they came to be that way, and they affirm the way in which they have "done" their life cycle. *Non-exploratory* persons are reasonably content, but they have purchased this contentment at the price of non-introspectiveness. Their lives are unexamined and they exist fairly comfortably within this constricted context. They are the least likely to express feelings of loss or despair. *Pseudo-integrated* persons seem to be trying valiantly (sometimes desperately) to hold things together with slogans and trite maxims that pass for an integrated life philosophy. There is a brittleness to them, a sense that much despair lies just below the surface and threatens to leak through the crust of bromides. *Despairing* persons are bitter, resentful, ungenerous, sad, and wish either to die or have a chance to live their whole lives all over again.

Stage directions: *A hillside with the dried-up bed of a stream beside which stands a ruined mill. The ground is rough, and the whole place is desolate.* Peer is back home, sitting on a rubbish-heap composed of his belongings to be auctioned off. The end is near for him and Despair is creeping into his heart. The Man in Mourning says: "This is the end of the song. It's over." The world-weary Peer responds: "All songs end in the self-same way. And they're old . . . ." Of the products of his life he says: "There's gold and there's trash, they were bought at a loss, so I'll let them go cheap." Even a symbol of the once-cherished Solveig is discardable. He says, "Here's a dream of a prayerbook with clasps . . . I'll let it go for a hook and an eye!" Then, while peeling an onion layer by layer, Peer undertakes a review of his life, only to exclaim at the end: "What an incredible number of layers! Don't we get to the heart of it soon? (He pulls the whole onion to pieces). No, I'm damned if we do. Right down to the center there's nothing but layers—smaller and smaller . . . ." There was no identity core to Peer, only a series of roles.

Stage directions: *A fir-tree heath at night. It has been ravaged by a forest fire, and blackened tree-stumps stretch for miles. Patches of white mist lie here and there among the stumps.* PEER GYNT *comes running across the heath.* There follow now a series of inner reproaches for a life incompletely lived given voice by objects on the heath. The thread-balls (like tumbleweeds) blocking Peer's path say to him: "We are thoughts, you should have formed us . . . ." The withered leaves exclaim: "We are a watchword, you should have proclaimed us . . . ." The dewdrops, falling from the trees, murmur: "We are tears that were never shed; we might have melted the ice-spears that wounded you. " Broken straws call out: "We are deeds, you should have performed us; doubts that strangle have crippled and bent us . . . ." And, most poignantly, I feel, A Sighing in the Air intones: "We are songs, you should have sung us, a thousand times you curbed and suppressed us. In the depths of your heart we have lain and waited . . . . We were never called forth—now we are poison in your throat."

After this, Peer meets the Button-Moulder whose task it is to melt down and re-cast faulty buttons into shiny new ones. We learn that this is to be Peer's fate. Mistakenly, Peer thinks it is because he has been such a great sinner. "Not so." says the Button-Moulder: "You are not . . . what they'd call an exceptional sinner—not even a middling one— . . . you took sinning lightly . . . you just dabbled in the mire . . . so you'll be melted down." What was Peer's transgression then? " . . . you were designed as a shining button on the coat of the world . . . but your loop was missing, which is why you must go in the pile with the throw-outs to be . . . 'reduced to an ingot'." Peer was "bright as a button" in the beginning as a child, but he failed to attach himself to a life, to commit to an identity. Again, we hear the Button-Moulder: "Up till now, you have *never* been yourself, so it's all the same if you die completely." Peer is unable to convince him that he was either good enough, or bad enough, to escape re-moulding. In a nice Rogerian twist, a century before Rogers, Ibsen has the satanic Thin

One say: "Now don't get upset—it's your sins I'm belittling, not you . . . ." The decision of the Button-Moulder seems final: "Look, I have it in writing: 'Collect Peer Gynt; he has utterly failed in his purpose in life—as defective goods, he must go in the ladle'."

As Peer twists and turns to avoid the inevitable consequences of a half-lived life, only the most judgmental of us wants the story to end this way. There has been something lovable about this diffuse character, something redeeming. Erikson, at least gives us some hope. Not only are past stages remediable, but the final stage of Integrity has many elements that recapitulate the initial one of Trust, the one that Peer's mother helped him to negotiate successfully. Not the least of these recapitulated elements is a return to the arms of a providential mother. Hermann Hesse in *Narcissus and Goldmund* has Goldmund, as he lays dying, tell his alter ego, Narcissus: "But how will you die when your time comes, Narcissus, since you have no mother? Without a mother, one cannot love. Without a mother, one cannot die." Before the end, before the Button-Moulder claims his raw material, comes the faithful Solveig to enfold Peer Gynt in her arms:

> Sleep now, dearest son of mine.
> I will cradle you, I will guard you.
> Child, you have nestled on your mother's knee all the livelong day.
> God bless you, my joy.
> Child, I have held you close against my breast all the livelong day.
> You are weary now.
> Sleep now, dearest son of mine, I will cradle you, I will guard you.
> I will cradle you, I will guard you; sleep and dream, dearest son of mine.

It appears that the Button-Moulder will have to return another day.

NOTE

1   The Boyg, a very large, practically shapeless and slimy troll-like character, is psychologically rather like a combined personification of Freud's Id, Kierkegaard's "void," and Sartre's Nausea.

BIBLIOGRAPHY

Bradley, C. (1992) *Development and Validation of a Measure of Generativity-Stagnation*, unpublished masters thesis, Department of Psychology, Simon Fraser University, Burnaby.
—— (1997) Generativity-stagnation: Development of a status model, *Developmental Review* 17: 262–90.

Bradley, C.L., Kowaz, A., and Marcia, J.E. (1990) Industry and generativity: new directions in psychosocial developmental research, in C. Vandenplas, H. Holper, and B. Campos (eds.), *New Directions in Interpersonal, Psychosocial, and Identity Development* , pp. 113–17, Louvain: Academia.

Erikson, E. (1959) Identity and the life cycle, *Psychological Issues*, monograph no. 1.

—— (1982) *The Life Cycle Completed: A Review*, New York: Norton.

Hearn, S. (1993) *Integrity, Despair, and In-between: Development of Integrity statuses*, unpublished doctoral dissertation, Department of Psychology, Simon Fraser University, Burnaby.

Hearn, S., Glenham. M., Strayer, J., Koopman, R., and Marcia, J.E. (1997) *Integrity, Despair and In-Between: Toward Construct Validation of Erikson's Eighth Stage*, manuscript submitted for publication, Department of Psychology, Simon Fraser University, Burnaby.

Ibsen, H. (1966) *Peer Gynt: A Dramatic Poem*, trans. P. Watts, London: Penguin.

Kowaz, A. and Marcia, J.E. (1991) Development and validation of a measure of Eriksonian Industry, *Journal of Personality and Social Psychology*, 60: 390–7.

Marcia, J.E., Waterman, A.S., Matteson, D.E., Archer, S.A., and Orlofsky, J.L. (1993) *Ego Identity: A Handbook for Psychosocial Research*, New York: Springer-Verlag.

Orlofsky, J.L., Marcia, J.E., and Lesser, I.M.(1973) Ego identity status and the intimacy versus isolation crisis of young adulthood, *Journal of Personality and Social Psychology*, 27: 211–19.

Index